CALLED BY
MOTHER EARTH

CALLED BY MOTHER EARTH

A Father's Search for His Son

GREG F. NATERER

Breakwater Books
PO Box 2188, St. John's, NL, Canada, A1C 6E6
www.breakwaterbooks.com

A CIP catalogue record for this book is available
from Library and Archives Canada.

ISBN 9781778530142 (softcover)

We acknowledge the support of the Canada Council for the Arts.
We acknowledge the financial support of the Government of
Canada through the Department of Heritage and the Government
of Newfoundland and Labrador through the Department of
Tourism, Culture, Arts and Recreation for our publishing activities.

Printed and bound in Canada.

Breakwater Books is committed to choosing papers and
materials for our books that help to protect our environment.
To this end, this book is printed on a recycled paper and other
sources that are certified by the Forest Stewardship Council®.

 Canada Council   Conseil des Arts
for the Arts   du Canada

Newfoundland
Labrador

CONTENTS

In memory of Jordan Philip Naterer.
Forever a family of five.

FOREWORD

I first met Jordan Naterer through mutual friends in high school. We became good friends while studying engineering together at Memorial University. During the first few weeks of undergraduate studies we often worked together, primarily as lab partners and studying for courses. We shared a love of science and engineering that prompted long discussions and debates over topics we had recently learned. We also volunteered together in the Memorial University (MUN) chapter of Engineers Without Borders (EWB). Here, Jordan's knack for problem-solving and his desire to help solve global issues were on full display. He worked diligently to help organize events and educate the public on EWB's work.

Jordan had a fun, competitive spirit, and always aimed to improve and perfect everything he did, whether in sports, games, or other areas of his life. I recall, while applying for our first work terms, talking with Jordan about writing the best cover letters, to which he staged a debate on the best salutations for professionally closing out the letter. He asserted that a combination of "sincerely" and "regards" covered all bases the best. In any case, it worked out well and we were both granted our first work terms at companies in downtown St. John's. Though working for separate companies, we would often meet with other students in nearby offices for lunch in the food court of Atlantic Place, where we talked about our work and enjoyed a break from jockeying spreadsheets.

Jordan was academically keen in a number of other areas outside of engineering, such as sociology and philosophy in particular. He took courses in those subjects and could deliver speeches on any sociological topic on command. His line, "Now that is putting Descartes before the horse," became a regular quip during these semesters, among his arsenal of puns and other wordplay that he enjoyed so greatly.

Our interest in engineering led us both to continue studies after our undergraduate degrees. Jordan left for a master's degree in electrical engineering at UBC, while I remained at Memorial University for a master's degree in process engineering. Despite the distance and the 2020 pandemic, we remained in touch, discussing the woes of the graduate student and sharing jokes.

Hearing of Jordan's disappearance in October 2020 was shocking. I took part in the extraordinary search efforts by the Naterer family and other organizers. These were immense efforts that family, friends, and volunteers contributed to finding a loved one, or in some cases, a stranger. Processing and writing these experiences and emotions was no doubt a great challenge; however, Jordan's father, Dr. Greg Naterer, and family have skillfully summarized them in this book. The stories of the journey, ranging from the physical into the spiritual aspects, provide a personal insight into this kind of effort that is seldom written about and reflect a deep dedication to their love for Jordan.

Throughout the ten months of the search, there was an outpouring of support and help from friends and co-workers at Memorial University. Updates were reported often in the local media. St. John's is a tight-knit community that helped the Naterer family in various ways. From analyzing drone videos, to intelligence gathering online, and supporting private search and rescue efforts from a GoFundMe fundraising effort, the community came together to help the Naterer family.

On the surface, this book is the story of the search for Jordan after he didn't return from a hiking trip. But it's really about much more than that. It's about what the Naterer family discovered while they were searching for Jordan. It's a book about choices, perseverance, friendship, and learning. It's about coming to terms with life and loss when terrible things happen, discovering what really matters in life when such things happen, and finding support and comfort in places you expect and in places that surprise you. It's a book about loving Jordan and losing him. It's a book about finding Jordan and saying goodbye to him, for now. It's a book about humanity—trust, deceit, compassion, endurance, openness, judgment, and love.

Jordan's efforts to survive and the Naterer family's determination to find him are inspirational. Their courage to continue searching under the most difficult of circumstances stemmed from a deep love for each other. This book serves as a testament to their resilience and fortitude. It also provides helpful strategies for others facing similar tragic circumstances.

Not more than a few days go by in which I don't have some thought of Jordan—a memory brought up by running by his old neighbourhood, or hearing or seeing something that makes me think of his jokes and sense of humour. While difficult to lose him, I am grateful for the time we spent together as friends and can only think to extend the same positivity he had to others moving forward in the future. I send my continued love and support to the Naterer family, and all those who helped to support the search effort to find Jordan.

Sincerely and regards,

David Hopkins
November 10, 2023

PREFACE

The mountains are calling and I must go.
—JOHN MUIR

American outdoor enthusiast John Muir wrote those words in a letter to his sister in 1873. He had been hiking for over five weeks in eastern California, a trek that included several climbs in the Sierra Nevada mountains. Not long after returning from that experience, he went back again to hike in high terrain. Mountains had a magnetic attraction for Muir, as they have for many people who enjoy the beauty of the natural environment.

My son, Jordan, loved nature hikes, mountains, and forests. When he was a young boy, he took up rock climbing. Later, when he was a student at Memorial University in St. John's, Newfoundland, we hiked together as a family along the Avalon Peninsula's beautiful East Coast Trail. After moving to Vancouver to pursue engineering graduate studies at UBC, Jordan hiked with friends in the mountains of

British Columbia and Alberta. He was continually called back to the mountains.

But on the Thanksgiving weekend of October 2020, he disappeared after losing the trail in an unexpected snowstorm on Frosty Mountain, in E.C. Manning Provincial Park. For the next ten months, my family and I, along with hundreds of other kind-hearted individuals, searched for Jordan at various times and in different ways. This book describes our shared journey to find Jordan, and particularly my personal experience. This time and these events had profound impacts on me—psychologically, spiritually, physically, and mentally. It changed my perspective on nature and it helped me find deeper meaning in Indigenous teachings. I came to believe in the nature spirit of the forest, and that a forest is much more than just a collection of trees.

The Indigenous people of the area of British Columbia in which Jordan was hiking that fateful weekend use the word Tmxʷulaxʷ or "Mother Earth" to describe the sacred life and forces that comprise the spirit of the natural world. During quiet times of meditation in the forest, I sensed a spirit there, and it helped me to call it by its local name. When I hiked off-trail, if the background noise of the forest was normal, with the sounds of birds and other wildlife, I felt an inviting presence and that I was welcomed there. But if the soundscape suddenly changed and became quiet, I felt unwelcome, as if Tmxʷulaxʷ was watching to assess my intentions. I tried to listen carefully to Tmxʷulaxʷ, seeking signals, conscious or subconscious, that might point me in the direction of my son.

When I meditated during this time, I often had flashbacks of Jordan. I imagined conversations with him about things he had described to me. Sometimes I felt I heard his words and voice, as if he was speaking to me again. As the months of our searching wore on, I felt like Jordan's presence was merging with the surrounding forest. I also sought practical guidance during these inner conversations with him—half-remembered, half-imagined. Should I turn right or left at the next lookout?

Although this book largely focuses on my personal experiences in Manning Park over a ten-month search period, elsewhere, and at the same time, my wife Josie and daughters Julia and Veronica were playing their own critical roles in the search for Jordan. Josie stepped away from fundraising work at her growing business in order to work full-time on our search. She led all aspects of the coordination of the search efforts—finding more volunteers; writing and sending endless communications, prompts, pleas, and reminders on social media; preparing printed materials; and much more. Our daughter Julia led a major online fundraising effort to support the expenses of hiring search and rescue, helicopter, and drone companies in 2020. Throughout the search, our daughter Veronica helped analyze the vast amount of information posted online, as well as witness reports. Both of our daughters showed great fortitude, continuing their academic studies, while we all did our part to search for Jordan.

I would like to thank the hundreds of individuals who contributed in significant ways to that search: those who looked on the ground; volunteers who spent countless hours examining drone videos and other aerial imagery of Manning Park; colleagues at Memorial University and dear friends in St. John's who helped with intelligence gathering; donors who contributed financially through Julia's GoFundMe initiative; and all the other individuals who sent in important information about Manning Park.

My particular thanks go to our most dedicated supporters, volunteers, salt-of-the-earth people. They include the core search group—Trevor Tory, John Leblanc, Bob Jackson, Kevin Palardy, Mike Bergan, Lynn and Stan Hussey, Jennifer Travis, Tom Moyle, Keira Eavis, Dean Perez, Olga Sawatzky, Pascal Szeftel, Alejandro Rojas-Bernal, Mikaela Hallett, Alessia Rodriguez, Andrew Schuldt, and Mike Manuel; the targeted ground searchers—Marko Naterer, Ed Secnik, Lutz Lampe, Rune Melcher, Kristin Ohm-Pedersen, Max Aleksandrov, Mike Smitham, Igor Tchouiko, and Jennifer Brown; the map managers—Rastko Cvekra,

Sidney Donaldson, and Maria Yulemetova; the video team—Catherine Wanczycki, Lauren Howell, Lindi Braund, Cindy Saunders, Betty Rebellato, Sheila McFarland, Ani Bek, Eva Zhu, Jordy Ydse, and Sue Davidson; the St. John's core search group—Elizabeth Whelan Hollett, Celina Stoyles, Julie Sinnott, and Allison Chislett; the Canadian Canine Search Corps team—Karen Somerville and Nick Oldrive; our media liaison—Andrea McDeer; and the special advisers—Mike Allison, Sandra Allan-Wagnitz, and Susan Flanagan.

Community help and support extended across Canada beyond our immediate volunteer group. The Pattison Sign Group graciously displayed our Missing Person signs as large billboards from Vancouver to the Alberta-BC border. Many people called to volunteer or share helpful trail information about Manning Park after seeing those signs. Even after our pay period for the signage was completed, Pattison continued to display the Missing Person billboards in prominent locations.

There is a well-known Newfoundland phrase that indicates the "best kind." It means "great" or "couldn't be better." This aptly describes the faculty and staff members of Memorial University's Faculty of Engineering and Applied Science.

Special thanks to all who helped with the publication of this book, especially Sandy Newton and Samanda Stroud for their valuable editorial contributions to the written manuscript, and David Hopkins for his heartfelt tribute to Jordan in the Foreword. The assistance and support of the publishing team at Breakwater Books, particularly Claire Wilkshire, Nicole Haldoupis, Rebecca Rose, and Rhonda Molloy, are gratefully acknowledged.

Initially, I was reluctant to relive the memories of this journey to find Jordan. But after Josie and my two sisters-in-law, Karol and Yvonne, encouraged me to write a book, I decided to start the project. I could see that it would be a special way to keep Jordan in our hearts and create a lasting legacy for him. Once I began writing, it soon became a labour of love. I hope *Called by Mother Earth* will be a valuable keepsake that my family will cherish for years to come.

I believe Jordan's heroic efforts and determination to survive were extraordinary. The search efforts, too, were remarkable. I hope the strategies we used will be helpful to people facing a similar crisis, and that our journey together will serve as an inspiration: to follow your hearts and take courage—even in the midst of tragedy—from the love of others.

Greg F. Naterer
November 2023

ACRONYMS

CCSC	Canadian Canine Search Corps
FRS	Family Radio Service
GMRS	General Mobile Radio Service
GPS	Global Positioning System
JRCC	Joint Rescue Coordination Centre
KML	Keyhole Markup Language
NFL	National Football League
NSERC	Natural Sciences and Engineering Research Council of Canada
PCT	Pacific Crest Trail
RCMP	Royal Canadian Mounted Police
SAR	Search and Rescue
SIM	Subscriber Identity Module
UBC	University of British Columbia
VPD	Vancouver Police Department

LAND ACKNOWLEDGEMENT

The Similkameen Valley is the ancestral, traditional, and unceded territory of the Syilx Nation, and is home to the Upper Similkameen Indian Band—the Upper Smelqmix People—and the Lower Similkameen Indian Band—the Lower Smelqmix People.

For reasons of privacy, names in the text with quotation marks around them on first use are pseudonyms.

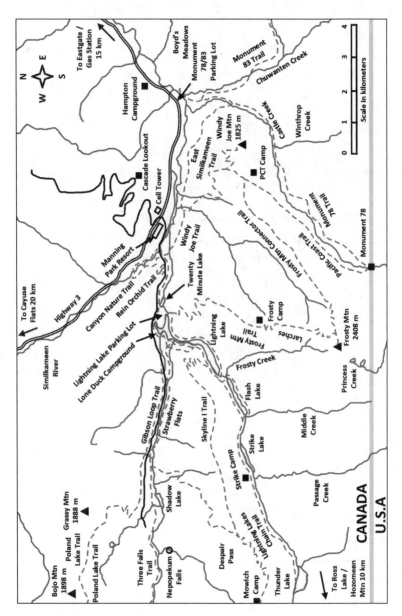

Hiking trails in E.C. Manning Park.

E.C. Manning Park search area (Shutterstock Photo ID: 1666419778).

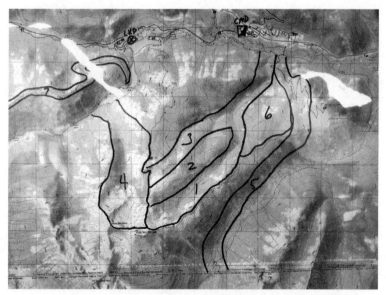

Search regions in E.C. Manning Park (as prioritized in the Vancouver Police Department search, October 2020); CMD: *command centre;* LKP: *Lightning Lake parking lot.*

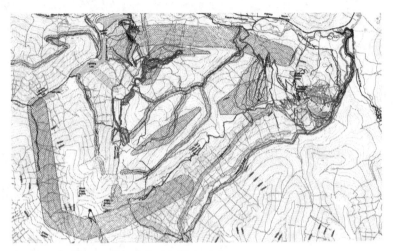

Areas searched by ground and air up to December 2020.

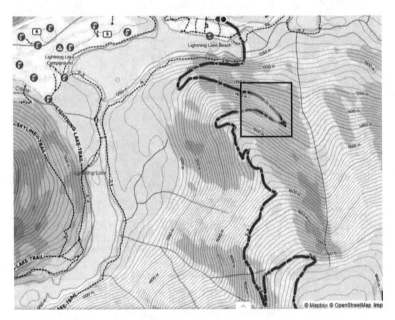

Frosty Mountain Trail second switchback: Location of Ethan Morf's reported sighting.

one

AN OCTOBER
CALL

Into the forest I go, to lose my mind and find my soul.
—MUIR, LIMBAUGH, 1986

HE WEEKEND OF THANKSGIVING IN 2020—OCTOBER 10 TO
12—was peculiar for the Naterer family. My wife, Josie, and I had
recently purchased a property to rent out in the city in which
we lived, St. John's, Newfoundland. After installing some new
bedroom and living room furniture on the Saturday, October 10, we
went out for dinner.

As per our regular routine, before we went out, Josie called Jordan,
our twenty-five-year-old son, to see how his week had gone. Jordan
had moved to Vancouver a few years earlier to pursue a master's degree
in electrical engineering at the University of British Columbia (UBC).
To our surprise, Jordan didn't pick up the phone that Saturday night.
Josie left a voicemail but sensed that something was wrong.

The following day, Sunday, October 11, it was time to cut the grass at our own house. Our neighbour Ted was also outside working. Usually, Ted and I are friendly and talkative when we see each other, but not that day. For some reason I felt miserable and unsettled. I pushed my lawn mower by Ted without speaking or even looking up to greet him. I am generally pretty self-aware, but that day I couldn't pinpoint what was bothering me.

Our daughters, Julia and Veronica, were busy doing homework that Sunday. Julia had just started her first year of the engineering program at Memorial University, while Veronica was in her last year at Gonzaga High School. They had talked with Jordan a week earlier and learned that he was planning to go hiking and camping overnight during the Thanksgiving weekend, although he hadn't yet decided on his specific destination. Jordan had described some new hiking gear he'd bought and explained to them how bear spray worked.

We had invited our friend Alice over for our family Thanksgiving dinner on Monday. Alice and I worked together as deans at Memorial University. Josie was a fundraising specialist at a growing business that she had launched several years earlier. To all appearances, we were a happy family leading a normal life. However, an undercurrent of anxiety was running because, by the end of the evening, Jordan had still not returned Josie's weekly phone call.

The moment that changed our lives forever came the next morning. Tuesday, October 13. I was away from the house doing chores. Our daughters were still at home. Josie answered the phone when it rang, and an unfamiliar voice identified itself as a police officer from the Vancouver Police Department (VPD). The officer informed Josie that Jordan had been reported as missing. It was a brief call.

Josie hung up, horrified and speechless. When I arrived home, she was sitting beside the fireplace in the family room. Veronica was sitting on the couch. Josie shared what she'd been told.

This is how it happens: Your world shatters in an instant.

My own first feeling—beyond shock—was that the police team would quickly find Jordan. But I had so many questions. Where had he last been seen? Where did he disappear *from*? Josie said the police seemed to be unsure. This was clearly very serious.

She had learned from the police that Jordan had planned to join a group of friends in Vancouver for Thanksgiving dinner on Monday. When he didn't arrive, one of his friends called the police, as he too had not been able to reach Jordan. As we would soon find out, that call set in motion a perplexing process involving several organizations and individuals.

My shock quickly turned to a state of panic. Josie and I decided that one of us should fly to British Columbia immediately while the other followed up with the police and collected more information. I booked a seat on the next flight from St. John's to Vancouver and notified my office that I would be gone until further notice.

I left St. John's that same day and Josie booked a ticket for the next day, Wednesday. Before she flew out, she contacted Jordan's bank for permission to access his bank records. She found a record of an October 10 purchase in the store at E.C. Manning Provincial Park, about two and a half hours east of Vancouver. Through the friend of Jordan's who had initially contacted the police, a wider group of friends was quickly mobilized. They drove to the park and soon found Jordan's black Honda Civic in the Lightning Lake parking lot, near the start of the Frosty Mountain trail. That confirmed the park as the focus of the search for our missing son.

Manning Park had no search and rescue (SAR) plan for missing persons. Normally this would be were managed by the local Princeton Royal Canadian Mounted Police (RCMP) unit. But the VPD, the first police authority to be alerted, decided that their agency should lead the search for Jordan, even though our son was missing far away from his home in Vancouver.

The VPD retrieved Jordan's computer from his apartment. Without access to it (yet), Josie had created a detailed timeline of Jordan's activities prior to and on the Thanksgiving weekend using his bank records. It appeared that Jordan had planned an overnight backpacking trip that passed through a beautiful larch forest area on the Frosty Mountain trail. It was easy to see why this destination would attract him. The Larch Meadows (more commonly known as the Larches) near the summit of Frosty Mountain has ancient trees—among the oldest in Canada. Larch are deciduous pines. Their needles change from a verdant green to a stunning gold colour in October. The larch plateau and summit backdrop would not only be spectacularly beautiful at this time of year, but they likely would have reminded Jordan of eastern Newfoundland, where larches are common.

Jordan was an experienced and speedy hiker. He understood what it takes to complete a long hike in mountain terrain. He was physically fit and regularly passed others when hiking. We believed that he had lost his way or perhaps had fallen and was injured. Nothing worse could have happened to our son.

Although we didn't know specifically why Jordan had chosen that destination, we speculated that the beauty of the mountains and the Larches, the challenge of the terrain, and his interest in photography could have been the motivation.

We were alarmed to learn that Manning Park is huge. It covers over 80,000 hectares of protected area in the North Cascades mountain range of southern British Columbia. The trail to the summit of Frosty Mountain, the highest mountain in the park, is also one of the most spectacular and challenging of the park's many trails. It's about an eight-hour trek up and back from the top of Frosty Mountain—and the trail connects with other routes to make a ten- or even twenty-kilometre loop. There's also a path from an area near the summit of Frosty Mountain that leads west to the heights of Windy Joe Mountain and then down, which makes a looped route of thirty kilometres (and usually requires camping overnight).

So...which path had Jordan taken? We had no way to know.

From witness accounts, we also soon learned that a snowstorm had unexpectedly swept through the sub-Alpine areas at higher elevations. From photos taken by hikers on October 10, there had been some fog in the morning at the base of the mountain. By the late afternoon, it was snowing at higher elevations. Not only was visibility poor, but it was likely that hikers were caught off guard by the snowy conditions.

———

Flying across Canada with no idea of what was happening with Jordan was agonizing. Throughout the flight, I envisioned positive outcomes, hoping that by the time I touched down, Jordan would have been found. Or we'd have some clue about what had happened and the police authorities would be able to quickly find and rescue him.

After landing in Vancouver, I stayed with friends, Linda and Bill, until Josie arrived. Early on Wednesday morning, Bill drove me to Manning Park, where we booked into the park's ski resort. Four of Jordan's closest friends in British Columbia—Alejandro, Mikaela, Alessia, and Andrew, all graduate students at UBC—met me there. They had already helped spread news that Jordan was missing and called for more volunteers to come and help with the search at Manning Park.

The VPD had started to coordinate the SAR efforts in the park. By the time we arrived, they'd set up an SAR command centre at the far western side of the resort, with a helicopter launch site nearby. On a large map, seven search areas had been prioritized, numbered according to the probability of finding Jordan within them. Regions one, two, and three covered all the drainage basins[1] on the "inside" of the Frosty

---

1   A drainage basin is the land area drained by all waterways and tributaries that flow down a mountain to a common outlet (for example, a pond, lake, or river). Drainage basins often contain several watersheds, with each stream and tributary having its own watershed area. Smaller watersheds and waterways drain to those of ever-increasing size. Mountain hikers often…

Mountain trail loop—these "interior" basins were considered the most promising areas, but also among the most treacherous. Region four took in the Frosty Creek drainage basin west of the Frosty Mountain trail. Region five followed the Pacific Crest Trail (PCT) to Monument 78 on the Canada-US border. Region six enclosed the base of the interior drainages west of the Windy Joe Mountain trails. And region seven followed the Skyline 1 trail.[2]

From Wednesday until Saturday, Josie and I worked closely with the VPD, who were assisted by SAR teams from the town of Princeton and the RCMP. The search effort also brought many SAR volunteers from other nearby communities. These were organized into teams of three to five members by an operations manager; they scoured the ground on foot. Each team had a defined purpose and a particular region to search.

While we waited nervously in the command centre, helicopters and search teams went off to their assigned areas. Each time they returned, we were on edge to know what they had learned. It was an extremely stressful, and frantic time.

Television and radio reporters came looking for interviews and to find updates. Despite some initial reluctance, I agreed to speak with them, with the hope of attracting even more volunteers to the park and the search effort.

Our own proactive fact-finding efforts were carried out at the same time and were critical during these initial days. As the news of Jordan's

---

...simply shorten the term for any of the waterways within a drainage basin to a "drainage."

2   The Skyline trail has two sections—1 and 11—which follow a series of mountain ridges above the Lighting Lakes Chain trail to the Canada-US border. The first section (1) begins near the Lone Duck campground and goes southwest, past Snow Camp Mountain and Lone Goat Mountain, until the Mowich Camp. Then the second section (11) continues past Mowich Camp and Hozomeen Mountain until it reaches Ross Lake at the Canada-US border. Hereafter the Skyline trail will refer to both sections, unless otherwise specified.

disappearance spread, more and more hikers who had been on Frosty Mountain the same day posted information on social media sites and hiking apps about what they remembered seeing and experiencing.

There were two groups of volunteers—one searching on the ground and another gathering intelligence online and from interviews with staff at Manning Park. The latter group combed through websites and social media postings to identify people who'd been in the park from October 10 to 12. They reached out to at least a hundred people who had posted information. The information they found was recorded in individual witness reports. These details were used to focus the searchers on the most probable areas of Jordan's disappearance. Since Manning Park itself and the number of possible scenarios were so large, we needed to prioritize search efforts based on accurate factual information.

As a result of the outreach and in addition to Jordan's friends from UBC, dozens of other volunteers and groups arrived at the Manning Park Resort to help us search for Jordan. Every morning we met in the resort's restaurant or in our room to lay out maps and discuss strategies. All relevant information was passed along to the police authorities, who then updated their own search strategies.

Each morning before the ground searchers set out, Josie and I greeted the volunteers to thank them for their efforts, especially in such difficult mountain terrain. They expressed hope and shared where and how they would search that day. Sometimes we viewed maps together and discussed possible scenarios of how Jordan might have lost his way. I also shared details from the timeline of Jordan's activities on October 10, as we learned them.

- 6:39 a.m.—Jordan checked a maps app on his phone for a route from downtown Vancouver to Manning Park.
- 7:00 a.m.—Jordan searched for the Frosty Mountain trailhead and viewed the area from Highway 3 to the trailhead at the Lightning Lake parking lot.

- 7:08 a.m.—A security camera captured Jordan (with a green backpack) leaving his apartment in Vancouver.
- 9:30 a.m.—Jordan arrived at the main entrance of the Manning Park Resort.
- 9:41 a.m.—Jordan bought a coffee at the Manning Park Resort Country Store.
- 10:18 a.m.—Jordan bought a back-country permit for one night, marking the Frosty campsite as the place he would stay overnight.
- 10:31 a.m.—A cellphone ping placed Jordan somewhere west of the Manning Park Resort cell tower, across the highway from the resort, and between the Frosty Mountain and Windy Joe Mountain trailheads.
- 12:32 p.m.—A second cellphone ping placed Jordan somewhere east of the Manning Park Resort cell tower, consistent with the trails southeast of the highway leading to Windy Joe Mountain, which ascend the mountain.

Since the highest-probability search areas were farthest away from the command centre, some search crews were taken by helicopter and picked up several hours later, so they could make the most effective use of their time. As the days ticked by, I remained optimistic that each helicopter that departed from the launch site would come back with Jordan aboard. Each time they returned without success, our spirits fell further and desperation set in deeper.

We had initially hoped that Jordan might be located by his phone. The VPD requested a ping from Jordan's service provider, Telus, in the initial days of the search to see if it could be located electronically. Telus forced a signal to the device and reported that Jordan's phone was no longer reachable or attached to the network—it was either turned off or the battery was dead.

Occasionally a search team arrived back with news that raised our spirits. When helicopter sweeps of the (fully exposed) north face of

Frosty Mountain revealed no backpack anywhere, we took it as posi-tive news. It was considered a significant possibility that this danger-ous area was where Jordan may be located, but the sweep suggested that an accident there was unlikely.

As the search continued, we continued to comb through witness reports and social media posts online for new information to share with the VPD and help strategize. Some of these details were found during the official VPD search while other information was uncovered later by our team of volunteers.

1. Between noon and 1:00 p.m. on Saturday, two hikers had lunched in their car, which was parked to the left of Jordan's. But one of them, Geneva, did not remember what type of vehicle (if any) was parked next to her Subaru. After eating, they set out on a three-day clockwise loop of the Frosty Mountain trail (via Windy Joe Mountain first). On their first day, they took a side trip to the Windy Joe lookout and camped at the PCT campsite. They did not see Jordan at any point during their trek.

2. Between 1:55 and 2:15 p.m. on Saturday, solo hiker Matthew Alexander parked in the same general area. He did not recall seeing Jordan's car, neither in the parking lot nor on his drive out to Highway 3.

3. Between about 2:37 and 2:47 p.m. on Saturday, fifteen-year-old Ethan Morf and his father saw someone who may have been Jordan a short way up the Frosty Mountain trail, near the second switchback. Ethan said this person was going up the trail while they were coming down. The Morfs arrived back at the parking lot at around 3:05 p.m. Ethan reported that he had talked briefly with the young man, who was enthusiastic

and cheerful. Ethan felt very confident the person was Jordan, based on his height and the description of his backpack.

Other than Ethan Morf, however, none of the hikers we traced specifically reported seeing Jordan. It seemed inconceivable to us that so many people had been on the trails that Thanksgiving weekend and yet no one had seen him. Also disconcerting was the fact that, despite several attempts to verify Ethan's report, his father never returned our volunteers' phone calls. The fact that no one else could confirm they had seen Jordan and the lack of corroboration from Ethan's father were troubling. Both factors—plus Ethan's young age—caused several of our search volunteers to doubt that Ethan's sighting was reliable. Nevertheless, Josie and I still took the report seriously, keeping all possible scenarios open.

Another hiker, Vincent, and his partner, who arrived at the Lightning Lake parking lot around 4:00 p.m. on October 10, remembered seeing Jordan's black Honda Civic there. But they also had not seen Jordan along the trail. Since Vincent was hiking down about an hour behind Ethan Morf and his father, he should have crossed paths with Jordan before Jordan reached the lower plateau of Frosty Mountain. This, too, suggested that either Ethan's sighting was incorrect, or something had happened to Jordan between the Frosty Mountain trail's second switchback (location of Ethan's sighting) and somewhere near the lower plateau approaching the Frosty campsite.

The ups and downs of possible clues followed by the searchers' failure each day were very draining emotionally. Josie and I both found it more and more difficult to sleep each night. But we remained strong, and we picked ourselves up, again and again, each morning to continue the search.

On Sunday October 18, Josie and I were called into a meeting at the command centre with senior authorities and members of the VPD,

RCMP, and Princeton SAR. An officer of the VPD took charge. There were brief introductions and then we were informed that the search for Jordan was being suspended.

Why?

"The subject was not responsive"—SAR jargon for "our search efforts have been exhausted." The official search, they added, could be reinstated only if new substantive clues turned up.

Josie and I were crushed. I nearly collapsed. In desperation, I relayed some new witness reports to the VPD, insisting that new information *had* been found. I also urged the officials not to call my son a "subject"— he was my flesh and blood, and he was still out there. Their curt reply was that the new information was insufficient to reactivate the search.

I thanked the SAR volunteers for their hard work but repeated that more had to be done. To make our case, I highlighted certain regions in drainage basins that needed more thorough checking—drones could be used more extensively, especially over the interior drainage basins. I had imagined that a complete search would have used all available technologies plus canine teams through the major drainages—but only a couple of dogs had been used for a short period of time. I offered to personally pay to continue the search. I insisted that little had been done. I was sure more could be done.

But their decision was final. After only four days, the VPD SAR team suspended the search for Jordan.

We were devastated. Their decision was incomprehensible to us. How could an unsuccessful search be concluded so quickly? Jordan was an extraordinary and resourceful young man who we felt was likely still alive out there and needing our help. He deserved our every effort.

There was only one choice for Josie and me. We were determined to continue searching, and to change the officials' minds.

Over the next few days, volunteer groups continued to hike the mountains in groups that Josie and I organized. One volunteer found a white cap and a pair of Oakley sunglasses in the Larches near the ridge leading to the summit of Frosty Mountain. We believed this was a major new clue leading us to the path taken by Jordan—he'd owned a similar cap and sunglasses. But the VPD was not convinced this was solid enough evidence and still would not resume the search.

Meanwhile, friends in St. John's contacted government and police officials, asking them to pressure the VPD into reactivating the search. Appeals were made to senior politicians, including to the premier of Newfoundland and Labrador and the prime minister of Canada. One of my dear friends at Memorial University, Syed, organized those efforts, which included a petition. Many Newfoundlanders joined this online petition to urge the restarting of the search. In a single day—by Monday, October 19—more than 3,000 people had signed the petition. Thousands of additional signatures would arrive in the coming days, soon exceeding forty thousand.

On October 21, while he was meeting with Memorial University, Prime Minister Justin Trudeau, participated in a virtual town hall Q&A session with students, staff, and faculty members. One of my co-workers (also named Justin) had initially prepared a question about climate change—but a thought that he couldn't shake hit him while he had the floor.

"With deep compassion and humility, may I ask: Is there any way you or your staff might be able to encourage additional support in the search for Jordan Naterer?" he asked.

The prime minister replied that he understood the heartbreak of our family. His own twenty-three-year-old brother, Michel, had been lost in the mountains in British Columbia in 1998. That official search effort was also called off before Michel was found. The prime minister explained that he didn't have the ability to reinstate a search, but he committed to looking into it.

On October 22, the VPD called Josie with news: they were reactivating the search for Jordan, effective the next day, Friday, and into the following week, since the weather forecast was good.

What a relief!

We were asked, however, not to allow any of our own volunteers to search simultaneously during this period. Our team of volunteers agreed to hold back. A number of people were staying with us at the resort, including Jordan's former supervisor from UBC, our friends Tom and Keira, my brother Marko and some of his friends from Ontario, as well as several other volunteers who stayed nearby and travelled each day to Manning Park.

From our cabin window, Josie and I could see the spot where helicopters arrived and departed with the search teams. In the morning of Friday, October 23, I was glad to see that helicopter search activity had begun.

But little or no activity followed from later in the day on Friday until Sunday.

When Monday began similarly quiet, we asked the VPD what had happened—where was the promised search activity? They told us they had suspended their search on Friday afternoon, shortly after it began.

Once again, we were devastated. It appeared that either their commitment to continue searching into the following week was not genuine—or SAR volunteers had not been found. If the VPD had informed us on Friday that they had again suspended the search, our own team of volunteers would have been able to resume searching on the weekend. This further added salt to our wounds, as Saturday and Sunday had been ideal warm, sunny days—agonizingly, now lost.

At this point, we expanded our own search team of volunteers. Our room became the new command centre and we filled its walls with maps. We also brought in food and supplies for everyone who was helping. To support our private search efforts, our daughter Julia began an online fundraising effort from Newfoundland. Her leadership allowed us to hire helicopters, private drone operations, and SAR companies to help us keep searching.

Soon after the VPD suspended their search for a second time, an unusual call woke me in the middle of the night. The phone rang around midnight and a man named "Jack" introduced himself. He had called, he said, to sympathize with our situation and share that he had extensive experience in dealing with federal agencies on SAR missions. He described how he could help get more federal assistance with helicopters and ground search teams—saying that, in his view, we were entangled in a jurisdictional predicament.

I was intrigued. We had felt that the overlapping of duties among the VPD, and the Princeton SAR and RCMP authorities was confusing. The Princeton RCMP and SAR teams had the SAR expertise in the mountain wilderness of Manning Park, yet the VPD had led the search process—even though this SAR mission, almost three hours away from Vancouver, was drastically different than one that would have been undertaken in the city.

As Jack spoke about the jurisdictional roles, I wondered why the VPD hadn't simply transferred Jordan's file to the Princeton RCMP. Both organizations were involved but our communications had always been directed through the VPD because they were the so-called "lead." Jack didn't have an answer but felt that more federal air assets were available and should be used. He left me with an offer to help that included free legal support.

The next morning, I searched Jack's professional profile and credentials online. On the phone, he had seemed sincerely touched by our circumstances and upset with how quickly the local authorities had suspended the official search. He had told me about his legal background and past experiences working with senior levels of government, and according to his online presence he seemed legitimate. So, I accepted his offer of support.

Jack then sent a letter to senior federal government officials, explaining our situation and requesting assistance in the form of further SAR support. Specifically, he asked why a federal Cormorant helicopter had not been forthcoming from the commander of the Victoria base of the Royal Canadian Air Force. The letter outlined why he thought the VPD didn't have jurisdiction in the provincial Manning Park and stated that coordination of the ground search with Princeton RCMP had created a confusing jurisdictional web.

In his view, the VPD's jurisdiction as a municipal police force ended at the civic boundary of the city of Vancouver. And it also hadn't made sense: the VPD did not, he said, have sufficient experience with SAR operations in the North Cascades. Although the VPD efforts had included helicopter support, they had fallen short with drone and canine support.

Jack stressed the importance of bringing more SAR air assets into the search. He listed specific examples that could be called upon: RCMP fixed-wing aircraft, Canadian Coast Guard rotary-wing aircraft, Transport Canada Dash 8 surveillance aircraft operated by PAL Airlines under contract to the Department of Fisheries and Oceans, or Royal Canadian Air Force military SAR aircraft. And, since we were now conducting our own private search, Jack asked for federal support to work with us in a coordinated manner.

His letter prompted several bureaucratic replies. After an initial response was received, he made a further request—to the appropriate provincial minister and also the federal Minister of National Defence. In response, Jack was told that Manning Park fell under provincial jurisdiction and thus BC SAR services—not federal. Also, since the RCMP operates separately from the VPD, and the VPD was a municipal entity, Jack was told, other federal authorities were not able to assist. We were caught up in a bureaucratic nightmare—it was unclear to me why federal support could not provide any aid, even if the situation was under provincial jurisdiction.

Jack responded by explaining that, though the outlining of jurisdictions was helpful, the VPD had *already* sent air assets into Manning
Park even though it was a provincial park under provincial authority.
He again questioned the VPD's level of expertise in mountain SAR operations outside the city and reiterated that the VPD's jurisdiction as a
municipal police force should have ended at that city's boundary. And
he again asked the Minister of Transport to make Transport Canada
Dash 8 surveillance aircraft available to assist in the search. He also
asked for the Canadian Coast Guard to make some of their helicopters
available.

The Joint Rescue Coordination Centre (JRCC) in Victoria is staffed
by personnel of the Royal Canadian Air Force, Canadian Armed Forces,
and Canadian Coast Guard. Jack believed the JRCC had air assets available to deploy at Manning Park and asked the various entities to make
a request to JRCC for air assets.

That's when the VPD weighed in directly. They sternly contacted
Josie and I, saying they would not seek any federal air assets to support
the search. And they warned us, for reasons that seemed believable,
not to continue communicating with Jack. Chastened and discouraged, we stopped our communications.

Some of our volunteers had also conducted more detailed background checks on Jack and they, too, warned us against aligning ourselves with him. We later learned that Jack's correspondence with
federal authorities, either directly or second-hand, was being shared
somehow with Manning Park staff, which could have compromised
our ability to continue searching for Jordan in the park—an unthink-
able prospect. So I told Jack not to contact us again.

From time to time, as our search continued, Jack would resume
contact. We didn't respond. Nevertheless, he continued to advocate for
further air support for our search efforts. None of these efforts mate-
rialized, but they left an enduring impression on me about just how
tangled the web of jurisdictions involved in SAR efforts can be.

It was now clear to us that the responsibility for finding Jordan rested solely in our hands. And we were certainly not going to give up. This meant, however, that Josie and I took on many new roles, including the major one of organizing the volunteer searchers.

Our cabin at the resort accommodated a large team. Every day, more volunteers (known and new) arrived at the park, attracted to help by news reports and our pleas for more volunteers. Some of them were put to work sharing information online about how the search activities were organized, and helping with other tasks like organizing files, images, and witness accounts in online folders.

Alejandro, Mikaela, Alessia, and Andrew moved into the cabin with us and helped to analyze search strategies and collect information from volunteers and hikers. They all had different fields of study in their graduate programs and had formed close friendships with Jordan at UBC's Green College, starting about two years earlier. Their efforts and support would turn out to be indispensable throughout the coming months.

An engineering alumnus from Memorial University, Mike M, also moved into the cabin with us. He provided valuable logistical support and leadership during our search operations. In my position as Dean of Engineering and Applied Science at Memorial University, I had hooded Mike when he had graduated a few years earlier. When he heard on the news about Jordan's disappearance and recognized him as my son, he decided to join our volunteer team. On several occasions, Mike organized and led groups of searchers near the Frosty campsite.

Several other Newfoundlanders living in British Columbia also joined our search efforts. I learned that a special kinship exists among Newfoundlanders—especially those far from home—that compels them to help each other when another Newfoundlander is in trouble. When I asked why they had decided to come to Manning Park, they explained that they had felt a sense of closeness and solidarity with fellow Newfoundlanders in need of help. Newfoundland and Labrador is a relatively small province, but its people have a big heart.

Our friends, Tom and Keira, were exceptionally helpful and kind-hearted during our initial search efforts in October. Both hiked many times into difficult areas that had not been adequately covered by the official SAR teams. With these efforts and their continual presence, Tom and Keira became steadfast pillars of friendship on whom Josie and I could always rely upon for emotional support. Tom and Keira's searches were all mapped; they became excellent records and reference tools in our later efforts.

Another key volunteer, Rastko, was our map keeper. He overlaid all the searches onto a master copy of a single map—an invaluable resource as our search continued.

Josie and I searched on the ground several times with Tom in mid- and late October, primarily along the Monument 78 trail. We discovered that you don't have to wander far off a Manning Park trail to become lost. We once diverted slightly to cross Castle Creek and connect with the East Similkameen trail. On our way back, we lost the path—even though it was only about ten metres away. We walked around in circles for some time until we found the creek and our prior path (and there was no snow on the ground!). In snowstorm conditions, as Jordan had encountered, finding one's way would have been far more difficult.

All of these events took place at a time when the COVID-19 pandemic was raging everywhere. This added another layer of complication to nearly every tactic in our search for Jordan. Physical distancing, masking, and self-isolation were ongoing requirements, and the pandemic had other implications, too. Some people were reluctant to help because they were worried about spreading the virus. Others were concerned about catching it, as outsiders came into the cabin to join our team. There were also logistical challenges in organizing search teams, plus the added overall stress and mental health implications that came with dealing simultaneously with a personal crisis and a global pandemic.

Despite the challenges, many volunteers helped in important ways as the days went by. A key support role was examining digital imagery, which was done initially on a single computer in the cabin (later, videos from drones and fixed-wing aircraft would be uploaded to a shared drive and could be accessed remotely). This was time-consuming but critical work. The footage had to be carefully examined for any possible clue: anything on the ground that looked unusual or had an unnatural colour.

One volunteer, Jennifer, was exceptionally dedicated in this effort. She spent countless hours searching the imagery as soon as it became available online. We hadn't known Jennifer before Jordan's disappearance, but she found out about our situation through an online post and soon became extremely devoted to our search. She was extraordinarily helpful and supportive to Josie.

So many volunteers—almost too many to count or list—helped us in this period. They searched the park's trails, offered map support, did intelligence gathering, reviewed drone imagery, and searched social media groups. They examined weather conditions and witness accounts, posting what they found on a shared drive. A social media group was created for the search and hundreds (later thousands) of people joined it. Within the larger group of volunteers, a few dozen people were consistently active on the ground and online. Several members of this core group came and went, while others remained until the end.

There were several logistical complications to learn about and sort our way through. One of them was related to the location of Manning Park—on an international border. Although there is a clear-cut line through the forest marking the end of one country and the beginning of the other, this forested boundary is overgrown in many places and can be undetectable on the ground, especially in poor visibility. If

Jordan had hiked the Monument 78 trail,[3] for example, but lost the path there (or elsewhere south of the Frosty Mountain trail), it was possible that he had unknowingly crossed into the United States. But Canadian search teams could not search across the border on their own, and the police authorities had not formally opened a missing person file in the United States.

Considering the terrain, air surveillance was key. We hired a local company, Hummingbird Drones, to do sweeps over areas close to where we thought Jordan may have lost his way. We kept records of areas already searched to guide the drone company on where to sweep next. But the vastness of the potential area—and not knowing exactly which trail Jordan had chosen or when during the weekend something had happened—meant guesswork was also used.

Hummingbird Drones began their searches a few days after the VPD suspended their search the second time. On October 20, they searched drainage areas near the Frosty campsite and around a small pond southwest of the Frosty Mountain summit and close to the border. Weather conditions then shut them down for a few days. They resumed their sweeps in late October and continued into early November, generating much footage to be analyzed by volunteers.

We also hired Valley Helicopters in late October. They conducted air searches around the Monument 78 and 83 trails (east of Windy Joe Mountain), which had not been prioritized by the official SAR teams. They also searched the Windy Joe and Frosty Mountain trail areas, including nearby drainages.

In the last week of October, thanks to resources raised through our daughter Julia's fundraising efforts, we asked Ascent Fraser Valley Guides to conduct ground searches north of the Frosty Mountain

---

3   Significant crossover points at the border have numbered monuments—
     usually some form of physical marker, post, or sign. Monument 78 is the
     closest one to the Frosty summit, while Monument 83 is farther to the east.

summit toward Monument 78 and other drainages. Subsequent searches were then continued by Berntsen Enterprises Limited (a professional SAR team with five members) up until November 21. We also coordinated a ground search with Whistler Coast Mountain Guides between October 29 and November 3, and again on November 19. Many more ground, helicopter, and drone searches were conducted from late October until December.

As for our own ground searches, volunteers arrived each morning ready to go out. The start time was usually eight o'clock. Josie and I developed maps and plans for every volunteer, outlining areas to check that had not been searched by the VPD teams. In assigning search areas, I asked people about their hiking skills and tried to match a search area with their comfort level and ability. Safety was paramount—we did not want anyone else to be hurt or lost. Only experienced mountaineers paired in groups of two could search off-trail. At the end of each day, volunteers returned to our cabin to summarize their findings. We collected and used the information to strategize for the next day.

One of the volunteers—Clayton, an experienced tracker (or "bush-whacker")—found a handful of synthetic down material near the Monument 78 trail, including two black hairs. This raised our hopes. Jordan's hair was black and he kept the same type of synthetic down in his apartment in Vancouver (he used it to make crafts and pillows). We felt this was a significant clue, and surely enough of a lead for the VPD to reactivate their search. They, however, decided it was not sufficiently compelling to either pursue DNA testing or resume their efforts.[4]

With this new discovery, we hired another private helicopter company to more thoroughly search along the Monument 78 and 83 trails.

---

4   Subsequently, I investigated laboratories that could do DNA testing. I sent the sample hair to a lab in Mississippi, which unfortunately determined that it was not a match with Jordan's.

But no further signs suggesting Jordan had been there were found, either in the area of the synthetic down or nearby.

As we undertook responsibility for the searching, I asked the VPD several times for copies of their maps of the areas they had searched and a full list of Jordan's Google searches on October 9 and 10, which the police had pulled from his computer. We were eventually given permission to access a police computer with that information. It greatly improved how we strategized and where we focused our searching.

What we discovered was that Jordan had searched detailed trail descriptions of Frosty Mountain on the Camping Canuck, AllTrails, and Vancouver Trails sites. He followed several paths virtually on the AllTrails site, and searched both front-country and back-country camping options at Manning Park. His final searches on October 9 included the Frosty Mountain and Lightning Lakes Chain trail (four searches), E.C. Manning Park (ten times, including its weather and wilderness camping), the PCT (three searches), Monument 78 (thirty searches, including the trail and campsite), Frosty Mountain (six searches), starting a hike late to camp (two searches), and several general searches on camping. We found Jordan's repeated interest and multiple searches of the PCT and Monument 78 noteworthy. Knowing him the way we did, we believed it indicated he had a serious intention to see Monument 78 at the Canada-US border.

Interestingly, Jordan had not reserved a camping space online. Instead, he filled in a camping pass once he reached the Manning Park Resort. It indicated his intention to camp overnight at the Frosty campsite, about seven kilometres from the Lightning Lake parking lot. Initially, this appeared to conflict with a desire to see Monument 78 because of the distance between the two places. However, after further thought, we felt Jordan may have changed his mind on the morning of October 10 or decided to hike to see both locations on a different day.

We could also see that when Jordan made his searches, the weather forecasts did not predict snow. It was early October, temperatures were still relatively warm, and there was no snow on the ground. We had learned by this time, however, that the forecast applied to conditions on the ground at the resort. The weather can be entirely different at higher elevations.

Having turned up just the one questionable sighting of Jordan in the park, our only solid evidence so far about which way he had set out from his car was the two cellphone pings at 10:31 a.m. and 12:32 p.m. Luckily, our crew of volunteers included two subject matter experts and engineers, Lutz (Jordan's graduate thesis supervisor at UBC) and Mike M. They did an in-depth analysis of the pings and helped us understand what they meant. (I also asked Telus to check back over the twenty-four hours after the VPD's initial contact. But the company said they found nothing from the device in that time period, either.)

A ping indicates a signal either to or from the phone that is searching for its network location. The phone responds to the network signal with information that can identify the phone's location. Any activity—an online search, a text, or attempted call—will generate phone signals that communicate with the network.

Since Jordan's bank records indicated that he bought a coffee at the resort store, the earlier (10:31 a.m.) ping likely occurred when he was at the restaurant or in the resort parking lot. The tower is located across the highway from the resort, about forty metres north of the intersection of Last Resort Road and Chickadee Lane. Technically, the start and end angles (of the phone from the tower) indicated the phone was in an area west of the cell tower. Unfortunately, we could not determine what kind of phone activity generated the ping from Jordan's phone.

The start and end angles of the second ping (12:32 p.m.) placed his phone east of the same cell tower. The VPD confirmed this second ping was consistent with the location of the trails southeast of the highway that led hikers to and then up Windy Joe Mountain. If the information from the later ping was correct,[5] it would be consistent with a scenario in which Jordan bought a coffee at the resort, parked at the Lightning Lake parking lot, then started on a clockwise loop of the Frosty Mountain trail, heading for Windy Joe Mountain first. That route would give Jordan a gentler climb during the elevation gain toward the Frosty Mountain summit—but that scenario would have invalidated Ethan Morf's reported sighting.

So we were still left with questions. If Jordan was heading first for Windy Joe Mountain, what did it mean that his camping permit indicated he planned to stay overnight at the Frosty campsite? This location could be reached on his first night out only if he did the loop in a counter-clockwise direction—or at least it would be much more easily reached that way, considering the time he set out. But if he hoped to finish the loop on Sunday, he might have thought he could push up Windy Joe Mountain and go on to Frosty Mountain on Saturday, reaching the campsite that night.

The information we had was tantalizing, but none of it added up to a clear picture of what happened.

This period was the most stressful time of my life. Josie and I were uplifted and supported by many people—friends, family, and strangers who had goodness in their hearts, empathy for our situation, and skills

---

5   Signal information is imperfect and subject to errors that can be caused by reflections off objects and physical obstructions blocking the transmission. In addition, there is just one cell tower at Manning Park; without a second tower, a signal cannot be properly triangulated. The uncertainty of the data from the algorithms used to assess Jordan's pings was estimated to make them accurate to within 150 metres. Telus also indicated that their records of Manning Park could have been outdated, so a sector (a triangular region of signal uncertainty) might have changed but might not have been updated in their records.

and energy to help us in our search. We discovered, however, to our great surprise and dismay, that not everyone who comes forward to act in a crisis has the best intentions.

After the VPD search finished, it was brought to my attention that someone had deleted all the files on our shared drive that volunteers were using to collect information and gather intelligence. The deletion, we could see, had been made by someone who was not known by any of our volunteers. I searched their name online and learned that they had a criminal record that included physical assault and attempted murder. Searching further, volunteers determined that they lived in Vancouver and had somehow accessed the shared drive from information about our search that was available online.

Why would someone erase such critical information, including witness reports and contacts?

It was highly unlikely that Jordan knew this person, but their nefarious actions raised in our minds the possibility that Jordan was missing because of foul play. We shared what had happened with the VPD, and asked them whether we could determine their location during the Thanksgiving weekend. Had they been in contact with anyone who went to Manning Park on October 10 through 12? The police decided not to investigate, and these questions remain unanswered.

This wasn't the only person we encountered who exhibited disturbing qualities. Volunteers searching for witness reports online found hiking photos posted by a young man in Manning Park on the day Jordan went missing. It was soon discovered that Jordan had communicated with this person in the past year. They shared an interest in computers, coding, and software. He worked at a company that was a competitor of the database security firm in Vancouver where Jordan worked.

This man apparently knew Manning Park (and all the areas of the park near the Canada-US border) quite well. One of his social media accounts claimed he logged hundreds of kilometres a year, and that he hiked in the mountains near or in Manning Park every weekend between April and October. But when we contacted him, something about the information he provided about his whereabouts on the Thanksgiving weekend and his knowledge of Jordan did not seem completely truthful.

Online records showed that he had communicated with Jordan before his disappearance. He was listed as a friend on one of Jordan's social media pages, which couldn't have been a coincidence because we knew that Jordan did not accept friend requests from people that he didn't know. We also had reason to believe that information about photos the young man had posted (such as when photos were taken) was not truthful.

When a volunteer reached out to this man, he explained that he had hiked in Manning Park on the dates shown on his social media account—the first week of November. He also said that he'd hiked in the North Cascades on Thanksgiving weekend near the international border (on the PCT and Monument 78 trail), but in a subsequent conversation, he said he had not been hiking on the Thanksgiving weekend. He also denied knowing Jordan. Some of the captions of his photos posted around October 10 were troubling. He wrote, for example, that two hikers can keep a secret only if one of them was dead.

Despite several requests, the young man refused to send his original geotagged photos of where he'd hiked in Manning Park on October 10, nor was he willing to answer basic questions about his hiking trip on Thanksgiving weekend. When the VPD asked him about his knowledge of Jordan's disappearance, he said he had no connection to Manning Park on the Thanksgiving weekend.

The experiences with both of these individuals, among others, made several of us increasingly concerned that something worse than what we had imagined had happened to Jordan.

After the Thanksgiving weekend, snow had fallen and melted at various rates and elevations. Some of the volunteers became reluctant to hike trails in the more snowy conditions. By the second week of November, even the hired SAR team was no longer willing to search on the ground. This was the last setback in a string of devastating events. It left us without a plan for going forward.

I could not bear to make the decision to leave my son behind. But it seemed that everyone was finished with the search except our family. Eventually I accepted the reality that hope and prayer alone, without a viable plan, would not reunite us with Jordan. And there were our daughters in St. John's to consider, who were alone and suffering emotionally while our search in British Columbia seemingly failed to achieve any progress. They, too, needed our support.

So, on November 10, Josie and I made the painful decision to return home to St. John's.

Linda and Bill came out to Manning Park and drove us back to Vancouver. It was unbearably difficult to leave the park behind. We still did not know what had happened on the Thanksgiving weekend. We had no closure and no plan. We knew it was very likely Jordan had not survived. But we still had hope.

I sat in the back seat as we drove away, looking through the window at the mountains and wondering if this was our final farewell to Jordan.

two

LIFE TURNED UPSIDE DOWN

*The term "panic" derives from Pan, the god of the
woods. People lost deep in the forest report a terror, as
though trees might conspire against them. Nature
has no special regard for humanity. Panic is our
brain's way of reminding us we should be humble.*
—QUACKENBUSH, 2020

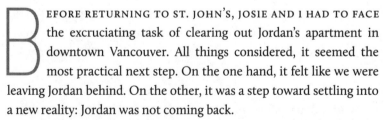

B EFORE RETURNING TO ST. JOHN'S, JOSIE AND I HAD TO FACE
the excruciating task of clearing out Jordan's apartment in
downtown Vancouver. All things considered, it seemed the
most practical next step. On the one hand, it felt like we were
leaving Jordan behind. On the other, it was a step toward settling into
a new reality: Jordan was not coming back.

After all we had just been through, we knew it was most likely that
Jordan was no longer alive. The hope we held onto was that maybe he

had *somehow* found a way to survive in the wilderness. And we knew we couldn't give up on finding him, whether the truth was the first scenario or the second.

We were determined to continue our search efforts from Newfoundland. Fortunately, we had an extraordinary volunteer, Trevor—a staff member at Manning Park—who had committed to continue helping us search on the ground, even after we were back on the other side of the country.

Staying in Jordan's apartment before our return felt surreal. Our task was to clear out his home and close his lease agreement. Josie called a lawyer to begin the legal process of obtaining curatorship of Jordan's possessions. She also made the necessary contact with the landlord, the bank manager, and Jordan's employer to settle his affairs. We packed away his books, clothes, and other belongings.

Everything we touched was precious. We picked up his clothing, smelled and kissed it, and immersed ourselves in memories of our son.

News of our unsuccessful search had been reported several times in the local media in St. John's. When we returned to Newfoundland, we were met with abundant support, emotional and otherwise, from friends. Our kitchen overflowed with the food they brought by. St. John's is a tight-knit community.

It was a strange feeling to have our personal family crisis so widely known in the city and my workplace. Not only could we hardly manage the tragedy ourselves, but it all happened in the public eye. Reporters often called for updates. People we'd meet while we were out and about were compassionate but curious. It was difficult to continue explaining the dreadful details, especially when there was still no conclusion about what had actually happened.

And, of course, people had their own ideas of what should or could have been done. Some couldn't understand why we didn't try this or that approach. They offered ideas of what else could have been tried. But due to the terrain, how events unfolded, and what was (or wasn't) in the witness reports, their suggestions couldn't have worked—or we had tried them and they *hadn't* worked.

As November turned into December, we held onto our steadfast determination to find Jordan. We remained hopeful that he might still be alive—somewhere and somehow—despite the time that had passed. Our continuing sign of hope was a candle we kept lit on the front porch. Although winter was coming and each night became colder, the candle still shone brightly. Neither snow nor freezing temperatures would extinguish our candle of hope for Jordan.

———

In all our spare hours during December and January in St. John's, we did what we could to keep searching. Since we were no longer able to search on the ground ourselves, our efforts shifted to more carefully analyzing the imagery that had been collected during October and November in Manning Park. We also obtained other software tools to examine the imagery in more detail.

With help from Bill and Linda, we made contact with Kisik Aerial Survey, a company that specializes in aerial imagery taken from fixed-wing aircraft. They had taken high-resolution ground imagery of Manning Park in both August and October that we were able to purchase and geo-reference. Other aerial images could be overlaid and accurately tagged with GPS coordinates on a single digital map made from the Kisik imagery.

We decided to ask for a third set, to see if there were any noticeable changes. The company agreed to survey a larger area around Manning Park. This time, they went beyond the region of the previous SAR searches, farther to the south, west, and east of the Frosty Mountain trail. We decided to extend the boundaries of the aerial search in case Jordan had moved farther away than the search teams had assumed was likely.

We received the new imagery on November 14, then it too was geo-referenced and imposed over the previous sets of maps, all of which were available online for volunteers to view and search for clues.

In December, we also connected with Paul, a professor at UBC, who developed software that could interface with our aerial imagery. The software enabled comments to be added to specific GPS coordinates on the maps. This allowed volunteers to mark a location if they spotted a potential clue—a tent-shaped object or colours that matched Jordan's jacket or backpack, for example—and then checks could be performed on the ground using exact GPS coordinates. The resulting maps with tagged imagery earned the name "heatmap" among our volunteers. It didn't necessarily show heated areas of higher temperature, but because the clues were marked with red dots, the name stuck.

Throughout December and January, the focus of our efforts shifted to searching the Kisik imagery and all the videos taken by drone surveys during October and November. Volunteers reviewed the footage and looked for any possible clues that might signal Jordan's whereabouts, marking points on the heatmaps for further investigation. The depth of snow had changed between October and November, but many of the same areas were photographed. We hoped that any significant differences between the images might indicate human activity.

I sent potential clues—such as images of unusually shaped objects— to John, a volunteer in Abbotsford, British Columbia, and he would check out the clues on the ground himself. John had been one of our most dedicated volunteers right from the start of our search in October. He was an avid outdoorsman and a highly experienced mountain climber and hunter. I would form a close friendship with and deep admiration for John over the coming months.

The volunteers identified many promising clues. In more remote areas where John was unable to search, we would hire a private search company and helicopter to check the locations on the ground. However, these search efforts were costly, ranging up to about ten thousand dollars per day. So we checked the imagery very closely to ensure that the clues were substantial before we arranged a helicopter and search team.

We also supplemented the ground searches with periodic drone searches near the areas of promising heatmap clues, particularly around the slopes of Windy Joe Mountain. We hired Hummingbird Drones again in early December to perform a sweep of some larger areas. If promising images were found, Hummingbird Drones was sent back to do a more thorough sweep or else we hired a private search group with a helicopter to check more carefully on the ground.

We wanted these searchers to look thoroughly—not only near the GPS coordinates, but also beyond them into the surrounding areas. If Jordan had been there and moved on, we hoped they might find signs of human activity. To my disappointment, they were only willing—because of the extent of the snow cover—to go to the specific GPS point on the hillside, and not also search the surrounding area.

This was hard to accept. It seemed to us like their approach was losing us both precious time and important opportunities. We did not want to chance missing critical information within our grasp that may have been just beyond the GPS point. I wanted them to search an area of about fifty metres in all directions around the specific coordinates, to offset the uncertainty inherent in GPS mapping. Coordinates are subject to error when they are translated from one map to another and georeferenced from imagery. We felt that even though the ground was now snow-covered, if Jordan had died, then animals would have torn at his body and clothing, which may have created clues in the form of unusual colours in the surrounding area or branches among trees.

I was frustrated that the private search company wouldn't search more extensively—I felt that they had given up on Jordan. I remember thinking: If you had lost your son in this way, would you give up? I was not going to give up.

In drone video footage that had been taken on October 25, volunteers spotted a previously unidentified clue that looked particularly promising. Some images appeared to show a person moving off-trail on aWindy Joe Mountain hillside. We examined the footage carefully many times to confirm it was a person. It seemed highly unusual that anyone would be wandering around steep terrain off-trail on the mountain in the snow. The figure appeared to be wearing dark clothing and a red backpack or jacket.

During a few seconds of the video, we thought we could make out a person facing away from the camera toward a tree. We studied the image carefully but could not definitively conclude it was a person. We had already mistakenly identified a person when looking at other images—it was as if our eyes were helping us see what we wanted to see. But when imagined human shapes were viewed in relation to the surroundings, relative size often confirmed that what had seemed promising was actually a stump or an unusual pattern of fallen trees, and not a human at all.

We knew, too, there had been searchers near this particular location on October 25, so this new "clue" could have been one of them. My brother Marko and friends Ed, Greg, and Roger had come from Ontario in late October to help us look for Jordan, and they had searched areas off-trail on Windy Joe Mountain on that day. But we didn't have GPS coordinates to confirm their exact locations. We also knew they had searched in two groups of two and always stayed close together. It seemed unlikely that the image was one of the searchers, because the suspected person was moving alone with no one else nearby.

In general, we always looked for footprints in the imagery. But, oddly, when the figure in this imagery "walked" away from the camera, there were no visible footprints in the snow. Nevertheless, we called the private search company and a helicopter and asked them to search the area around the GPS coordinates. Mountain climbers also searched on the ground for any evidence of human activity and found none. But it was unclear to us how thoroughly the surrounding area was searched, so this clue remained an unresolved mystery.

Although most witness reports were logged in October, additional new information continued to arrive after we returned to St. John's, either directly or indirectly through volunteers or other channels. Volunteers continued to connect online with hikers who had been in Manning Park that Thanksgiving weekend. They searched social media sites and any other conceivable sources for even the smallest of possible clues about where Jordan had gone, what had happened, and where he might be found.

Some hikers also responded to the Missing Person posters that had been circulated in Princeton, Hope, and other communities near the park. People contacted us with information from hiking apps online. We were particularly interested in information from people who had been hiking between October 10 and 12. We carefully scrutinized and cross-referenced their information against other records to see if the new information enhanced our overall understanding or conflicted with other reports.

We also had more time available to thoroughly analyze the reports and cross-reference them against each other while searching imagery in December and January. During these winter months in St. John's, we examined each piece of information in more depth than we had previously been able to in October. We also studied how weather reports may have influenced Jordan's decision-making and observations in the aerial imagery.

One of our earliest reports had come from a hiker named Jody. At about 8:30 a.m. on Saturday, October 10, she and two others in a group started up the Frosty Mountain trail, reaching the Larches at about 12:30. Jody remembered seeing four groups of campers at the Frosty campsite on her way back down the trail. Some were packing up to descend as well, while others were hiking up to the summit. She did not recall seeing anyone who matched Jordan's description. This gave us specific times and places where Jordan had *not* been.

Another report came from Josh, a solo hiker on October 10. Between about 9:00 a.m. and 2:00 p.m., he had hiked to the summit of Frosty Mountain and returned to the parking lot. He reported that snow had been falling hard at higher elevations, on and off around 12:30 and then consistently in the early afternoon. As he'd gotten closer to the parking lot again, the snow had changed to rain. Josh had passed through the Frosty campsite between 10:30 and 11:00 on his way up and remembered only one group there, who had been packing up at the time. Other hikers also reported a large amount of snow past the Frosty campsite on Saturday.

Solo hiker Matthew spent the night of Friday, October 9, at the Frosty campsite. On Saturday morning, he reached the summit at about 10:00 a.m., returning to the campsite about fifteen minutes before noon. He packed up his tent and continued down the trail to reach the parking lot by 1:55. He did not remember seeing any sign of Jordan or his black Honda Civic.

As previously mentioned, fifteen-year-old Ethan Morf was the only person who reported seeing a young man who matched Jordan's description. Ethan reported that on their hike, it had begun to snow heavily on the Frosty Mountain trail around 3:00 p.m. This suggested that, if it had been Jordan that Ethan had seen, they had met somewhere between the second switchback and the Frosty campsite while Jordan was heading *up* the Frosty Mountain trail. It had started to heavily snow soon after Jordan passed the boy and his father.

Vincent was another key witness who had hiked that Saturday. He had hiked down the Frosty Mountain trail and returned to the parking lot around 4:00 p.m. He reported that conditions at the top of the mountain near the summit had been extreme—very snowy and gusty.

Similarly, Ricky, who spent Saturday and Sunday in the park, reported that the storm had not let up on the 10th. According to him, it snowed from the summit right down to the lake. At 8:56 a.m. on Sunday, Ricky had taken a photo of the Lightning Lake parking lot. In it, Jordan's black Honda Civic was parked beside a white Subaru owned by a hiker named Geneva. Neither Ricky nor the two people hiking with him recalled seeing Jordan.

Ryan, who also hiked on Saturday, said that he had been caught in a snowstorm while on the trail and felt he could not climb to the summit of Frosty Mountain. Tristan, another solo hiker, noted how snow on the ground made her lose the trail that day. She hiked to the campsite and made the woodshed. But she lost the trail before the summit because it was covered by snow. She eventually found her way back to the path on her descent. These reports suggested that something went wrong for Jordan due to the unexpected snowstorm on Saturday afternoon, probably at a higher elevation.

Unfortunately, we had no witness testimonials from hikers who took the Windy Joe Mountain trail or its connector trail toward the Frosty Mountain summit on Saturday afternoon. Nor were there any reports that could corroborate the cellphone pings that placed Jordan closer to Windy Joe Mountain shortly after noon on Saturday. So, given the difficulty of ignoring what the technology told us, we kept both scenarios—that Jordan had either hiked clockwise or counter-clockwise around the Frosty Mountain trail loop—under consideration in our search strategies.

We leaned toward thinking that, if an accident had occurred, it probably had happened on Saturday. Knowing about the camping gear and clothing that Jordan had bought, we felt he was well prepared for overnight camping in sub-zero temperatures. We analyzed all the witness reports for the following day, Sunday, looking for clues that would lead us to him.

Rosalie hiked the Frosty Mountain trail on Sunday, from roughly 9:00 a.m. until 2:00 p.m., and climbed all the way to the summit. She was fairly certain that there were a couple of people ahead of her on the trail, including a group that was packing up their camp at the Frosty campsite. Ariadne, who had also hiked that day, reported no tents at the Frosty campsite on Sunday afternoon. She likely hiked past the campsite later than Rosalie.

Alexandra hiked the Frosty Mountain trail between 9:40 a.m. and 5:00 p.m. on Sunday. She remembered a large group led by a staff member from the resort. There were about twenty people in that group. Three men passed her on their way down the trail. They mentioned that they had camped overnight.

Kos sent us a detailed report about the trail conditions on Sunday. He and his group had started their hike that day around 9:30 a.m. The snow and slippery sections began about seven kilometres beyond the Frosty Mountain trailhead sign. At about the eight-kilometre mark, which they reached at around 2:00 p.m., a snowstorm hit. They continued to the summit, but on their way down they found their route covered with snow and very slippery. When they reached the Frosty campsite, they saw two other groups they didn't recognize, who had set up their tents for an overnight stay. They had no cell coverage in the area (their phones used the Fido and Freedom networks).

Nikolai and the three other people with him had decided to shorten their hike on the Frosty Mountain trail on Sunday because of the snow conditions. They waited in their car for two and a half hours (until 6:30 p.m.) for two of their friends to finish their hike. They could not recall seeing Jordan's car, as it was snowing with poor visibility. They did recall seeing three groups of hikers at the campsite earlier in the day.

Another witness, Konstantinos, reported seeing a group at a higher elevation than the Frosty campsite on Sunday afternoon. They told him they would camp overnight and hike to the summit the following day, Monday.

Still another witness, Alex, was on the trail between 9:40 a.m. and 5:00 p.m. on Sunday. Alex hiked to the edge of the Larches and decided not to summit because of the poor weather conditions and visibility. In his opinion, the only way for hikers not to have seen Jordan (if he had been hiking that Sunday) would have been if he had diverted off the trail or, if at the top of the mountain, he'd taken the alternate route down.

Alternate route? Alex's report was the first I'd heard about an alternative route down from the summit of Frosty Mountain. It introduced new, possibly treacherous, areas west of the summit that would need to be searched, including drainage basins that had not been covered by the SAR teams.

Like the others who had been hiking on Sunday, Alex also reported that it had snowed all Sunday afternoon. He remembered one solo male hiker: young with long hair, wearing jeans. We determined this wasn't Jordan. This hiker passed Alex on the way up and again on the way down the Frosty Mountain trail. A group of three male hikers also passed Alex on their way down.

Tabitha and Ryan reported that on their hike on the Lightning Lake trail on Sunday, which they traversed between 1:00 and 6:30 p.m., once past the lake itself, they saw no one except a group of six mountain bikers travelling together (whom we were never able to make contact with).

One hiker posted on social media about hiking with a group in a clockwise loop of the Frosty Mountain trail on Sunday, starting up Windy Joe Mountain. They reported seeing no shelters on the route but heard a loud sound about three or three and a half kilometres from the trailhead. They described it as like a falling boulder smashing into a tree, somewhere down the mountain northeast of the Windy Joe Mountain summit. Could this have been Jordan trapped on a ledge in the mountain, trying to send a signal?

Fewer people hiked the Manning Park trails on the last day of that Thanksgiving weekend, Monday, October 12. Nonetheless, it was a critical day for us to collect more information about trail conditions. We were fortunate to get reports from several hikers.

Allison hiked the Frosty Mountain trail on Monday, beginning in the late morning and finishing around 7:00 p.m. She recalled that sometime before 5:30 p.m., her group stopped at the Frosty campsite.

It was already dark. There was one man inside the cabin, but she couldn't recall what he was wearing. There was also a couple at the campsite—both people were tall and wearing red; they stayed longer than Allison's group.

Another hiker, Anna, was on the Frosty Mountain trail with her partner on Monday. She also recalled a solo male hiker in the shelter of the Frosty campsite. They remembered his hair was brown and he was about 170 to 175 centimetres tall. He had collected water for heating food with a camping stove inside the shelter. They also remembered that he had a beard at least a few days old. Several aspects of this report were consistent with Jordan's appearance: hair colour, height, specific brand of camping stove, and a few-days-old beard. However, several other people who fit the same description had also passed through the campsite over those few days. It could have been Jordan—if he had arrived there on Monday after camping out elsewhere (for instance, at Monument 78)—although we felt it was unlikely that Jordan would have gone unnoticed at the campsite.

Mike G described the ground conditions on Monday past the Frosty campsite toward the summit, as well as the hiking conditions in areas through the forest up to the Larches and the boulder field near the top of Frosty Mountain. It would be particularly easy to lose the trail in the boulder field, he explained, because there are only occasional spray-painted markers on a few rocks to guide hikers.

Suman provided a similar description of Monday's conditions between the Frosty Mountain trailhead and the summit (but in the opposite—counter-clockwise—direction of the loop). He noted that the last one-and-a-half-kilometre stretch prior to the summit was noticeably steeper.

A narrow ledge with a stunning view of the surrounding mountains connects the first and second peaks of Frosty Mountain. There is a wind shelter between the two peaks where hikers can rest and eat lunch. Suman mentioned that for anyone with a fear of heights, this route is not a good choice. And very windy conditions were reported at the top that day. Suman provided our first account of conditions near the summit, although he was not able to provide any details of surrounding features of the terrain or peculiar observations.

There were many other observations and details that didn't seem to have any bearing on Jordon's whereabouts. One person saw a red-and-white tent tucked inside the emergency shelter high on the Frosty Mountain trail, for example. But that description didn't match any of Jordan's known camping gear.

A hiker named Lewis reported seeing a few people coming down with big backpacks on Monday, but no one was wearing a jacket matching Jordan's. Lewis also noted that he passed people nearly every fifteen minutes. His group saw three or four other groups on the way down, as well as a young man running past the Larches. As dusk descended around 5:45 p.m., he passed the campsite and remembered a young man inside a little tent in a camping area.

Another hiker, Mel, said he noticed four solo hikers separately but was not sure if any of them was Jordan.[6]

Kristin reported that when her group reached the summit on Monday, she could see snow cornices developing along the ridge. Because of these potentially dangerous formations, they didn't hike all the way to the summit. She reported that the snow was knee-deep on the upper half of the hike and observed that many switchbacks and false trails could deceive hikers, some of which just led down to gullies and drainage basins.

Aside from Ethan Morf's report, none of the witness testimonials from Saturday to Monday seemed to suggest anyone had specifically seen Jordan. But they did paint a consistent picture: An unexpected

---

6   Some people wondered why Jordan hiked alone. We felt his decision to do so was neither uncommon nor unusual. We believed he was simply looking for quiet and peace by himself in the beautiful surroundings of the Larches.

and severe snowstorm on Saturday afternoon had brought poor visibility. This would have made it easy to lose the Frosty Mountain trail in the snow somewhere between the initial switchbacks and the summit. It was reasonable to assume the same would be true had Jordan hiked in a clockwise loop, starting up Windy Joe Mountain.

With each report—especially those that stressed the severity of the snowstorm—I kept imagining Jordan's predicament, which left me emotionally drained. Even when he realized that he'd lost the trail in the snow, it may have been impossible to correctly backtrack, since his footprints would have been already covered with more snowfall. I felt Jordan's panic and despair, imagining those moments, and my heart ached.

Although snow cover made searching exceedingly difficult from December onward, our team of dedicated volunteers was determined to continue. Josie reiterated many times to the media that we were not going to give up. We knew in our hearts that we would find Jordan and bring him home.

Countless scenarios about what had happened to Jordan were still possible. Some were more likely than others, but due to the lack of definitive evidence, it still seemed that Jordan could have become lost anywhere in Manning Park or even south of the international border. The witness reports were mostly focused on the Frosty and Windy Joe Mountain trails—but what did it mean that Jordan had searched online so many times for Monument 78? We felt more attention was required in that area.

In December, a new volunteer, "Claire," became more actively engaged in the search process. I first became aware of her involvement when she volunteered to help inform American authorities about the possibility of Jordan's disappearance south of the border near the Monument 78 campsite. She had learned about our search for Jordan through social media and presented herself as a compassionate, caring individual who was sincerely trying to help out.

Claire offered to place posters in communities on both the Canadian and US sides of the border near the Monument 78 campsite. She asked for payment to print posters and we were happy to cover those costs.

Normally, I am careful about who I trust. I want to know a person well before trusting them with important responsibilities. But working from St. John's, it was difficult to confirm to what extent any of the volunteers were actually helping on the ground at Manning Park. We decided to trust Claire enough to make payments and grant her administrative access to our online files.

Perhaps the outpouring of sincere help from so many volunteers, particularly Newfoundlanders, coloured my judgment—not to mention that these were not normal circumstances and time was working against us. It was unimaginable to us, despite the nefarious erasing of the hard drive earlier, that anyone else would take advantage of our vulnerability.

I would soon discover this was not how the world works.

Our contracted private searches were costly, especially the days involving a helicopter. So we had limited funds to pay volunteers for their expenses. People came to the park to take drone footage without our knowledge and then afterwards asked for payment in exchange for the footage. We were warned by our friends Keira and Tom to be careful about fraudsters who take advantage of people in a crisis situation.

Online fundraising for SAR efforts can yield great benefits. It can secure resources to extend the searching and it spreads the word about a missing person. What we did not know before this happened to us, however, is that it also carries risks. It can attract people who show up specifically to take advantage of a situation for their own personal gain.

Over time, we developed a trustful relationship with our most dedicated volunteers in British Columbia. They were the ones on the ground who warned us about suspicious individuals on the team. Their trusted advice became critical for dealing with the fraud attempts that began to unfold.

Unfortunately, Claire was a case in point. Over time, her messages to us became increasingly disrespectful of other volunteers. Her behaviour became unprofessional when she dealt with people who expressed opinions different from hers about where to prioritize our searches. Soon, prominent volunteers began to leave the search effort because of Claire. Others warned us that she was a fraudster and trying to scam us. Her requests for payments for posters increased and became more expensive. Then she recommended that a friend of hers should investigate possible foul play—provided we make further payments.

Claire told us what she did for a living, but other volunteers who worked in the same profession reported that the information was inaccurate. It gradually became clear that Claire's motives for engaging with us were probably not transparent.

When we began to suspect something was suspicious about her behaviour, she backtracked to make a more positive impression. In early December, after Claire had stirred up a conflict among the volunteers, Josie suspected that she had texted as someone impersonating another volunteer to smooth over the situation and regain our trust.

We learned that technology exists to send impersonated messages from illegitimate phone numbers. We suspected that Claire (or someone associated with her) was sending us messages through false phone numbers.

When these dishonest manoeuvres continued throughout December, for the sake of maintaining our group of volunteers and returning our focus to finding Jordan, we decided to disconnect Claire's administrative access to our shared folders. She had previously told us that the search was causing her stress, so we tried being diplomatic and suggested that she take a step back, at least temporarily.

She had previously committed to travel to Manning Park for the upcoming New Year's weekend to help search for Jordan. She expected reimbursement for her expenses. When a major storm dumped more than a hundred centimetres of snow on Manning Park on December 31, we urged her not to go. To our surprise, she travelled to the park anyway and took a room. Then, around midnight our time, she sent us a series of disturbing emails to make our own New Year's Eve go from bad to worse.

Claire explained how she had been crying all morning because we'd disconnected her administrative access to our online accounts. She also claimed that one of the volunteers was sending threatening emails to her, for which she blamed us. And then she threatened us: We would be liable for covering her lost salary, she said, if she was dismissed from her job for travelling to Manning Park during the pandemic to search for Jordan.

And that wasn't all. She wrote that the loss of her administrative access to our accounts made her so upset and ill that she required emergency services at a nearby hospital (from where she claimed to be writing). In her view, despite all of her help to find Jordan, we had betrayed her by restricting her administrative access to our accounts.

It was a brutal note—but we were skeptical about many of its points. We called the front desk at the Manning Park Resort to see if anyone was in Claire's room (which we were partially paying for). A staff member knocked on her door and, when it opened, could clearly see that Claire and others were gathered in the room.

That report erased all remaining doubts. We were indeed being scammed. Not only were we devastated by Jordan's disappearance, but now we would have to deal with a (vengeful, as it turned out) fraudster who had infiltrated our team.

We never determined if Claire realized that we had checked on her at the resort. We did contact the police in Vancouver and St. John's and explained our situation. They recommended a no-contact order. We informed Claire and hoped communication from her would stop.

But Claire would find other devious ways to burden and deceive us in the coming months.

Claire's actions added more stress on our beleaguered family and distracted us from our search for Jordan. Our now heightened awareness of fraudsters led Josie to deactivate the existing social media group and reopen another site shared only with a much smaller, trusted group of volunteers. We became much more careful about who we welcomed into the group.

———

In December, we encountered another peculiar character who made surprising commitments to search from Ross Lake through selected drainages to Windy Joe Mountain. We felt grateful but, because his promises didn't seem physically possible, I remained skeptical.

This man told Josie that he had past experience as a survivalist in the wilderness. But my radar went off when I heard that he had asked a volunteer if there was much snow at Manning Park at the time—an odd question in December for an experienced survivalist from that area.

Given our desperation to find Jordan, we were then pulled into an (unrealistic) promise: He would search over Windy Joe Mountain with his own human-powered helicopter. Some volunteers thought this was actually possible. We were told he had received permission from park authorities, so we went along with the idea.

But the helicopter search didn't happen. Being in Newfoundland, we didn't know if this man had actually arrived in the park or not. After a few weeks of bold promises, he disappeared from the effort and we never heard from him again.

———

On December 10, based on some heatmap clues, a group of five volunteers, led by Mike B, searched on Windy Joe Mountain, specifically areas south and southeast of the summit, covering about twenty-seven kilometres. In the morning, another volunteer, Sheila, forwarded them some drone imagery that showed a human figure off-trail. It looked like a person wearing black and some sort of cape. But the team found nothing there. We concluded the heatmap clues were just unusual colours on fallen trees.

It was now winter and the snow had arrived to stay in the park. The private companies were no longer willing to help us search for Jordan. Eventually I realized that if I wanted the ground to be more thoroughly searched, I would have to go myself and search. There were too many significant clues accumulating from the heatmaps that could not be left unchecked.

It was also becoming more and more unbearable to stay at home in St. John's when numerous images were being flagged with places to check but there was nobody on the ground to do the follow-up searching. Despite the time of year and the deep snow we knew would blanket the park for months to come—and after discussing the situation at length with my family—I decided that I must return to Manning Park.

Josie and I kept our plans confidential, at least initially. We were concerned about backlash from some volunteers who were searching online imagery but felt that we should wait until the snow disappeared (June or July) before continuing to look on the ground. And there would be other naysayers, we knew. But this was a personal decision. How does anyone know what they would do until they find themselves in such a situation? What if they still had a hope, as I did, that somehow a miracle was possible? People lost in the wilderness *have* survived for months, even during the winter—Jordan might be one of them.

Waiting until June felt unbearable to me. Unless I searched every square metre of Manning Park myself, I would always feel like I had given up.

I knew, as some of the naysayers did not, that winter snowshoeing was common at Manning Park. I had confirmed with Trevor, a volunteer who worked in the park, that the Windy Joe Mountain, Frosty Mountain, and Lightning Lake trails were popular with snowshoers throughout the winter. I'd also learned that cross-country skiers go up the same trails, but often return off-trail down one or more of the mountains.

Once my decision started to become more widely known, a very kind-hearted couple, Lynn and Stan, offered to let me stay in their cabin in Eastgate, a small community about a ten-minute drive east of Manning Park. Lynn and Stan lived in Vancouver and visited their cabin periodically, so I would stay there mostly alone.

I booked my ticket for February 14.

three

INDIGENOUS REVELATION IN FEBRUARY

Trees are sanctuaries. Whoever knows how to speak to them, whoever knows how to listen to them, can learn the truth. They do not preach learning and precepts, they preach, undeterred by particulars, the ancient law of life ... Trees have long thoughts, long-breathing and restful, just as they have longer lives than ours.

—HESSE, 2014

MANNING PARK WAS NAMED IN MEMORY OF ERNEST Callaway Manning, the Chief Forester of British Columbia between 1936 and 1941. During his time as Chief Forester, Manning helped develop the idea of setting land aside for future generations to enjoy. Four provincial parks—Tweedsmuir, Hamber, Wells Gray, and E.C. Manning—were created through the combined efforts of Manning and Arthur Wellesley Gray, the Minister of Lands. Over the years, Manning Park decreased in size, most noticeably at the park's eastern boundary.

Manning Park has stunning mountains and carpets of forest. It protects an awesome natural landscape. But it was also a cruel opponent in our search for Jordan. I often felt both awed by the vastness of its unbroken forest and fearful of its power.

Upon the resumption of ground searches in February, Mike B became a key volunteer. Previously, he had visited us at our cabin in October and periodically helped with ground searches during that time. With his military background, Mike had valuable logistical knowledge on search strategies and interactions with police authorities. He also suggested that I reach out to the Upper Similkameen Indian Band and seek a blessing for safe passage through their land.[7]

Josie followed up and contacted Mike A, a Band council member and Indigenous community leader from Hedley, a small town about an hour east of Eastgate.

In the Okanagan traditions, Siwɬkʷ and Tmxʷulaxʷ are treated with utmost reverence. As I learned from Mike A—and also through reading *The Seven Sacred Teachings of White Buffalo Calf Woman*—Siwɬkʷ is the lifeblood that connects Tmxʷulaxʷ with animals and humans. The Syilx word Tmxʷulaxʷ refers to sacred life and forces that encompass the spirit of the natural world that represents all life forms and their relationships with each other.

Learning more about the local Indigenous traditions after I came

---

7   In 2014, the Band had endorsed a *Siwɬkʷ Declaration*. It stated: "The Okanagan People have accepted the unique responsibility bestowed upon us by the Creator (Ḱʷuləncútn) to serve for all time as protectors of the lands (Tmxʷulaxʷ) and water (Siwɬkʷ) in our territories, so that all living things return to us regenerated. When we take care of the land and water, the land and water take care of us."

back to Manning Park in February—and then spending so much time in the forested mountainsides in the park—changed my perspectives on and appreciation of nature. Instead of considering what I saw around me in terms of taxonomy and plant names, I began to see them more in terms of revered Indigenous concepts, expressed through a word that I couldn't even pronounce correctly. I came to *believe* in a nature spirit.

Before Jordan was lost, I had suspected that a nature spirit existed and I admired it, but I didn't fully appreciate its dynamic character as a living protector of the land. Once I began to comprehend the active role of this nature spirit, I increasingly came to adopt more Indigenous ways of thinking about it. As the weeks went on, my understanding of and relationship with Tmxʷulaxʷ would evolve in unexpected ways.

I felt inadequate and apologetic for the ways by which I, as a non-Indigenous person, expressed Indigenous beliefs. In my limited and incomplete understanding, I was unaware of how the nature spirit connects all forms of life in the forest. It has its own language, which it uses to communicate with trees and animals. I also learned from Victorino Saway's writing that, for Indigenous people, the forest has a range of purposes—it is an area of worship, a market, a pharmacy, and a shelter, among many others.

I often prayed and meditated while searching in the forest, asking for help in any form—even something as small as a random thought—anything that would point me in a direction leading to useful information. During these quiet times, I began to inwardly converse with Tmxʷulaxʷ about Jordan. I slowly gained an unexplainable sense of the nature spirit's personality and moods. And I began to recognize that each mountain and drainage basin had its own character. Some were compassionate, forgiving, and helpful; others were unwelcoming, deceitful, or even malicious.

Initially, I felt that Tmxʷulaxʷ was an adversary. I felt that the nature spirit knew what had happened to Jordan and I very badly wanted it to share that information with me. I would urge Tmxʷulaxʷ to reveal its secrets about Jordan. I thought that I deserved an answer about what had happened. Over time, I developed a more stoical attitude, even one of reverence.

I believed that Tmxʷulaxʷ was able to communicate with me. Peter Wohlleben's fascinating *The Hidden Life of Trees* explained how trees are social beings that work together. They share and nourish each other in ways similar to human communities. There were hidden signals in the forest that I continually tried to decipher.

I grew to feel more deeply connected to nature—that nature was part of me and I was a part of nature. I recognized, too, that I was only a small part of nature—a junior partner in my relationship with Tmxʷulaxʷ. I became ever more curious about other Indigenous cultural beliefs, thoughts, and practices related to nature and wildlife.

Rereading *Aesop's Fables* reminded me that philosophies and stories about nature are ancient. They guided my own thought processes. Oliver Luke Delorie's book on forest bathing explained the ancient Japanese beliefs of Shinrin-yoku. The concept looked to nature in a healing way for comfort in times of grief.

Deepening my intellectual understanding of such practices was useful, but as I spent more time searching in the forest, I felt an inner transition—less thinking and more experiencing, living, and feeling. My hiking partners also shared their own philosophies about nature, mountains, and wildlife. They, too, added to my understanding of the forest. I hoped that all of these new ways of thinking and understanding would guide me on the path toward Jordan.

———

Jordan's UBC friends had stored his car in Vancouver. I picked it up when I arrived, drove to the cabin, and began settling in. Eastgate is mostly a summer community, so there were only a few neighbours nearby in February. Lynn and Stan introduced me to a few of them.

Their kindness and generosity helped me keep a positive mental and physical state despite the darkest of circumstances.

It didn't take me long to realize the full extent of the daunting task ahead. How could I, with little prior winter mountaineering experience, search such an enormous area of mountain wilderness? Most of the volunteers who had done ground searching earlier had stepped back from taking on snowshoeing at Manning Park.

Fortunately, two extraordinary individuals, John and Trevor, agreed to go out with me regularly on my searches until Jordan was found. I had met both men for the first time in October. Each was an experienced mountaineer. I would not have been able to search off-trail without partners like them.

John lived in Abbotsford, a few hours west of the park. Although he had a family and demanding full-time job, he committed to come out every weekend, Saturday and/or Sunday, until Jordan was found. He had hiked the park solo from the start in early October, and had kept it up throughout the winter, often in the most difficult terrain. We had remained in contact after I had returned to St. John's in November. Now, in early February, he committed to stay the course with me until Jordan was found. I had never imagined anyone would be so generous and unwavering in their support to help us find our son.

Trevor was an award-winning employee at Manning Park. With his kind-hearted and caring demeanour, I could understand quickly why he deserved such recognition. Trevor used his vacation time and managed to get other time off from work to search a few days each week with me. He was deeply moved by Jordan's disappearance. Trevor was about the same age as Jordan, and like my son, loved the peace and serenity of nature. His companionship on our hikes together continually reminded me of Jordan.

John and Trevor's commitment meant I could search three or four days a week with a steady and trustworthy partner. This was more than just fortunate—it was a godsend. I could not have gone out searching in the winter without them, particularly in the most critical off-trail areas. I had no previous experience with off-trail hiking or snowshoeing in mountainous terrain nor how to search for a missing person in such conditions. They taught me how to navigate the difficult topography and search in the forests of Manning Park.

Josie was able to arrange another one or two volunteers to go with me every week. On days where no partner was available, I restricted my searches to only safe on-trail locations.

On Tuesday, February 16, John arranged a day off work to go snowshoeing with me—the first of many days together to come. We snowshoed around Lightning Lake and then went off-trail between Lightning Lake and Flash Lake. Previously I exercised regularly, but the muscles and joints used in mountain snowshoeing are entirely different than those used in treadmilling and weightlifting. My pace was slow and my stamina was low. It took me several weeks (truthfully, months) to build an endurance level that could keep pace with John's.

A bird swooped down in front of us. I had been feeling Jordan's presence, so the motion of the bird in the woods, and the forest itself, became charged with memories of Jordan. I remembered an episode from when Jordan was about ten and in Grade 5. On his return home from school one day, Josie had asked how his day was. Jordan said he was sad and told her how he'd started out excited because he had money to buy a hot dog for lunch. He sat on a bench to eat with a friend, put the hot dog down for a moment, and turned away. A gull quickly swooped in and snatched it. It upset him and he threw his hat at the bird as it flew away.

The snow on the Lightning Lake trail had been packed down by other hikers. Gauging by the amount of snow piled on Rainbow Bridge, which crossed Lightning Lake, we estimated there were two to three metres of snow on the ground (a snow probe later confirmed it was nearly three). This depth of snow would last until May in most areas of the park and posed a continual risk of sinking deeply when we were snowshoeing off-trail, especially around snow-covered waterways, holes, or tree downfall or blowdown.

My first experience with the hazards of off-trail snowshoeing came when John and I detoured off the Lightning Lake trail toward Flash Lake. At first I found it unnerving to go into the forest in the deep snow. But I entirely trusted John as a hiking partner. With more than three decades of mountaineering and snowshoeing experience, he was the best person to teach me safe off-trail snowshoeing techniques.

As we crossed over some fallen trees, I stepped into a sinkhole. Suddenly I was in snow up to my hips. I had sunk about a metre and one of my legs had got caught amongst buried tree branches and plunged into the water below. Whenever I tried to move my legs, I sank deeper. Then one of my snowshoes became stuck under the branches.

I felt panic, but John remained calm. He urged me to be calm, too, and told me how to move my body and legs to stabilize my position. Following his directions, I twisted and leaned back while he used his poles to clear the snow away from my leg. Then we scooped more snow away with our hands. Soon, I had a little room to manoeuvre. With John's help, I was eventually able to lean back far enough in the snow to gain stability and pull myself out.

Despite my wet sock and boot, we continued on, as per our plan. I learned that day the importance of packing extra socks (and gloves and a hat). Although it was uncomfortable in wet boots, once we regained the trail, the terrain was relatively easy and we finished the remainder of our route.

The encounter with the sinkhole was unnerving, but it was also a valuable first lesson on how and where to place my feet, each and every step. When trees fall in the forest, there are often gaps beneath the trunks and the ground. Once these trees are covered by snow, stepping on or near such gaps is hazardous, especially if the trees lie over water, rather than rock or frozen earth. The gaps usually extend about a metre on either side of a fallen tree. I soon learned how to predict where such sinkholes would occur by the alignment of the trees on the ground.

On February 16, I had quickly learned how weak footing can be created and obscured by tree downfall. Knowing I would have experienced partners at my side, such hazards could not deter me from my goal of finding Jordan.

On February 17, I reconnected with Trevor. Since the first days of our search, he had been immensely helpful, including by providing valuable insight into topographical features across the park. Between October and December, he had hiked off-trail into difficult and inaccessible areas where other searchers were unable or unwilling to go.

Our first hike together on that day in February took in outlying areas of the park, where volunteers had speculated there might be abandoned private cabins that could have provided Jordan with shelter. The first area was several kilometres east of the Monument 83 trail, which we felt Jordan could have taken, either by mistake or because he was seeking a way off the mountain.

We searched near the Blowdown Picnic Area, a five-minute drive east of Manning Park Resort, and then in Sumallo Grove, about a twenty-minute drive in the other direction. The terrain south of the Blowdown Picnic Area was covered by dense forest, and deep in snow. We often sank to our knees in the snow as we searched there. After a few hours of covering the area side-by-side and a few metres apart, we found no sign of any cabin.

When there on the ground, it was difficult to imagine how Jordan could have reached the Monument 83 trail—it would have required him to pass over several other trails east of Windy Joe Mountain. It seemed unlikely that he would have crossed those gaps and continued eastward rather than heading north or south along other trail openings in the forest (which he would have assumed or known would take him in the right direction). We decided to move this area farther down our list of search priorities.

In the afternoon, we shifted our efforts to Sumallo Grove, at the far northwest edge of Manning Park. We kept track of the area we covered using GPS. My unit could show and record our positions, as well as trail locations and previous searches, in separate files. After snowshoeing a few hours along the Skagit River trail, we noticed something unusual some distance off the trail. It appeared to be a sharp edge protruding out of the snow. We approached cautiously.

"Trevor, it appears to be an old truck. It's buried deep."

We approached closer and were shocked to see not just the remnants of an old truck but also a stone-walled cabin.

"I can see through the roof," Trevor said as he got closer. "There's a pile of broken wood inside, along a dirt wall."

It appeared as if the roof of the structure had collapsed inward. But we saw nothing inside except broken material from the roof and walls.

Discovering an old cabin was uplifting—it indicated there were possibilities for shelter, on which Jordan's survival would have depended. We thoroughly searched the area and found no evidence of any recent human presence there, however. I realized that any chance of finding traces of Jordan in this spot were remote at best.

Farther along the Sumallo Grove trail, we reached a waterfall covered in icicles and snow. There was a hole in the cliff beside it, about two metres high and covered by wood—apparently an abandoned mining shaft. We could make out its shiny brown walls leading into darkness. But here, too, there were no signs of human activity.

Trevor offered to go inside and have a look. I had reservations but gave him my cellphone and he squeezed into the shaft and moved farther into the tunnel. He crawled and searched for some time, finally returning back safely. He'd seen nothing promising, but also had not reached the end of the tunnel. We were both encouraged to learn that abandoned mining shafts existed in the park. These, too, represented possible shelters for survival (and explained the truck's presence). We estimated that, by the age of the truck, mining operations had been conducted in the area about six or seven decades earlier. We speculated about other mine shaft entry points closer to the resort.

Continuing on a little farther, we soon noticed another unusual object off-trail and deep in the forest—a small spot of unnatural colour. We snowshoed through dense tree cover toward it. As we got closer, it took form as another abandoned cabin. This one had an outhouse and storage shed. One of its walls was demolished, mostly hidden by snowdrifts, but we found indications that the cabin had recently been occupied. On the lower floor, there were chairs, tables, and a refrigerator, while upstairs there were two small rooms. In the shed, some workshop tools appeared to have been recently used, perhaps within the past year.

Why would there be an abandoned cabin in such a remote and inaccessible area of dense forest? We had no answers but were even more encouraged—if we'd found two cabins in one day, perhaps there were others that Jordan might have discovered just when he needed one.

After returning to my own cabin each night, I often found various problems to be solved, many of them in my email inbox. Sometimes they were from volunteers saying they would come on a particular day (who might then not confirm or arrive, which spoiled the next day's plan).

New issues not encountered in the fall in Manning Park also appeared—but some old issues returned or were still unresolved. Jack was in the latter category. He had continued to contact us to offer assistance by advocating for additional helicopters and fixed-wing aircraft to search the park and collect aerial imagery. After our decision to stop communicating with him in October, we hadn't responded to his inquiries. But his influence, I learned in February, was still being felt.

During the fall, several staff members at Manning Park had kindly assisted us by joining volunteer search groups. When I returned in February, however, they seemed no longer to be able or willing to assist. As it turned out, because of Jack's involvement, staff employees had been told not to lend a hand. I learned that some of them were unhappy about it and helped search anyway.

Jordan's Missing Person poster had been displayed on the main front door of the resort restaurant in October and November. But it was no longer there when I returned in February. I was told it was because resort policies had changed. That upset me, but I kept my feelings to myself because I could not afford to jeopardize my working relationship with park staff. I hoped they would come to realize that a father searching for his lost son was not a threat to anyone in the resort or their business operations. (Park management may have been worried about losing business by posting "bad news," but in fact the opposite happened—so many volunteers came to help in the search, people who would not have otherwise come to Manning Park.)

Eventually, staff again allowed me to place Jordan's poster in the resort—on a benchtop around the corner from the resort restaurant door. Not a prominent location, but better than nothing. Soon that poster disappeared, too. It seemed to me as if someone was trying to erase the memory of Jordan's disappearance.

Deflated but not defeated, I planned another strategy. I knew that the kitchen staff were supportive and empathetic. One of them told me she had gotten lost in the park herself a few years earlier, but luckily found her way out after about three days in the wilderness. Other staff members were also kind to me. They discounted some meal costs, knowing my expenses were piling up with every day I searched for Jordan. So I asked one of the kitchen staff if she might watch over the benchtop to make sure that Jordan's poster remained. She kindly agreed and from that day forward, there were no longer any issues.

I remain sincerely grateful for those kind-hearted staff members in the kitchen of the Manning Park Resort, especially the young woman who watched over my son's poster. She put aside her own work pressures to keep alive the awareness of our ongoing search efforts.

———

There were many logistical challenges and preparations involved in the days when I hiked with new or occasional volunteers. Sometimes more than one person offered to volunteer on a particular day. I would have to ask if one of them could reschedule to a date when no one else had volunteered to come, to maximize the number of days I could go out with at least one hiking partner. Having someone hike with me was critical—it allowed me to search off-trail and in difficult areas, such as drainages and beneath cliffs, where I was not comfortable venturing alone.

Rather than discussing plans the night before over the phone with a new volunteer, we would meet in the parking lot early in the morning and go over what lay ahead. This was mainly because I was just too exhausted, physically and emotionally, to speak with volunteers at night. I would show them a map and explain the priorities for that day's hike. Usually, I gave them a couple of options, so they could choose the path that best matched their winter trekking ability.

———

Hiking days were typically very strenuous. The off-trail terrain would typically include dense forest across the mountains' flanks, water crossings, massive tree blowdown (including broken trunks or whole trees that had been uprooted by the wind), and steep-sided drainage basins, all covered in deep snow. I often needed rest days after such outings, both to recover and take care of housekeeping work, such as grocery shopping, which was normally done in Princeton, eighty kilometres away.

While learning more about snowshoeing from John during our hikes, I soon realized that my hiking gear and clothing were not appropriate for these rugged mountain outings. Mountaineering in the snow is hard physical work, and the body generates a lot of heat and sweat. A good approach is to wear several layers of clothing made of wool or synthetic material (and none made of cotton). On rest breaks or in cold or windy conditions, extra layers should be added. The base layer should be insulating and made of moisture-wicking material such as merino wool, the middle layer should be fleece, and the outer layer should be water- and windproof.

I also learned that the boots I had brought lacked adequate support—proper footwear is critical to support ankles and knees and help avoid injuries. Also, my coat was too heavy and my socks were not the right type. I needed new gear. Hope and Princeton were both about fifty minutes away by car (each in a different direction). I decided to wait for a few weeks, until I'd accumulated enough reasons to drive into Abbotsford—a larger centre that offered the right kind of shop, but about two hours away. Once I had better clothing and footwear, I was able to snowshoe faster and over longer distances.

––––––

Manning Park is in the North Cascades mountain range, whose slopes where we were searching generally rise at angles between 35 and 45 degrees. We often encountered steeper inclines, where we had to use extra caution or search indirectly (from the sides or bottom, for example, or by climbing by switchbacks up the slope). For the most challenging terrain, such as cliffs, we called in rock climbers. Many of the off-trail areas we were searching have bands of cliffs. Several areas on the east and south sides of Windy Joe Mountain, for example, have complex terrain and can only be accessed by rope by experienced rock climbers.

Although most areas we searched had steep terrain, a few trails were actually relatively flat. These included the Monument 78 and Lightning Lake trails. Major drainages often end in steep cliffs along the banks of the waterway that drain the area. So hikers following a waterway upriver sometimes need to ascend the drainage slopes to skirt cliffs. This treacherous landscape made many parts of our search areas, particularly within drainages, very difficult to thoroughly check.

To further complicate matters, although topographic maps and elevation contours displayed in GPS units show the overall features of the terrain, they do not fully capture micro-topography. Sudden gullies, or short, steep faces of a hillside, and other rapid elevation changes (such as cliffs) are generally smoothed out on such maps. The terrain of Manning Park is much more rugged than it appears on paper or a GPS screen. And this truth often affected our planned off-trail hikes, particularly around Windy Joe Mountain and Frosty Mountain. What seemed passable when we looked on a map and planned a route often had more difficult micro-features that prevented further progress in the desired direction, once we were on the ground.

I usually hiked five or six days a week. Each outing totalled about twenty kilometres on average. These were usually tough kilometres that were often off-trail in deep snow and involved elevation changes of six hundred or more metres. When hiking days were more than thirty kilometres long, I needed a rest day afterward.

Time management is key to effectively searching as much ground as possible in a day. In winter, the days are shorter and none of us could risk getting caught in the mountain wilderness in the dark. We established a careful plan with a defined turnaround time every day, to ensure that everyone arrived back at the parking lot before sunset.

Knowing how fast we could hike over different types of terrain fed directly into our choice of turnaround times and destinations. My own hiking speed varied from three to four kilometres an hour in unobstructed areas to as low as one kilometre (or less) in more difficult terrain. On steep ground, it could be only a few hundred metres an hour. Hiking on a trail was much faster than off-trail searches, but less useful because the trails had already been searched extensively.

I also learned about how different snow conditions affected snow-shoeing. When the top layer of snow cover is soft, the most effective way of hiking down a steep slope is to kick in the heel of your boot and avoid placing weight on your toes. This technique becomes more difficult when the snow cover is hard, icy, or crusty. In those conditions, it is safer to zigzag down (or up) a slope. When slopes became exceedingly steep, we either zigzagged up in switchbacks, if space allowed, or kicked our toes into the snow to create "stairs."

The trail to the Frosty Mountain summit has four sections: an initially steep ascent of about four kilometres in dense forest, followed by about three kilometres of relatively flat meadows leading to the Frosty campsite, then a moderate ascent to another plateau at the Larches over about two kilometres, and then a final steep ascent of about one kilometre up to the (lower) summit along a rocky ridge.

Elevation change was an important factor when planning and strategizing hikes. The climb from the base of Frosty Mountain at the parking lot to the summit covers about 1,200 metres of elevation change, from about 1,200 metres above sea level to 2,400 metres.

While I was getting my snow legs under me in British Columbia, Josie was busy in St. John's pursuing different ways to raise awareness about Jordan's disappearance in communities near the park. She contacted stores, churches, and community centres, asking if they would put up posters in prominent locations. These efforts definitely brought wider attention to our search.

I took my first rest day on February 18. My next search area, on February 19, was the Rein Orchid trail, a relatively short trail close to the resort that I had chosen because I didn't have a hiking partner on that day. It was useful terrain to check since it hadn't been searched by any of the initial SAR teams, although my search did not turn up anything.

Then, on February 20, I hiked up the Frosty Mountain trail for the first time with John. It was heartbreaking to pass the second switchback myself, which was where Ethan Morf had reported seeing Jordan. I had imagined many possible scenarios here in my mind over the past five months. But when I actually hiked the trail myself, it shaped a much more realistic understanding of what actually might have happened.

On my first hike up Frosty Mountain, initially the path was packed down with snow. After a few kilometres, trails started to branch off in different directions. There were no signs indicating which way to go to reach the summit, so people here made various choices. In general, their routes did not follow the actual trail. This was the first time I experienced what Jordan also likely faced in that sudden October 10 snowstorm (if he had taken this route at all). Misleading tracks or apparent trail openings that went in the wrong direction may have diverted him off the main trail, after which fresh snowfall could have quickly covered all tracks—his own and others'—so that he eventually completely lost the main trail.

If Jordan had hiked up Frosty Mountain, it was important to understand where he may have veered off the trail. Considering Ethan Morf's reported sighting in the context of a witness report by a hiker coming down an hour or so behind him (who had not seen Jordan) suggested that something had happened between the second and sixth switchbacks. Possibly Jordan went off-trail in this area, to take photos or relieve himself, after which an accident occurred or he could not find the path again? Had he gone far enough off the trail in this area that he could have fallen and no one saw or heard him? Or had an animal diverted him off the trail? Many sightings of bears have been reported at Manning Park, primarily black bears but occasionally grizzlies. Or had he simply taken a wrong turn at a false spur trail and then something had happened?

On the 20th, John and I hiked up to the third switchback. Muscle fatigue meant my endurance for this type of mountaineering in the snow was still low. Climbing mountains over fallen trees and through deep snow had stressed all parts of my body. On our way up and down the mountain, however, I continually looked through the trees on each side of our route for any possible clues or unusual colours. On this day (and most days), I also periodically called Jordan's name. I knew the probability of his being alive and able to hear me was low. But he was my missing son and I could not give up hope.

My first experiences of snowshoeing east of the Frosty Mountain trail came on hikes up Windy Joe Mountain on February 21 with John, and then on the Monument 83 trail on February 23 with Trevor.

We passed several snowshoers heading up and down Windy Joe Mountain on February 21. Everyone I spoke to was aware of Jordan's disappearance. They offered to help by searching nearby along trails and letting us know if they found any clues. I gave them a card with my email address or directed them to one of the posters at the resort or trailheads for contact information.

We had heard rumours that someone was living off-grid in the Monument 83 trail area. Trevor and a helicopter had briefly searched the area in October and found a tent and other items. The SAR teams had not searched that far east of Windy Joe Mountain, so that area was potentially important new ground to be covered.

On February 23, Trevor and I hiked on relatively flat terrain. But we found massive tree blowdown along the Monument 83 trail and again snow at least two metres deep. As we moved along, I thought about how Jordan might have arrived there. If he'd opted for the clockwise loop, he could have been on the Frosty–Windy Joe Mountain connector trail when he lost his way and went down the wrong side of the mountain and across Castle Creek, missing the Monument 78 trail and arriving in the forest between the Monument 78 and 83 trails. It seemed unlikely that Jordan could have missed the Monument 78 trail because of the gap in the trees. But we did find that there were long sections between the Winthrop Creek bridge and Canada-US border that were not marked or cleared. With fresh snow cover, it would have been possible to cross the trail without recognizing it.

And, of course, fear and panic would have been dominant emotions by then. Jordan's sense of self-preservation could have caused him to move rather than stay put. The farther he went, and as his food supply dwindled, the more likely it would be that he would make irrational or unusual decisions. Or maybe continuing to move might have given him a sense of purpose and productivity. It was so hard to know.

———

After each day's hike, my knees and ankles were usually very sore. One evening, John and I drove back to the resort for dinner together. I was limping so badly on the way in that he said I walked like a penguin! Remarkably, despite the pain each evening, after a good night's sleep I was fine and ready to go the next morning (although that was harder when my dreams of Jordan kept me awake at night). I was astonished at my body's ability to recuperate so quickly after a good sleep. A supplement of glucosamine helped to ease the joint pain and prevented inflammation in my knees and ankles.

The first and last hours of each hike were the most difficult for me. Early mornings were challenging until blood flow had circulated enough to reduce the stiffness in my joints. At the end of the day, it was my knees that caused issues. Coming down the trail, the pounding with each step was painful. I had injured my right knee playing football in my youth—a player had blocked me at the knees from the side with his helmet. When hikes went beyond twenty-five or thirty kilometres, the pain in my right knee increased sharply. I tried to hide all this from my hiking partners—I didn't want anyone to find any reason to cut back on their hiking commitments.

I sometimes used a knee brace, but it wasn't too helpful. I was concerned that it might weaken my supporting muscles relative to my other knee. So I preferred to gradually build up strength in my thigh and calf muscles to lessen the strain on my knees. Over time, I gained strength and endurance for increasingly longer and more difficult hikes.

Especially in the coldest months of February and March, one of the most painful emotions each day occurred when I opened the door and stepped outside in the morning. The freezing air hit me like a ton of bricks and my mind immediately went to Jordan. How could he survive another night at such temperatures with no shelter beyond his tent? Could he create a heat source? Was it even possible to survive overnight at this temperature?

As I cleared the snow off my car, I would manage to convince myself that, although very unlikely, it was not impossible to find a method of survival. Jordan was resilient, courageous, and not to be underestimated. Why couldn't he be one of the lost souls who overcame all odds and survived?

Then I would force my thoughts away from emotion to a more pragmatic attitude. I'm here to do a job—find Jordan, dead or alive, no ifs, ands, or buts.

four

SCENARIOS AND STRATEGIES

*Only those who risk going too far can
possibly find out how far they can go.*
—ELIOT, 1931

N FEBRUARY, WE WOULD START HIKING BY AROUND 7:00 A.M.
(when the days grew longer, we moved the start time to six o'clock).
We wanted to use all the daylight hours we could.

One of the topics that often came up in the morning meetings
was how the day's search strategy related to the expected behaviours
of someone who had lost their way and of Jordan's possible behaviours
specifically. Several people had recommended books to me about lost
person behaviour. Given the nature of our efforts to find Jordan, my
time for reading was limited, but I did try to scan them and other
sources for helpful ideas and strategies.[8]

---

8   I learned useful insights from several books and articles, which are included
     in the reference section at the end of this book.

I often wondered, for example, how fear might have affected Jordan's ability to survive. I found studies[9] that explained how, if you find yourself lost, fear disturbs the body and disrupts normal mental functioning, concentration, and decision-making. Losing your way can be so terrifying that you may not recognize simple, normally well-known landmarks. If thirst and hunger also set in, a person can also lose their sense of direction.

I would discuss with my partners and other volunteers whether it was more likely that Jordan, once lost or injured, had kept moving—either randomly or with a plan—or hunkered down and stayed in one place. Conventional wisdom advises staying put when you are lost, but even if Jordan had done that, he eventually would have needed to move to find food and, more importantly, water. In general, an adult can survive for two to three days without water, but much longer (thirty to forty days) without food.

Potential food sources in the woods in and surrounding Manning Park included mushrooms, berries, and possibly meat—grouse live in the area and are relatively easy to catch. With these possible options, Jordan would have quickly realized that his highest priority was a water source. Although he would have had snow, it was not a viable water source unless he had a steady source of heat to melt it.

Jordan's need to find water suggested to us that our search plans should prioritize areas off-trail along both sides of waterways within the major drainage basins. There were about a dozen of these waterways in our search areas of interest, and each had many tributaries. These included the basin "inside" the Frosty Mountain loop (bounded on all sides by the Frosty Mountain trail), three basins west of the Frosty Mountain trail (the Frosty Creek, Middle Creek, and Passage Creek drainage basins), and one basin south of the Frosty Mountain summit (the Princess Creek drainage basin). Each one captures all the surface water from rain and snowmelt, as well as groundwater.

---

9   See Coble et al. and Heth and Cornell.

The remote and off-trail drainages at Manning Park are the most treacherous and dangerous terrain that I had ever encountered. Hiking through them can be relatively easy near the top, but then it becomes progressively more difficult—often nearly impossible—as you move downhill. The sides of the drainage become steeper the lower you go, sometimes creating embankments that are as abrupt as cliffs and may be dozens or up to a hundred metres in height. The drainages often have massive swaths of tree downfall, making travel even more difficult.

We realized that if Jordan had become lost and had tried to find his way by hiking down a drainage, he would have eventually gotten to slopes that were too steep to traverse. And then he would have known that he had to hike back up the sides to reach passable terrain.

We also felt that, irrespective of where he was, if Jordan had recognized a geographical feature or heard sounds from the highway, he might have decided to move toward them. He also may have placed a unique marker at a distinctive intersection, so he could explore a nearby area for water or food and be able to find his way back to that position. So it was important that we kept our eyes out for markers—an unusual rock pile or something colourful tied to a tree.

As we snowshoed on- and off-trail, we did periodically notice flagging tape on some of the trees. It was unclear whether it indicated a path on the trail or a previous search by rescue hikers, or something else. I added our own orange flagging tape up high on tree branches to distinguish our path and avoid other searchers repeating the same tracks. I also hoped that it would provide a marker for Jordan if somehow he was still alive. Periodically, I also placed loving notes with a granola bar in a plastic zipper bag in the hopes that he might find them.

To orient himself, Jordan might also have tried to gain a vantage point from a higher area. This, too, had its challenges because Manning Park is heavily forested and the trees are typically between thirty and fifty metres tall. There are few open lookout areas in the woods, and if visibility is not obstructed by trees, it can be blocked by drainage basin walls or adjacent mountains.

The heavy snow on October 10 could definitely have contributed to Jordan's disorientation—both initially, and if he had strayed from and then tried to regain the correct path. When you reverse your direction on any trail, your surroundings can look completely different. Side paths may appear more prominent from one direction than another, which would have made Jordan question whether he was on the right path or not.

If he had intentionally camped off-trail overnight, his route to regaining the main trail would have been covered by a fresh layer of snow. He may have thought he was backtracking correctly, but actually moved farther away. And this could certainly have happened if he'd camped when he became lost. It was also a real possibility that Jordan may have walked in circles without realizing it,[10] feeling like he was making progress, unable to see that he was not.

There are two main types of ground searches: targeted and grid searches. Our targeted searches focused on clues identified by volunteers examining the heatmaps or following up on tips. Grid searches are more systematic and are designed to cover all the terrain in a designated area.

In a grid search, people in teams hike back and forth spaced ten to thirty metres apart (staying within sight of each other), moving in a parallel fashion in the same direction and generally at a constant elevation. When the edge of the designated search area is reached, they shift

---

10   Unintentionally walking in circles when lost is a known phenomenon. To avoid obstacles, such as to go around a tree, a disoriented hiker might aim for a point on the other side of it that appears to be 180 degrees from where they start. But using only a visual approximation often leads to some degree of offset. Repeat this many times, and soon enough the hiker arrives back in the same area they set out from.

down- or uphill then traverse back in the opposite direction, again in a parallel formation. This back-and-forth sequence is repeated until the search area is thoroughly covered.

Unfortunately, and for reasons we never understood, the October SAR groups did not perform grid searches. Instead, searchers were sent out on designated paths through areas of interest. But without a systematic grid search, vast areas next to the trail routes were not covered in any comprehensive way. This was one of the things I set out to address when I returned to British Columbia in February.

However, it wouldn't be easy, or fast. The grid-search method covers the ground as thoroughly as possible and so does not follow a path of least resistance. A prescribed direction can lead through difficult or impassable terrain, so the intended grid line might have to be deviated from so the searcher can get around an obstacle. Even if the searcher deviates from a prescribed path, they should nevertheless inspect the area for possible clues.

———

From Manning Park's website, I learned that almost a million people visit the park every year. Many of them come to hike in the mountains. There are dozens of publicized hiking trails, but it is important to know how to navigate in the woods in order to stay safe. Another thing I realized as I explored more of the park was that, other than at the trailheads, there are generally very few or no signs along trails to point hikers in the right direction. There are only a few signs at trail junctions. I found that distance markers on some trails are hardly visible and many were dislodged.

With so many risks and hazards along the hiking trails, I felt that a stronger safety culture was needed at Manning Park. Over time, I became aware of several other people who went missing in the park. For example, several went missing in 2021 alone. A nineteen-year-old Montreal man (a new employee at Manning Park) was lost overnight—the second time in a month he'd gone astray in the park. Fortunately, he was rescued from a mountain ridge by a helicopter and a RCMP SAR team. Also later that year, a vehicle owned by a man named David Greatrix remained parked at the Monument 78 trailhead for weeks. His body was later found by Princeton RCMP a few kilometres from the trailhead. The cause of death was never determined. Also in 2021, Andriy Fendrikov, a fifty-two-year-old avid back-country hiker went missing and was later found dead near Snass Mountain in Manning Park. And on October 8, 2020, surprisingly close to where Jordan would go missing just a few days later, another man named Alexander Pisch was reported missing at Ross Lake, near the southwestern edge of Manning Park. The man has still not been found.

Signs and markers along any trail are important for safety reasons, but this is especially true in Manning Park. A path can be hard to discern among fallen trees—and tree blowdown may not be cleared for years. Three or more layers of blowdown have accumulated in some places (such as on the East Similkameen and Boyd's Meadows trails, among others). The many false and spur trails branching off the main trails can also deceive and endanger hikers. Several routes that appear on maps are either not maintained or no longer exist—it would be best to warn hikers rather than continue to have them portrayed as viable trails.

We found that broken tree branches sometimes covered the opening of a spur trail, but it was hard to tell if they were placed there intentionally by someone to block the way (since it was a false detour) or natural tree blowdown. On a false trail, the terrain can quickly become treacherous and unforgiving.

Another factor to consider while we were out searching was the lack of cellphone coverage on most trails—there is either none or just a sporadic signal, depending on your location or cellphone carrier.

Taking all these factors into account, it was easy to see that even the most experienced hikers could get lost in Manning Park. I travelled with several expert hikers with mountaineering experience who had become lost either during the earlier search for Jordan or previously on other hikes. I could clearly see how this could have happened to Jordan, even with his own solid experience, especially if caught off guard in an unexpected snowstorm.

———

On February 25, I solo hiked the Shadow Lake trail and the Steamboat trail (adjacent to the resort). If Jordan had lost his way while he was on the Skyline trail and come down the north side of Frosty Mountain, or gone down into a drainage between the Skyline and Shadow Lake trails, then he may have possibly ended up in the Shadow Lake area. That route and direction would have been unfamiliar to him, but he may have hoped to eventually arrive at a location he recognized. If he missed the Shadow Lake trail or descended from higher up the mountain and had not found something familiar, it wasunlikely that he would reverse course and go back up the mountain. I felt that he would have continued downward.

We made sure that a poster of Jordan was displayed at the trailhead of all trails and campsites at Manning Park. At Strawberry Flats (near the trailheads of the Shadow Lake and Skyline trails), there was no display board, so his poster was pinned high on a tree. To my surprise and dismay when I arrived at the trailhead on a day after I placed the poster, someone had poked out Jordan's eyes in the picture. It was deliberate vandalism—and quite disturbing.

Though episodes and discoveries like this cut me sharply, my spirits were lowest when I was looking off-trail, under fallen trees and in the snow for unusual formations—which could have been hiding something important. Other snowshoers may have noticed such things, too, but they would have ignored them unless they were aware there was an ongoing search for a missing person. I visualized what might lie beneath the snow and occasionally poked in with my hiking poles, both hoping and dreading what they might touch.

At some point on each hike, I would need to pause and ease my sadness with tears. This release usually came when my partner ahead of me would not notice if I fell behind for a few minutes. I let the tears flow, picked myself up, called Jordan's name, then continued on. Many hollows in the park became valleys of tears for me.

I gained strength from the eternally positive attitude of my wife, Josie. Although she was over 7,000 kilometres away, I could feel her strength and encouragement. Together, we felt that we would find our son. We avoided speculating on any possible scenario of Jordan's death. No matter what difficulty was posed by the trails and mountains, we both shared and fed the candle's flame of hope that we might find Jordan alive.

We had a few techniques to help us stay positive, especially as there were some volunteers who tried repeatedly to convince us that Jordan was certainly dead and that we should stop searching. These negative views drained us of energy, so we tried to surround ourselves with people who had a proactive attitude—they didn't necessarily believe that Jordan was alive, but they kept negative thoughts to themselves and conveyed a can-do attitude. They made positive suggestions of how and where to move the search forward rather than spending precious time speculating on Jordan's demise.

When talking about Jordan with hiking partners, I always used the present tense—"Jordan is," not "Jordan was." Careful use of words and actions that demonstrated what I wanted to be true—such as shouting Jordan's name on our searches—were important for several reasons. They helped me and Josie continue holding onto hope, and they helped inspire and motivate other hikers. I didn't think volunteers would be interested in returning again and again if I held a negative attitude or was in a continual state of depression.

My determination to find Jordan, perhaps surprisingly to some, grew stronger over time. Jordan was an incredible young man who deserved to be found. People should never give up on those they love, no matter how hopeless a situation may appear.

So I let volunteers wonder about the man shouting "Jordan!" in the trees. I knew it looked hopeless to most of them. But at least they would see that I and my family were not giving up. And I knew that Jordan knew that we would never give up.

On February 27, I did my first "loop hike" with John. This involved snowshoeing up the Frosty Mountain trail to the fifth switchback, then dropping off the trail and traversing down the mountain off-trail toward Lightning Lake and then back to the parking lot.

Snowshoeing off-trail down the mountain for the first time was unnerving. The distance was short—only about five hundred metres— but the slope was steep. There was at least two metres of snow-covered dense tree downfall, making the conditions unlike anything I had seen before. John had hiked several of the highest mountains in the world, including glaciers in Alaska. He explained why there was no avalanche risk (one of the many things I was worried about). Despite my nervousness, I felt entirely safe with John. And luckily, after two weeks of snowshoeing in the mountains, I had become stronger and more capable in off-trail terrain. I had also picked up my new hiking gear by this point and gained enough stamina to better keep up with John.

Each step down was carefully planned to avoid sinkholes and tree wells. One of the most common dangers on a descent was sinking one leg into the snow while momentum carried the rest of my body down the mountain. In some scenarios, this momentum could break a person's leg. So extra caution was taken whenever footing was uncertain.

To my surprise, when we reached a spot that appeared too steep for snowshoeing down, John simply sat down, lifted his legs, and started sliding through the trees. When he'd come to a stop, he encouraged me to do the same.

"That looks like fun," I shouted back, "but I'm nervous about losing control!"

"No worries, Greg, it's safer than hiking down. This snow is unstable. Follow my path down. I'll wait here and stop you if you lose control."

So I did what he'd done, sliding[11] at least fifty metres along his path. John grabbed me when I approached him to slow my momentum. As I cleaned myself off and regained my footing, he explained that it's sometimes safer to slide on steep slopes because it increases your surface area on the ground, giving you better stability.

There were some implications for my ability to search while glissading down these and other slopes. I was not able to poke or search around, since my focus was taking a safe path down. But at the top and bottom, we thoroughly scanned the area enough to feel confident that nothing important was located there.

As John and I continued down the mountain, we discussed possible scenarios in which Jordan could have found himself in this area.

"He could have lost the Frosty trail by going off a false spur trail," I offered. "Or a bear could have scared him of the trail, or he couldn't see any tracks on the real trail and was confused?"

"If he veered east off the trail, he would have gone into the interior drainage basin and eventually arrived at Similkameen Creek," John said. "If he veered west off the trail, he'd be diverted into the Frosty Creek drainage basin below us." This was the area we were searching.

"There's also a possibility that he could have aimed for a higher position to gain visibility," I said. "If he wandered down to Frosty Creek, he could have climbed up again on the other side to improve his view."

---

11 Mountaineers call this sliding "glissading." With your snowshoes on, you sit, tilt back on your butt with knees bent and legs elevated. You hold your poles upside down and push them into the snow to slow down (or you slow down by digging in your heels). To steer, you push harder on one or the other pole. If you have tight-fitting clothes, the snow does not infiltrate the back of your jacket or boots.

"It would have been hard to cross the creek. It's more likely he would have followed the drainage down to Lightning Lake."

"But if it didn't look familiar, could he have tried to climb up again to spot a landmark and reorient himself? In that scenario, he might have gone farther in the wrong direction and become lost even deeper in the forest."

We talked it over until we eventually reached the parking lot, with nothing certain determined and no clues found.

Later, back at the cabin, I replied to emails and uploaded photos and maps for Josie to share with volunteers. As I had started to do every night, I looked out the window into the forest behind the cabin. I imagined Jordan walking out of the forest. My desire to bring Jordan into the cabin was so strong that I would have given anything for the loving embrace that would follow. Maybe if I concentrated and stared long and hard enough into the forest, a miracle could happen?

No miracle would happen on this night. But tomorrow was another day to hold onto hope.

five

SNOWFIELD MOUNTAINEERING IN MARCH

You are not in the mountains. The mountains are in you.
—MUIR, 1986

A S A NEW MONTH BEGAN, I CONTINUED TO PONDER THE BASIC questions. Why had Jordan decided to climb *Frosty* Mountain specifically (assuming that was his ultimate destination)? Why had he hiked alone?

I knew Jordan felt a spiritual connection with nature when hiking. The mind and body are joined as one when you push yourself to the limit, and Jordan understood this. Josie had hiked with him in British Columbia. He often hiked with a group of friends from UBC. I'd hiked with him in Newfoundland, as a family and alone (times I always looked forward to).

Jordan enjoyed both solitude in nature and the physical challenge of tackling increasingly difficult hikes and higher mountains. He also loved the beauty of mountain views and was an avid photographer. The panorama from atop Frosty Mountain would certainly be a spectacular draw. It would take in mountain ranges on all sides and include Mount Winthrop to the east, Castle Peak to the south, and Hozomeen Mountain to the west. Plus it was fall, and the Larches would have been in their magnificent fall colours.

But were there other reasons he made the choices he did? Reasons that might lead us to finding him?

My first snowshoeing trek in March was a solo hike on the 1st along the looped Canyon Nature trail and the Little Muddy trail. Both were near the resort and safe to hike without a partner.

I knew Jordan had viewed the Canyon Nature trail online, so it was an important area and had not yet been searched. About halfway around it, I noticed a few campsites—which could have been a possible diversion if Jordan had arrived there. Although this area was relatively accessible, a mishap could have happened off-trail and out of sight of casual hikers. The campsites, too, were off-trail and I was alone, so I did not risk snowshoeing in. But I made a note to return after the snowpack receded.

The Little Muddy trail is near the bottom of the drainage area inside (as in, bordered by) the Frosty Mountain loop. Anyone lost in that drainage would most likely be funnelled downwards by the terrain and exit at the Little Muddy trail. On this day, I met a family with their teenage daughter. When I asked if they had heard about Jordan, they said they were aware. In fact, virtually every hiker I met in the park knew of Jordan's disappearance—mostly due to Josie's tireless communication efforts.

On every hike, I used my GPS unit to track my location on a map that was overlaid with the locations of heatmap clues. We would divert off-trail and, as we got close to the spot, we'd push our hiking poles into the snow. Given that heatmap clues were based on aerial imagery from October and November, it was possible—even likely—that later snow-fall had covered the curious objects that had shown up in the images.

On March 2, Trevor and I hiked the East Similkameen trail. Partway along, we veered off-trail to check two heatmap clues. One was in the shape of a tent and the other had traces of a colour that matched Jordan's jacket. When we reached the target locations, we found an unusual pattern of tree downfall, which explained what we'd seen in the imagery.

We hiked next over to Boyd's Meadows. Neither the East Similka-meen trail nor the trail out to Boyd's Meadows were maintained by park staff. Multiple layers of massive tree downfall covered them. They were obviously unmanaged back-country areas and not the "fami-ly-friendly" trails of the park's promotional materials. For most of this hike, Trevor and I created our own tracks through the snow.

Trevor was ahead of me and close to Boyd's Meadows when he noticed something unusual. It appeared to be human footprints cross-ing the trail. My initial reaction was that they were moose tracks. But looking more closely, they had the same shape, size, and stride length of human footsteps. If a person had made them, they likely would not have realized they were crossing an old trail—a trail that led out of the woods.

I followed the footprints with my eyes, back into the forest, until they went below some low, thin, unbroken branches. At that point, my heart began to race so much that I could feel all chambers pumping. It did not look possible that a moose could walk beneath those branches without breaking off the smaller ones. Trevor agreed with me, so we turned and followed the footprints off-trail.

The terrain eventually became difficult, but the footprints kept going deeper into the forest. We decided one of us should wait while the other continued to follow the tracks. Because Trevor was more experienced than me, he snowshoed farther in. We periodically shouted each other's name. He kept going until eventually I couldn't hear him anymore.

Like me, Trevor carried a GPS unit, but I was still concerned that if we became separated we would have to find our way out independently. I toned down my panic by taking off my backpack for a drink of water. But I was greatly relieved when I finally heard him call out again.

"I followed the footprints as far as I could," he reported when he got back to me, "but eventually lost them in the snow."

"On the other side of the trail, the branches are unbroken about a metre above the footprints. A moose seems like a logical explanation, but there should definitely be broken branches above those tracks. It's a mystery what happened here."

We had established a working relationship with the Upper Similkameen Indian Band by this point. We sent off photos of the tracks to their office and asked for their opinion. Their thought was that the tracks were likely made by a young moose, so we decided not to pursue it any further. But I couldn't forget those unbroken branches.

———

With each passing day, I became more aware of the vibrant life existing all around me in the apparently "sleeping" winter forest. I learned how trees communicate with each other from several writers[12] and how they share nutrients through their roots and mycorrhizal networks. If a tree is under distress from insect attacks or disease, it sends scents and other signals that nearby trees receive to alter their behaviour.

While hiking and particularly during breaks when I was resting off-trail, I tried to tune in to the forest and feel the presence and spirit of Tmxʷulaxʷ. Somehow, mysteriously, I began to sense signals that seemed to indicate whether Jordan had passed nearby or not.

———

12   See Simar, Wohlleben, and Worton, particularly, in the References.

When I slowed down, quieted my mind, and connected with my senses, I began to notice the smallest of details in the forest. I watched how leaves blew in the wind and listened to the sounds of their swaying for messages or patterns of significance. I opened myself to deeper thoughts and communications with Tmxʷulaxʷ.

"Speaking" with Tmxʷulaxʷ did not take the form of hearing voices. Rather, I saw or felt an image in my mind. I would get a mental image or symbol of what I felt a tree was attempting to communicate to me. I also sensed that trees had different attitudes. When asking a question, I could feel a response by tuning in—sometimes there was an unfriendly hostility in the form of obstacles (such as a steep rocky cliff) that prompted me to turn back.

On other occasions, I felt chills throughout my body due to fear. If I imagined a question for the tree—such as, "Is this a potential search area?"—then sometimes I was able to feel anxiety or tension about the usefulness of hiking there, or I would get a mental image of an event connected to Jordan that might have occurred nearby.

Another type of feeling that I experienced with Tmxʷulaxʷ was smelling an odour that was not otherwise present in the surroundings. A pleasant smell was like a message of "yes" or an indication that something was right. An unpleasant odour gave me the opposite message.

Paying attention to the details of my surroundings was critical if I was to sense signals and signs from Tmxʷulaxʷ. So I carefully observed changes between the time I first sat down near a tree and a while later, to notice whether I felt differently or heard anything unusual.

Weird experiences with unsavoury individuals continued to distract us from our search efforts in March, particularly involving the fraudster Claire. We received an email from someone named "George" who claimed to be Claire's partner, saying that she was upset and stressed after being disconnected from us because she was so committed to finding Jordan. He felt that he needed to step in on her behalf. This appeared to be a new tactic (and probably a false persona) that Claire had developed to regain communication with us.

George also wrote that other volunteers had sent Claire insulting messages. He acknowledged that Claire's behaviour had contributed to why some volunteers wanted her to leave the search group. But he felt she didn't deserve those hurtful messages. He was also upset that we had issued a no-contact order against Claire. He urged us to give her the benefit of the doubt. And he apologized for the trouble she'd caused and how it distracted us from the search for Jordan. He asked for an opportunity to speak with us about the situation.

We were unwilling to reconnect with Claire. We advised George to contact the police with any concerns about volunteers sending hurtful messages to her.

On another occasion, someone claiming to be Claire's sister sent us messages on her behalf. Again we felt it was Claire herself behind them. These notes explained that volunteers had contacted and insulted Claire several times via social media. She urged us to stop them from sending harassing messages to her. We couldn't control what others were writing on social media, so we suggested that she contact the police.

Nevertheless, the person went on to spin a long story about what had "actually" happened between Claire and other volunteers. Then she warned *us* not to contact Claire anymore—which made no sense, since we had issued the no-contact order and were not currently in contact with her. She told us also to ensure that no volunteers contacted Claire either.

It appeared that Claire's prior treatment of volunteers on social media had unleashed an angry response back. Perhaps this too had not actually taken place. But the person claiming to be Claire's sister felt it was our responsibility to control the situation. We had no control over what others were saying to or about Claire— especially when many of them, too, were now disconnected from our search team.

We suggested that she report cyber-bullying or any other criminal activity to the police. If those messages actually existed, it was
unknown to us who was sending them to Claire. It was exhausting for
us to have to deal with these conflicts between Claire and the other
volunteers on top of our search efforts. The presence of these unpleasant individuals diverted us away from the priority of finding Jordan,
and added even more stress to the search for our missing son.

In March, I bought a drone and it soon became a valuable tool in the
search for clues on the ground. I practised and operated the drone
manually in an open field near my cabin in Eastgate, usually in a basic
grid pattern. Near significant geographical features like a creek or
areas with a clearer line of sight to the ground, I made repeated passes
and flew the drone lower.

Before operating the drone in Manning Park, I had received permission from the BC Parks Area Supervisor. Flying a drone is generally
not permitted in the park, so I kept the supervisor updated regularly
on where and when I was going to deploy it. He was aware that it was
a special circumstance, as I was searching for my lost son. In general,
whenever I flew the drone, there were no people anywhere nearby.

After I began flying the drone in Manning Park, I soon discovered
that when wind gusts pushed the drone around, it affected the video
footage and the images were jumpy because the drone camera was rig-
idly attached. A better-quality drone was needed with a more flexible
camera head, so I could acquire smooth video footage irrespective of
wind gusts.

On March 4, I was ready to put the drone to use in our search. I flew
it in forest areas adjacent to the Little Muddy trail (where the Windy
Joe Mountain trail starts). Afterward, I uploaded the drone imagery
onto a shared drive so volunteers could review footage for any substantial clues.

Although we had aerial footage and heatmaps, those images were taken from aircraft with relatively low resolution down to the ground. Drone videos provided higher resolution images and allowed us to check larger areas over a shorter time period than ground searches. If noteworthy clues were found in the drone videos, then those areas were prioritized for searches on foot.

In the early afternoon that day, I took a water break near a bridge over a stream. The line of sight up the drainage basin was obstructed by tree downfall in the water. But enough flowing water was exposed to possibly show clues, such as pieces of coloured fabric that could have flowed down the drainage.

Tmxʷulaxʷ, I'm searching here for my missing son Jordan and need your help. I would be grateful if you could provide any signals or clues about his location.

I listened and carefully watched my surroundings.

The water here has arrived from up high in the mountains. Despite the snowpack and tree downfall here, this flowing water is always able to find a way down through the obstructions. It moves through, over, and under fallen trees. Like the water finding its way here through challenging obstructions, Jordan too has found his way.

It was an inspiring message from Tmxʷulaxʷ, but without any tangible clues or new information, it didn't provide much help.

———

Since the fall, Mike B had reached out periodically to Josie while the video review team searched aerial and drone imagery. And earlier in the winter, he and his friend Stan had searched on the ground at Windy Joe Mountain. Josie recommended that I reconnect with Mike, so I called in early March to share our latest updates about the ground searches. I asked him how he might be able to assist. He suggested primarily with strategy and intelligence gathering, because of his military background, and that his detailed knowledge of Manning Park would provide useful insights.

On March 5, Mike, Stan, and I searched off-trail between the second and third switchbacks of the Frosty Mountain trail. Another friend of Mike's, Aaron, also joined us with his drone. He flew his drone off-trail between the third switchback of the Frosty Mountain trail and Lightning Lake (about two kilometres up the trail from the parking lot).

As the four of us hiked up the Frosty Mountain trail, I continually looked downhill for possible clues in the branches. We trekked off-trail between switchbacks in new areas that had not been searched on the ground before. On our way down, we separated ourselves ten to twenty metres apart and searched individually along parallel tracks. We shouted each other's names when we lost visual contact. Occasionally I noticed piles of snow that looked unusual. I poked around with my poles but found nothing odd underneath. Nothing was found on this day, but it was productive nonetheless. We collected imagery from Aaron's drone and uploaded it to be examined by volunteers.

When I returned from a hike, I usually passed a Missing Person poster of Jordan. In a daily routine, I would touch, kiss, or otherwise hug the tree holding the poster. Anything bringing a sense of closeness with Jordan was an inspiration to continue searching.

I often mourned and decompressed with tears once I returned to my cabin. But these feelings passed like clouds in the sky. When a dark cloud moves overhead, the darkness is distressing, like sadness. But darkness is temporary and then it passes on. So, too, did the darkness of emotion with Jordan's disappearance—despair and weeping came periodically, but then passed by like a dark cloud departing.

Right from the initial searches in October, areas deep in the three main interior drainages were high priorities. By March, several of them had still not been thoroughly checked. I heard from volunteers that the terrain was treacherous and possibly the most difficult to search on the ground.

I wanted to hike into the most difficult drainages because I felt there was a higher likelihood of finding Jordan in one of them. But few hiking partners were willing or sufficiently experienced to go there. Fortunately, John was willing to hike anywhere with me.

I asked him if we could hike into the interior drainages from the bottom up toward the higher levels of Frosty Mountain. To my knowledge, nobody (except Trevor) had been able or willing to do that because of the extreme terrain. John agreed, so we met early on the morning of March 6 to begin the hike.

We started in relatively flat terrain but on a deep snowpack. The drainage basin quickly became steeper and soon so steep is was nearly impassable. In several places, the snowpack could not support my weight and I often sank knee-deep. I became exhausted by mid-morning, but there was still a long day ahead of us. We needed to make faster progress.

A clear area along the waterway ahead appeared flatter and like it would offer a more direct path up the drainage. So we descended from above the drainage and began snowshoeing along it—a serious mistake. After some smooth hiking, I noticed the hills on both sides growing steeper around us. Our waterway path appeared fine, however, so we continued on. Then we turned a corner and faced enormous tree downfall, flanked by steep cliffs on both sides, with confined visibility and deep snow.

We stopped to contemplate our options. Sometimes a path is safe in one direction but not when returning by the same route. Eventually we decided that our safest option was to climb straight up the cliff and out of the drainage.

"How can we climb that?" I asked John. "I don't know how to climb vertically in snowshoes. It's a long way up to the ridge."

"One foot in front of the other, one step at a time," replied John. "We kick each foot into the snow with our toes to create steps that we will climb up like stairs. I'll lead the way and create the steps."

"But how will I balance myself? It's so steep."

"I'll pick a route with branches we can grab with one hand," said John. "Stay calm and it will be fine."

And so we began the climb.

After a few kicks into the wall of snow, I learned the technique and could make good steps for myself or use John's. In several places, I was able to grab onto branches. Where I couldn't, we changed direction, or I somehow managed to keep my balance. The climb was like going up a ladder, except that each step was draining and physically demanding, and especially hard on my ankles.

When we reached the top, John applauded my efforts and reminded me how an obstacle can appear insurmountable at the beginning but manageable when taken step by step. To avoid feeling overwhelmed when looking from the start to the end point of our next difficult passage, John suggested I instead just focus on putting one foot in front of the other. The objective is to subdivide the trek into smaller manageable steps rather than being "an entire cliff." Any challenge can be overcome, he said, one step at a time, or one day at a time.

These words of wisdom paralleled my search philosophy. There were countless places where Jordan might have gone astray in Manning Park. When I looked out over the mountain ranges extending in all directions, I needed to focus on the next few steps ahead and not the enormous magnitude of the terrain. Any other way of looking at it, and I would sink into despair at the hopelessness of the situation.

John and I continued to follow the route of the waterway uphill, but no longer along its banks to avoid other traps. The search area presented a difficult dilemma in terms of strategy. It was important to thoroughly check this drainage, but the terrain could quickly become treacherous, slow to hike, and blocked by impassable barriers.

As we went on searching, I sensed Jordan's presence. I often meditated and thought about enjoyable times with him. On this day, I thought of times when we would compare our views on recent movies or books. Jordan and I shared an interest in science fiction and action films. I started a "conversation" with him and it felt like Jordan's presence had merged with the surrounding forest and was right there with me.

Jordan, you are so dearly loved and missed. Remember our debates about movies and books?

Dad, I enjoy the peculiarities in reading science fiction short stories. I see sci-fi and fantasy as ways of getting lost in a particular universe. You can relate to any characters.

My favourite sci-fi show is Star Trek Voyager. Maybe because it's the furthest ahead in the future and on the other side of the galaxy. Which are your favourites?

I sensed an interaction with Jordan's spirit, but it was not complete. He was there but not graspable. It was his spirit but not the same as if he was actually there. He didn't answer my question but offered something else.

You can really find yourself enjoying those genres, for the odd ways they bend reality. When that's in a novel, you can just get lost in that universe. When I'm looking at them through the restricted lens of a short story, I don't get lost as much.

I agreed: *I love how science fiction allows us to wander and dream outside the normal bounds of reality. I like how they open our minds to other new possibilities, too. They awaken our curiosity and imagination about some of the big questions of our existence. Like the meaning of life and death.*

Sci-fi short stories do bring odd ideas into your life and small forms of creativity, and sometimes make you able to see certain things in your life in different ways. And, instead of getting lost in these fantasy universes, sci-fi is a way of gathering inspiration from the regular things that you see every day. I imagined him in conversation.

I was listening so hard, holding onto this reverie, that I stumbled over some fallen trees. I shook myself and refocused on the terrain. But I still felt Jordan's presence.

When we got back to the car that day, we had discovered no clues, and made no breakthroughs. But we had gained experience in this important region and it remained a high priority area for future searches. We would return, taking other routes into the drainages. We would find ways to hike up a trail to a higher elevation and enter the drainage basin from the top. We had learned that starting from the bottom and climbing up was not very effective.

After a much-needed rest day, my next search was a solo hike around Lightning Lake. Although this trail had been searched many times already, there were countless areas adjacent to the path and directions into the forest off-trail that had not yet been carefully scrutinized.

In the quiet solitude of hiking by myself, I paused often and looked into the forest, scanning the trees and the spaces beneath and between them. I tuned in to the smallest features of the forest to find any possible form of clue.

The mountainside near here could have offered a route downhill if Jordan had lost his way west of the Frosty Mountain trail. Maybe he'd veered off the trail and been injured. And if he'd fallen and not made it to shelter, surely by now there might be bits of torn fabric—from a tent or backpack or clothing—that might have been caught in branches? This was what I sought as I scanned.

Once again, on my own in the woods, I shouted Jordan's name and paused in silence. I listened carefully but only heard the echoes of my voice receding through the valley. There were no signs of Jordan anywhere on this hike. I returned to the cabin to plan my next move.

On March 9, I went back to the Lightning Lake trail, on my own again but with a route that went farther out and around Flash Lake. In November, volunteers had noted clues that looked like a tent south of the trail where Frosty Creek drained into Flash Lake.

Using my GPS unit, I found the exact location where the volunteers saw possible evidence of a tent. It was relatively close to the trail. Two massive trees had fallen there—one on top of the other—and several more had also come down at different angles near the two big trees. There didn't appear to be any particular reason why this many trees had fallen here, other than natural downfall. All of them were snow-covered but some had unusual discolouring on their exposed surfaces—in varying shades of red—perhaps where the trees had struck and scraped each other. I suspected that, from above, the odd alignments and the discolouring could have given the appearance of a shelter. Still, I poked around under the branches—but there was no sign of a person or tent.

Returning to the trail, I continued to the next promising location on the heatmaps. In this case, I discovered as I got closer, the target was on much steeper off-trail terrain. I was not prepared to risk going in alone. This one would need to wait for another day to be checked. Nevertheless, I had a fairly good line of sight through the tree downfall from the trail to the location of the identified clues. Again the odd shape that had struck the volunteers appeared likely to be tree downfall lying in a triangular pattern.

I returned to the cabin after another unsuccessful rough outing, holding onto hope for a better outcome on another day. There was always a bit of relief on these "unsuccessful" days, too: any hike on which we had not found Jordan's remains meant we did not have to extinguish the hope of finding him alive.

On the following rest day, I investigated another new tool—a digiscope, which is a digital camera connected to a spotting scope—that could potentially scan more ground than hiking alone. A digiscope uses a cellphone camera to record distant images and videos through the eyepiece of an optical telescope. When I connected my cellphone to the eyepiece, I could create videos of far-off locations, which then could be uploaded to a shared drive so volunteers could search the imagery.

The digiscope offered a valuable new ability to scan territory, but its size (forty centimetres long and ten centimetres diameter, plus tripod) and weight (three kilograms) made it a considerable addition to my backpack, which already contained a number of essentials such as food, water, extra clothing, and navigation and emergency items.

Like droning, digiscoping could give us a closer look at the ground in locations that were difficult to get to. Its other advantage was that it allowed us to search from lower elevations upward. But it is difficult to fly a drone to elevations higher up a mountain than where you are standing, because you have to keep the drone low enough to capture views of the ground, yet high enough to clear the treetops. Judging aerial clearance from a lower vantage point is not easy.

So, from this point on, I would evaluate the pros and cons of each approach for a given hike, and factor in the distance to be travelled, the weight of the pack to be carried, and the nature and location of the areas we were going to search.

————

On March 11, I returned to the Lightning Lake trail. I wanted to spend more time on the north side of the lake, where a few locations had an excellent view up the Frosty Creek drainage basin, including all the way up to the Frosty Mountain summit.

As I passed Jordan's Missing Person poster at the start of the trail, I asked for his help.

Dear son, today I'm hiking along the Lightning Lake trail by myself. Please show me a sign or clue.

I love you, Dad. I'm with you in spirit. I will be taking care of you so that you stay safe during the hike. And I did feel his presence with me, like a spirit that lingered, waiting for closure.

I hiked on until I came to a good digiscoping location near the bridge across from Flash Lake. I pulled out the digiscoping gear and focused on the slopes around the Frosty Mountain summit, which were about eleven kilometres from where I had set up. I could clearly see, and recorded videos of, large snow-covered areas below the Larches. I sat down for stability and carefully scanned the sides of the mountain.

Most of the ground was covered in deep snow, but the resolution was high enough that I would be able to spot any unusual or unnatural object. And, after some time scanning, I did identify some unnatural features. I could also see tracks in the snow—but could not tell if they'd been made by animals or people, nor determine whether imprints that looked like tracks were actually made by snow chunks falling from trees.

This scanning exercise was my first experience actually searching near the Frosty Mountain summit. I had been unable to snowshoe there myself because of the treacherous and deep snow conditions. Looking up now, I felt a sense of awe. The mountain looked mighty and fearsome. I wondered why climbers—including Jordan—were drawn to such an intimidating place.

After I had digiscoped and thoroughly scanned the terrain up the Frosty Creek drainage basin, I returned to the parking lot and drove back to Eastgate. A feeling of hopelessness overwhelmed me. The scale of the terrain I'd viewed through the digiscope was difficult to comprehend. How would we possibly check that vast wilderness on the ground? What would be the best strategy?

I drew on John's advice to shake myself out of my despair: "One foot in front of the other." His words of wisdom once again kept me focused on moving forward.

On March 13, John and I searched off-trail in areas below the second and fifth switchbacks of the Frosty Mountain trail where the private SAR teams had been unwilling to search in December. They said it wouldn't be useful because of the amount of snow on the ground. I felt, however, that if the worst had happened, there would be clues to be found.

Our map keeper, Rastko, suggested that off-trail areas between switchbacks should be prioritized as high-probability locations. John and I searched these switchback areas extensively. It was gruelling terrain but necessary work. Many others had hiked there and it was disturbing to see so many variations in their tracks through the snow. Between the third and fourth switchbacks, for example, there were at least a dozen different paths made by hikers. Even with a GPS unit, it was difficult to identify the actual trail.

We carried on to higher ground and, when we arrived at the Frosty campsite cabin, John searched the walls carefully to see if Jordan had signed his name—a common practice there. But we found no sign of Jordan in the cabin.

We also searched off-trail through a large meadow area between the final switchback and the campsite. We diverted several times in opposite directions to check locations of heatmap clues.

At one point, to get through some tree blowdown, I crawled on my hands and knees beneath the fallen trees. As I pushed my way through the branches, I had flashbacks of a game Jordan and I played when he was still a child, before our daughters were born. We would fool around and then I would crawl on my hands and knees with him on my back. Sometimes, to make things more exciting, I gave him a bumpy ride. He would laugh and hold on tighter. He was an adorable little boy.

I also had a flashback of a trip we'd taken together when Jordan was about seven years old. Our friend Dan invited us to his cabin near Gimli, Manitoba. I showed Jordan how to fish at the nearby lake. Jordan tried the spinning reel. We used some lures and looked around for live bait—Jordan watched it all attentively. We had a grand time together without catching a single fish.

Then came flashbacks of Jordan's last visit home during the 2019 Christmas holiday. Josie and I were so proud of what a remarkable young man he had become and how he had matured during his first two years at UBC. As we drove around town, he asked to stop at Quidi Vidi, a beautiful little lake in St. John's. At its west end, near a bench, Jordan walked over to a gaggle of geese, pigeons, and gulls. Many landed and followed him. I'd captured this precious moment and it was a special memory of our time together on a beautiful sunny winter day. I now knew it was probably Jordan's last visit to St. John's and the last time we'd spend time together, just the two of us alone driving around the city.

six

ONE FOOT AHEAD OF THE OTHER

Therefore do not be anxious about tomorrow, for tomorrow will be anxious for itself. Let the day's own trouble be sufficient for the day.

—MATTHEW 6:34

A S I STARTED INTO MY NINTH WEEK OF SEARCHING, TWO new volunteers with prior SAR experience, Nicole and Richard, joined our search efforts. They had served on previous SAR teams that had come from Hope. I looked forward to learning more about the best SAR practices from them.

They told me that Jordan's disappearance was widely known and publicized among many SAR groups and communities in British Columbia. This broad awareness was mainly a result of Josie's communication efforts back in St. John's.

Nicole indicated that both she and her colleagues on the Hope SAR team believed the highest priority area to search, once the snow cleared, would be the Skyline trail, because it had been far less searched than areas near the Frosty Mountain trail. She had also heard about unidentified items and slide marks near Lightning Lake. She believed it would be worthwhile to send a dive team into Flash Lake and Lightning Lake once they thawed.

Nicole suggested that I contact the RCMP and ask them for a thorough ground search along the Skyline trail once the snowpack receded. When I followed up, however, I was told that the VPD was responsible for the case and the RCMP defers to the VPD. And the RCMP reiterated that the VPD would not authorize any further search activities unless substantial new information was found.

Richard and Nicole joined me on March 14 to search areas near Flash Lake where significant heatmap clues had been identified by volunteers. We set out along the Lightning Lake trail. When we reached the points of interest, we could see we'd have to go into the forest several hundred metres off-trail to reach them. Nicole and Richard both announced that they wouldn't snowshoe off-trail. They didn't explain their decision and I didn't ask.

We agreed on a turnaround time and I hiked in alone, shouting back periodically to stay in touch. Eventually we lost vocal and visual contact. I hiked close enough to several desired locations to feel they had been checked. Whether I reached them or observed them from a distance, I could see that the points of interest were all only discoloured and unusual formations of tree downfall.

A few key GPS points were more difficult to reach by myself. Snow levels were still at least two metres deep. The terrain was rising gradually but, as I searched farther, it suddenly became very steep. In the solitude of the forest, I reflected on Jordan and asked whether or not to push upward onto the mountain by myself. The heatmap clues ahead were compelling, but given the difficulty of the terrain and my turnaround time, I hoped to get signals from Tmxʷulaxʷ about what I should do.

Tmxʷulaxʷ, I can see that you have placed a wall in my path. This steep terrain has appeared so suddenly in front of me that I'm sensing you do not welcome me here.

I felt Tmxʷulaxʷ reply: *Your determination in this forest and resilience will teach you who you are and who you will become as a person.*

In my culture, a "real man" fulfills traditional expectations of masculinity in his behaviour, physical strength, or appearance. My view of a real man is something different. It's a man who will never abandon his child, no matter how difficult or hopeless a situation appears.

You have my admiration. However, my terrain is not a barrier, it is itself—unforgiving and more powerful than you may realize.

Tmxʷulaxʷ, you too have my admiration, but honestly, no mountain or drainage will stop me from searching. You know what is in my heart. You must understand that I, too, will not be deterred.

Understood. But you are wise enough to know that it is not prudent to take unnecessary risks when your objective can be achieved in other, safer ways.

I'm sensing from you, Tmxʷulaxʷ, that the path ahead is unsafe. The heatmap clue can therefore wait for another day. Our exchange shows me I need to go back.

I turned around, but even snowshoeing out to the trail had its challenges. There were several sinkholes and deep tree wells. Often it was necessary to snowshoe between two trees growing close together, along a narrow ridge between their tree wells.

When I arrived safely back, Nicole and Richard immediately asked what had happened. I told them I'd searched deep into the forest but found nothing to indicate human activity. I described how the grade had gradually increased but suddenly became very steep. We discussed various search strategies as we returned to the parking lot.

The next two days were rest days. I needed time to address car problems, buy groceries, and clean up the cabin. While I was running my errands, I mulled over what the last few weeks' experiences had taught me about the best areas to search. Nicole, Richard, and the Hope SAR team believed that the Skyline trail area should be prioritized. But other volunteers felt searching this area wouldn't be productive, mainly because Jordan's car was parked near the Frosty Mountain trailhead, so it seemed an unlikely scenario that he would have disappeared in this location. As time had passed with no clues found around the Frosty Mountain trails, however, our attention and interest, too, were turning to the Skyline trail area.

Several factors made it a realistic possibility that Jordan had gone missing near the Skyline trail. First, essentially no physical clues of Jordan had been found on the Frosty Mountain side of the park despite five months of intense searching. If Jordan had hiked up the Frosty Mountain trail, he could have changed his mind about going on due to either the deteriorating weather or the number of hikers coming down the trail, suggesting a lack of overnight space at the Frosty campsite. And if he *had* changed his mind, the Skyline trail would have been a logical and attractive alternative. He'd filled in the camping pass indicating the Frosty campsite as his overnight destination, but some unknown factor later in the afternoon may have caused him to alter his plan. However, the Skyline trail is not directly connected to the Frosty Mountain trail. Jordan would have had to return down Frosty Mountain and change direction to reach the Skyline trail.

There had been several helicopter sweeps over the Skyline trail area during the fall SAR operations. This told us that the official SAR leadership also believed that the Skyline trail area was a realistic possibility, even though the trail was not connected to the Frosty Mountain loop. The Hope SAR team believed that Jordan had changed his mind and hiked the Skyline trail instead of heading for the Frosty campsite.

On March 16, I hiked the Skyline trail for the first time with Trevor. We took a route from the direction of the Rainbow Bridge at the northeastern edge of Lightning Lake. It was soon apparent to us both that nobody had snowshoed this way over the winter—and it made our hike particularly difficult. We needed to kick in our own trail as we moved along the mountain. It is physically exhausting to kick each step into a fresh hard snowpack. We fought for every metre on those steep slopes.

As we climbed, I continuously scanned downhill off-trail, calling Jordan's name every now and then. If Jordan had been lost or injured in this area, he may have tried to return uphill to find the trail or continued moving downhill. We scrutinized areas between switchbacks more carefully, thinking Jordan might have attempted a shortcut off-trail between them.

On this first hike of the Skyline trail, we were only able to reach the trail's second switchback, but the outing helped us understand the terrain and imagine possible scenarios of how Jordan might have reached this location. We also laid down tracks in the snow that would be helpful to us if we were to return for another search. But we found no hard clues and returned to the car with only ideas and strategies for another day.

Considering the dense tree coverage on both sides of the trail, it seemed to us quite unlikely that Jordan had lost his way in the sections we'd covered. If he had opted for the Skyline trail and an accident had happened or he'd gone astray, it would more likely have been on the ridge at the higher elevation, where tree coverage was thinner. And if Jordan had gotten lost up there, his more likely path would be downhill through the forest along one of the drainages. Of course, the terrain itself might have led him down off the trail into a drainage, especially if snow had fallen. Below the ridge, it would have been much easier to make mistakes because there were no obvious landscape features for him to orient himself with.

As a result of Josie's ongoing social media recruitment efforts, two new volunteers, Bob and Pascal, joined our search in mid-March. They (and many others who joined) were moved to action by our family's unwavering determination to find Jordan so long after he had disappeared. Although she was not in British Columbia or searching on the ground, Josie made the initial connections with many of the new volunteers who would come to serve a critical role in the following months. Bob was one of these.

Both Pascal and Bob lived a few hours away from Manning Park. Pascal lived in Vancouver and worked as a civil engineer in water resources management, but he was on a leave of absence at the time. Bob was retired and served on the voluntary SAR team in Oliver, a small town at the south end of the Okanagan Valley, about two and a half hours east of Manning Park. Both men were experienced mountain climbers who had begun hiking in rugged terrain at a young age. Once we started hiking together, particularly off-trail, I could see immediately that they were much more skilled than me at mountain snowshoeing.

On March 17, Bob, Pascal, and I hiked up the Skyline trail, but started from a different location than my first hike there—this time from Strawberry Flats. After a few hours of climbing, we decided to divert off-trail to reach the Skyline ridge more quickly. When you break trail, the first hiker has the most difficult role. They create the first tracks in the snow. Following is much easier. Pascal kindly offered to lead the way up the mountain.

We reached the Skyline ridge around noon. The view was spectacular. We could see all the nearby mountain ranges and peaks, including Frosty Mountain (and the trail up to the Larches and summit), Windy Joe Mountain, Hozomeen Mountain, Three Brothers Mountain, and Mount Winthrop in the United States. We could also make out all the drainage basins between them.

The view from this vantage point gave me a new perspective on the possible scenarios of Jordan's disappearance. For example, if Jordan had changed his mind and hiked along the Skyline trail, then he may have taken the path along the Skyline ridge, and that would lead him southwest toward Ross Lake. If conditions were clear, he might have continued to the lake; but if the snowstorm had reduced visibility, he might have diverted off-trail from the Skyline ridge.

Under normal circumstances, it would be odd to continue hiking about twenty kilometres southwest and as far as Ross Lake. The Lightning Lakes Chain trail was a much more plausible destination, since it lies directly below the ridge. However, there was poor visibility at times that weekend, so Jordan could possibly have become lost on the opposite side of the Skyline ridge and, when he reached the high land, seen Ross Lake and mistaken it for one of the lakes on the Lightning Lakes Chain trail. Then he might have continued in the wrong direction in hopes of eventually coming down to what he thought was Lightning Lake. This scenario suggested that searching the area around Ross Lake might offer useful new clues.

Many or most of the possible scenarios, in fact, could much more easily be visualized from this vantage point on the ridge.

"I see the rationale of searching along this Skyline trail," said Bob, "but when I look over toward the Frosty Mountain trail and the Larches, I think that something wrong happened there." He pointed toward the mountain as he spoke.

"I can understand why you say that, Bob," I said. "But one of the problematic issues in that scenario is the 12:32 cellphone ping. We had experts analyze it and they concluded that Jordan hiked in a clockwise direction around the Frosty trail loop."

"Hmm. Well, I still think Ethan Morf's reported sighting at the second switchback was accurate. It's the only first-hand witness evidence and it places Jordan at a specific location on the trail."

Everyone who involved themselves in our search eventually formed their own likeliest scenario. We felt it was crucial that we stayed open-minded about everyone's opinion, regardless of whether we agreed or not. I told Bob that I definitely wanted to hear his thoughts, but that personally I was trying to keep all options open—including the scenarios that Jordan had taken either the clockwise *or* the counter-clockwise direction on the Frosty Mountain loop, or that he'd been on the Skyline trail or Monument 78 trail when things had gone wrong.

After searching along the ridge, we headed down the mountain along one of the major drainages. To cover more ground, Bob offered to go alone down one drainage, while Pascal and I followed an adjacent one. We agreed that although drainages were usually the most difficult terrain to hike down, they were also the most likely places or routes that Jordan himself would have taken—to get out of the woods or to find water.

Once again, snowshoeing off-trail down the mountainside was difficult. The terrain was steep, the snowpack was deep, and there were many tree wells and sinkholes. Pascal found the safest route down along a ridge between the drainages. I searched under trees, shouting Jordan's name, bringing images of him to mind—but I did not feel his presence in this area.

When we returned to the parking lot, I invited Bob and Pascal to dinner at the resort (as I did with all volunteers). It was a pleasure to offer this form of appreciation for their hard work after a long day of strenuous hiking. After we ate, Pascal departed, but Bob and I continued our conversation. We discussed Jordan and his past accomplishments. Then Bob spoke more personally, sharing that he could understand my pain as he had lost his son years ago under tragic circumstances. When he noticed Josie's posting on social media about the need for volunteers to help find Jordan, he felt a connection and special calling to help us find Jordan. I offered my condolences to Bob and dropped my head in sadness, tears, and empathy of his story. Even though it was only our first day together, Bob gave me a firm commitment that he would not leave my side until we found Jordan.

Thanks to Josie, who had connected me with Bob, I had found a great new friend. And Bob would help me in ways that others could never fully understand. How could I express appreciation to someone

I'd met only a few hours before, especially when that person was so willing to divert their own life to help find my son? No words could adequately express the depth of my gratitude.

Once again, I recognized that, if there was any positive outcome of this terrible situation, it was meeting exceptionally kind-hearted people such as Bob. He joined John, Trevor, Mike B, Stan, and Lynn in my closest and dearest circle of friends.

On March 19, Mike B, Stan, and I searched off-trail along the Monument 78 trail. It had been searched several times, but areas off-trail between the Monument 78 and Monument 83 trails had not been checked. Relatively little ground was covered that day because it was such slow going among the dense tree downfall. But it was a good opportunity to discuss strategy with Mike and Stan.

We talked about the best sequence for searching priority areas when the snowpack finally receded. We considered where and when that would occur first. We decided we would focus the search efforts in the initial snow-free areas, then move elsewhere as more clear ground emerged. With his military background, Mike was especially helpful in crafting strategies to best utilize our small core team of volunteers.

Areas that had been entirely neglected so far included the Middle Creek and Passage Creek drainage basins, which flowed north into Flash Lake and Strike Lake, respectively. Previously, we'd assumed that these valleys west of the Frosty Creek drainage basin were too far from the Frosty Mountain trail to hold promise.

As unlikely as these areas were, we could still imagine possible scenarios of how Jordan could have arrived in them. If he'd hiked near the Frosty Mountain summit, or veered off along one of the nearby ridges, he could have entered one of the drainage basins west of Frosty Creek. Alternatively, if he'd become disoriented above the Frosty Creek drainage basin, while deep in the forest, he could have headed in the wrong direction. Both of these scenarios were long shots, but I felt we could leave no stone unturned. They needed to be checked. Another benefit of snowshoeing to the ridge atop each basin, too, was the good vantage points we'd have for scanning the basins with binoculars. I sometimes preferred binoculars over the digiscope because of their higher magnification. Also, the reconnaissance would be helpful for returning to search more thoroughly by drone.

On March 20, John and I hiked along the Lightning Lake trail until we reached a viable point to enter the forest at the Passage Creek drainage basin, west of the Frosty Mountain trail. We followed a mountain path along the west-facing side of Passage Creek. It was a long day of extreme sidehilling, which involved hiking sideways at a relatively constant elevation across steep terrain. We were not climbing directly up the mountain but rather moving across it at gradually higher and higher elevations. We kept at it for a long time and it severely stressed my ankles.

We travelled far up this drainage basin in areas of the forest that had probably not been hiked by anyone for decades (or ever). Most of the time, we could not see beyond the tree cover, even at our highest elevation. As I hiked and searched among the trees, I was amazed by their size and beauty, on the one hand, but also their cruelty on the other, for they gave me no signs or clues of Jordan.

In the early afternoon, we finally reached a lookout point. As we approached the ridge that led to the summit, we could see east across the entire drainage basin to the west face of the adjacent mountain range. My heart sank at how massive this view of the forested area was. It was beyond intimidating to realize that such a vast area had not yet been checked on the ground. Volunteers had often said that our search was like trying to find a needle in a haystack. As I looked at the mountain wilderness from this vantage point, it felt like searching for one needle in a thousand haystacks.

I imagined that my feeling of utter despair was not unlike what Jordan might have experienced in the same mountain wilderness. But

I knew he would not have given up, so we, too, would not give up, despite the odds against us.

John showed incredible resilience. At no point did he ever indicate a feeling of despair while searching. Although nothing was found on this day, and despite the extremely difficult terrain, depth of snow cover, and amount of tree blowdown, his approach remained "one foot in front of the other."

———

As March wore on, there were more troubling email messages from people connected to the fraudster, Claire. Once again, someone claiming to be her sister wrote and warned our volunteer group to stop texting Claire. This time we also alerted the police ourselves—in St. John's—so they could connect the elements together if we reported contact with Claire.

The writer also alleged volunteer interference and questions at Claire's workplace, which had led to an investigation and her subsequent dismissal. The person felt we should be responsible for Claire's lost income. I was exasperated and exhausted with strategizing about how to make all the accusations and unsolicited contact stop. I hated diverting time and effort to Claire instead of the search for Jordan. We were cautious—not wanting the situation to escalate further—but I was also concerned about Claire confronting us in person at Manning Park. So far, we had not met Claire in person.

I had never discussed these problems with Trevor. When I finally brought them up, he was surprised. He had met Claire at the Manning Park Resort on New Year's Eve, where she'd said that she was unhappy in her current job and would be leaving it soon for a better opportunity—a much different story than what we had been told.

But there was another aspect to the conflict with Claire that was especially disheartening and complicated matters more. Early on, when we had still trusted Claire, we'd asked her for help to search through Jordan's phone for clues. We also gave her the SIM card from his computer—and she still had it. So we made efforts to keep relations cordial enough with Claire through March (while not alienating other volunteers) so that we could get that card back.

Unfortunately, we never were able to, and it profoundly grated on us that we'd made the mistake of trusting her.

Some of the volunteers, particularly John, felt that Jordan may have hiked the Frosty Mountain trail toward the summit but became disoriented somewhere west of the peak and headed down in a drainage that did not lead to a trail. From there, he may have entered a drainage basin to the west. It was difficult for me to visualize this scenario. I felt that I needed to see the summit area of Frosty Mountain for myself to assess the viability of this theory.

So on March 23, Pascal and another new volunteer, Mike N, hiked with me up to the ridge atop the west side of the Frosty Creek drainage basin. The mountain face below us was one flank of the drainage basin into Lightning Lake. It had not yet been searched on the ground.

That afternoon, I saw for the first time an enormous box canyon—a basin formation with only one way in or out. Except for the one opening out of which the waterway drains, it is enclosed on all sides by steep mountain walls. We could clearly make out the box canyon below us and the ridges connecting the summit of Frosty Mountain with the mountain peaks to the west of it.

Looking at this terrain up close, Pascal, Mike, and I agreed that Jordan would never have attempted to cross the ridge west of Frosty Mountain's summit—it was far too dangerous. Not even the most experienced mountain climbers would attempt this passage, which was extremely narrow and had steep drop-offs on both sides. If Jordan had become lost around one of the ridges at the summit of Frosty Mountain, it seemed most likely that he would have veered south into the Princess Creek drainage, north into the Frosty Creek drainage, or eastward, back toward the Frosty Mountain trail. I felt certain that he would *not* have gone west along any of the ridges toward the Middle Creek or Passage Creek drainage basins.

Although we found nothing to confirm Jordan's whereabouts on this trek, our decision to now exclude these possible scenarios was important. We could reduce the search area west of the Frosty Mountain summit. Our attention and limited resources could be better focused elsewhere and on more plausible scenarios.

On March 24, Trevor and I snowshoed up the Skyline 1 trail from Strawberry Flats. As on most days, I had flashbacks of Jordan and family time together. I sometimes shared these memories with Trevor as we hiked.

On this day and others, I told him about Jordan's talent and competitiveness in music, sports, and other activities. When we lived in Winnipeg, Jordan danced each year in Folklorama. This cultural event runs for two weeks each summer and celebrates the ethnic heritage of dozens of different cultures. Jordan dressed in a Slovenian national costume to reflect our family heritage. Josie and her family, as well as my own parents, had emigrated from Slovenia, once part of the former Yugoslavia, in the late-1960s and -1950s, respectively. Jordan liked performing the Slovenian polkas and waltzes with the dance group and had a natural talent for it.

Jordan was on his high school basketball team, played football, worked as a pool lifeguard, and competed in karate (Chitō-ryū). He was a fast learner and became skilled at a karate practice called kata. I remembered once being late to pick him up after basketball practice—a fresh wave of guilt broke over me as I related this anecdote, and it stayed with me. But I also remembered Jordan's efforts when he played sports, and determination to bounce back when a game—or life—knocked him down. I had no doubt that reflex was in action after something had gone wrong on the Thanksgiving weekend at Manning Park.

The area we hiked that day actually has two trails called "Skyline." It starts on Skyline I and then transitions to Skyline II farther southwest, closer to Ross Lake. We got as far as a major switchback below the Skyline ridge. Pushing ahead would have been even more strenuous because the tracks in the snow we had followed ended there and the terrain was steep. By that point it was mid-afternoon, and therefore time to turn back. We decided to return off-trail.

Our route down the mountain was one long, steep, uninterrupted drop about five hundred metres long. We spaced ourselves about twenty metres apart and scanned among the trees as we descended. It was pretty clear to us that Jordan could not have set up a tent in such terrain. But he could have passed through the area on his way down.

We were surrounded by endless imposing trees; the crisp mountain air smelled pure and fresh. Yet I sensed something sinister here, as if there was a phantom in the forest that had taken Jordan. It was elusive, without a physical existence—a ghostly presence.

Tmxʷulaxʷ, when will you show me signs or clues of Jordan?

My forest does not live in isolation of the other spirits of nature here. Our source of life and communications are all connected through the land, water, animals, sun, and air.

When I look around, your fallen trees are covered by deep snow. Some snow piles in the forest look unusual, like a tent could possibly lie beneath, buried by snow. But there are too many piles here to search. Please help. Please give me a sign.

If Jordan had set up a tent here, then imagine: he would need to clear away new snow each time it fell. I felt in response. For once, it seemed, Tmxʷulaxʷ was being helpful. *Clearing away snow from the tent would leave a separate pile next to the tent.*

You are right, but there are still so many piles to check. I must check every one that looks possible. If I check them all, we'd cover very little ground. But if I walk past one without checking, I feel guilt and regret because I might have missed an important clue.

Remember that guilt can work for you. Use it. When later you reflect on the day, think of those feelings as alarms in your decision-making mind. They can shed light on choices that made you feel dissatisfied. They can lead you to where you might find new ideas.

It was burdensome that—in both my searching and my memories on this day—feelings of guilt should arise. But I wasn't sure how to see beyond that guilt to deeper meaning of where to find Jordan.

I measured the effectiveness of each day by the amount of new ground covered, not on whether we had found a clue. This way, each day some progress toward our goal was made. The other way of looking at it would have meant failure every day, and eventually volunteers would be discouraged from helping me search. I needed their ongoing commitment. I hoped that the volunteers, too, might feel a sense of accomplishment, even though the ultimate goal of finding Jordan had not been reached.

So I counted this day as another success: We had covered a large area off-trail.

On March 26, Bob and I snowshoed up the Frosty Mountain trail and then off-trail in a grid search below the third switchback. Bob preferred grid searching as it covered more area on the ground. So when we dropped down off the trail, we spaced ourselves about twenty metres apart, with me farther down the mountain than Bob, and set a course parallel to the trail. We were snowshoeing virtually alone—we were each just able to see the other person.

I looked carefully under and around every tree and under piles of tree blowdown. In the quiet solitude, I cleared my mind in an effort to feel Jordan's presence or any other signals from the surrounding forest. On this day, I thought about Jordan as a child and teenager. He had excelled in so much. He'd learned piano at a young age and later taught music. He'd won a provincial physics competition in high school.

Jordan had a good sense of humour to balance his competitiveness. One of his friends at UBC told me how he liked to poke fun at how his pals ranked their favourite restaurants, bands, and sports teams. He'd also organized a survey and ranked each student's suggested name for their shared Wi-Fi network. If he thought their choice wasn't creative enough, he'd urge them to "step up their game."

Jordan was strong academically and an active community volunteer. He gave time to Habitat for Humanity and volunteered with the ReStore program, which raises funds for housing in third-world countries.

With all these thoughts of Jordan accompanying me, I traversed back and forth across the hillside until I reached the first switchback. But neither I nor Bob found anything. We then shifted to the second switchback, near where Ethan Morf had reported seeing Jordan, to again drop down off-trail. I tried to conjure my son at this point, as well. I so wanted to know if it had really been Jordan whom Ethan had encountered here. I needed to believe that at least one of the many people who'd hiked on that fateful October day had stopped and chatted with him. Had this been the location of Jordan's last conversation? I snapped out of this melancholy line of thought when I came to a sinkhole. We still had work to do before the sun disappeared behind the southern hillside and I needed to pay sharp attention.

This grid search took us through a drainage basin that flowed down the mountain into Twenty Minute Lake. The terrain was steep with many piles of snow-covered tree downfall obstructing our way down. As I climbed over the trees, more flashbacks of Jordan appeared in my mind. It seemed to me that these flashbacks came more frequently because Jordan was, or had been, somewhere nearby.

When he was a little boy, one of Jordan's favourite activities was sliding down an orange and purple playset in our back yard. I assembled it in the spring and took it apart at the end of the summer. Over and over, Jordan would climb up the playset and slide down into a small pool, where I'd catch him. It was a highlight of birthday parties with his friends.

When he was about nine years old, Jordan started indoor rock climbing. I took him for lessons and watched him improve each week. One of the activities was a competition: teams raced up and down the climbing wall. Jordan enjoyed the challenges of readjusting and twisting his body to reach for hand or foot grips, which were different sizes and scattered unevenly across the wall.

I think he enjoyed climbing mountain trails for much the same reasons he'd taken to rock climbing: the sense of accomplishment and the health and fitness benefits it gave him. We had climbed rocky trails together in Newfoundland. It was now unhappily ironic to me that our last hike together in St. John's, in 2018 before he moved to British Columbia, had been on a trail called the Deadman's Bay Path.

Winthrop Creek is a major drainage basin along the Monument 78 trail. If Jordan was lost somewhere to the east of the PCT or southeast of Windy Joe Mountain, it appeared from the map that the Winthrop Creek drainage basin was a plausible area to examine.

Nobody had searched this long drainage basin despite its potential, no doubt because the terrain was densely forested and hardly passable. I asked John if we could search up the waterway heading south toward Mount Winthrop. John was skeptical, but he was always supportive no matter where I asked to hike. So on March 27, we set out together from the Monument 78 parking lot.

After three or four hours we reached Winthrop Creek. We crossed over it via a bridge, then searched for a suitable place to hike off-trail up the drainage. Tree cover, particularly alders, became increasingly dense as we climbed in elevation along the drainage. But it was quite beautiful—everything was frozen and covered in deep snow, the air smelled fresh and crisp—and a route along the creek was visible.

Occasionally we would spot a few birds overhead. Sometimes we heard the strange call of grouse—a nasal squeal or hiss-like sound—or its distinctive low, cooing hum accompanied by a thumping it made by beating its wings. This starts slowly and builds to a crescendo that lasts about ten seconds.

After about an hour pushing up the drainage, the path became almost impassable. We encountered dense tree cover, blowdown, steeper terrain, and unstable snow conditions. No one could have been able to move much farther upstream here—or they would have needed to expend great physical exertion to move even a short distance. Once again we had to concede that, although Winthrop Creek had appeared like a possible scenario on a map, conditions on the ground clearly said it was highly unlikely that Jordan had passed through the area. Our time would be better spent elsewhere.

We left the Winthrop Creek trail and, since the south side of Windy Joe Mountain was quite close, we decided to see what we could see there. This area, too, had not been checked during the initial SAR searches and several intriguing heatmap clues had been identified near where we were. Finding a way to cross Castle Creek was a challenge, but we eventually used an ice bridge and then started snowshoeing uphill toward the clue locations.

The heatmap indicated the clues were not far from the creek. But the terrain was steep, so the actual distance hiked on the ground was much longer—and much of it was very difficult. We had to haul ourselves uphill foot by foot, using any alder branches we could reach. We managed to search a few locations (turning up nothing), but eventually progress became nearly impossible without ropes, so we reversed down the mountain.

But there was some good news: For the first time since October, I noticed some areas of actual ground. The continuous exposure to sunlight on this south-facing side of the mountain had fully melted some of the snow.

Family photo at Signal Hill in St. John's, 2017.

LEFT: Learning the basics of fishing with seven-year-old Jordan in Gimli, Manitoba.
RIGHT: Jordan visiting St. John's for the holidays, 2019.

Engineering Convocation at Memorial University, 2018.

Jordan hiking with UBC friends in Alberta, 2019.

MISSING PERSON
Manning Park, British Columbia

(not exact tent model, we only know its orange)

HAVE YOU SEEN JORDAN NATERER?
Last seen: Sat, Oct 10th
Eye color: Brown   Age: 25   Weight: 190lbs
Hair color: Brown Height: 5'11 Complexion: Fair

Were you in the **Frosty Mountain or Windy Joe** area on
October 10 or October 11?
Did you **see or hear anything strange** while hiking there?
**Jordan was wearing a burgundy red coat, green 60L
camping bag, black pants, white T-shirt, orange tent,
black hiking boots**

If you have any information, please email:
MissingPersonJordan@gmail.com
Phone: (604) 717-2530

TOP: Josie visiting and hiking with Jordan in British Columbia, 2020.
LEFT: Missing person poster, October 2020.

TOP: *On our way to search off-trail between the Frosty Mountain switchbacks with Mike B and Aaron, March 5, 2021.*
LEFT: *John approaching impassable terrain within interior drainages, March 6, 2021.*
BOTTOM: *With Pascal (March 23) overlooking the Frosty ridge.*

With John (March 27) struggling through the Winthrop drainage.

John and Bob overlooking the Frosty Creek drainage basin, April 3, 2021.

Searching through the Larches, with the Frosty Mountain summit in the background, April 3, 2021.

Sidehilling around the southeast side of Windy Joe Mountain, April 20, 2021.

Trevor crossing a tributary of Castle Creek, June 8, 2021.

LEFT: *Mike A brings welcoming words of wisdom to canine search team, Please Bring Me Home, June 11, 2021.*
RIGHT: *Finding an abandoned cabin with Marko, Ed, and Trevor, June 14, 2021.*

LEFT: Sidehilling with Trevor on the south side of Frosty Mountain, July 3, 2021.
RIGHT: Reaching the summit of Frosty Mountain, July 3, 2021.

Salt-of-the-earth core group of volunteers.

Then John made a discovery under some branches.

"Greg, I found a bone that seems to have had its meat recently chewed off!" he shouted.

The bone was about twenty centimetres long and wider at one end. There were no clues suggesting how it had arrived there. Maybe it had been dropped by a scavenging animal?

"With the ground exposed, I can see some food sources," I replied. "It looks like old berries have been recently pulled from branches here. So—evidence of wildlife?"

"There are bears, cougars, and deer in the park," John said. "We should hold onto the bone and check with police and see if it's human."

That last comment brought my stomach into my throat. Human? No, no, no. My thoughts had been going in an entirely different direction—it had to be an animal bone, and an animal bone that a human had eaten the meat from. I begged for this clue to be useful.

John speculated it was a deer bone, but neither of us could tell for sure. So we packed it away for an expert opinion and descended the mountain, returning to the car along the Monument 78 trail.

Here, too, things had changed on the ground. In the morning, the snow along the Monument 78 trail, packed solid, had been frozen from the night before. After the day's warm sunshine, it had become less stable. It supported our weight on some steps, but on others we sank to our knees. The trek out became slow and exhausting.

Once I was finally home, I sent the police and Upper Similkameen Indian Band photos of the bone. They both replied that it was from a young deer. I rejoiced. There was still a glimmer of hope for another day.

That said, we had found no new clues by this point. We needed new ideas. And we wanted to mobilize a larger team of volunteers to help with ground searches in May and June, as the snowpack receded. So, following Mike B's suggestion, we arranged a video conference call for March 28 with key members of the search team. We'd seek their advice and thoughts on new strategies.

The video conference was held on a Sunday evening at the Manning Park Resort. Josie and I welcomed the nine people who could attend and thanked them for their dedicated support and assistance. We updated them on our search activities and shared that no trace of Jordan had been found despite our efforts on the ground. We speculated that Jordan may have strayed outside the park.

Mike M mentioned the ground searches that had been done around the Larches in mid-October. Bob asked about the hat that had been found there during that time. Josie replied that Jordan's computer records showed he'd ordered a cap from Amazon, but it was different from the description of the one found. So the cap was likely not Jordan's.

Someone else asked about the sunglasses that had been found near the cap. Josie reported she could find no record of Jordan having bought sunglasses. She also thought they were a different brand than what she believed Jordan would normally wear.

Nicole asked if we'd found any more information to confirm if Jordan had been on Frosty Mountain. The answer was: nothing beyond the reported sighting by Ethan Morf in October. Mike B spoke about that sighting, adding some more timeline-based information from hikers who had been there between Friday and Sunday. Each bit of added intelligence raised issues when compared with Ethan's report.

Pascal questioned the sighting by Ethan—he wanted to hear how Ethan's father recalled events. Both Josie and I had tried several times to contact the man but he had never returned our calls.[13]

Pascal also wondered about timestamps on photos and whether daylight saving time could have mixed up aspects of the timeline. Josie

---

13 I called Ethan again after our video conference and asked him to urge his father to get in touch. Ethan confirmed that his father would do so—but still we heard nothing.

confirmed his suspicion: There were inconsistencies between reported times and timestamps on camera photos.

After going over the details again, we had a roundtable debate on possible scenarios. Each person was asked for their opinion on the two or three areas of highest probability for Jordan's location.

John was the first to weigh in. "I think the most likely scenario is either the lookouts around the Larches—they're areas where someone could easily slip—or beyond the Frosty Mountain summit along the ridgeline down to Strike Lake or another ridgeline down to Thunder Lake."

Kevin W, who was a BC Parks supervisor for Manning Park, thought Jordan had hiked in the Windy Joe Mountain direction to the East Similkameen trail. This clockwise loop of the Frosty Mountain trail was consistent with the 12:32 p.m. ping closer to Windy Joe Mountain.

"In my opinion," he said, "Jordan parked at the Lightning Lake parking lot, then went along the East Similkameen trail until he found that the bridge was washed out at Castle Creek. He wouldn't have known this ahead of time. I think he intended to hike along the East Similkameen to reach Monument 78."

Trevor also believed Monument 78 at the Canada-US border was a real possibility because of how many Google searches Jordan had done of that area. He also felt that Jordan could have crossed the border—there was no way to tell for sure since the border cameras hadn't been working the day he went missing. In fog or a snowstorm, Jordan may have unknowingly crossed the border through the forest at some distance from the Monument 78 landmark.

"I think the Skyline trail is the highest probability," said Nicole. "This is also the consensus view of my SAR team." In this theory, Jordan would have started up the Frosty Mountain trail, then changed his mind (possibly because of weather conditions or thinking there'd be no space at the Frosty campsite). He'd have turned back down the Frosty Mountain trail, choosing instead to take the Skyline trail.

This scenario opened the additional possibility that Jordan had gone as far as Ross Lake or the Hozomeen Ridge (to the southwest and across the Canada-US border). And these possibilities boosted my sense of hope because of abandoned cabins rumoured to exist at Ross Lake. If Jordan had gone that way, there was a chance he'd found shelter.

For his part, Bob believed Ethan Morf *had* seen Jordan. He had a permit for the Frosty campsite. He may have turned around after he saw Ethan and heard about conditions farther along, then camped off-trail. "Assuming a pace of about three kilometres an hour, I will be focusing up to three kilometres past the second switchback off the Frosty trail."

Kevin noted that the online back-country reservation permit form has an entry and an exit point, but not a place to indicate a chosen campsite. However, Trevor reminded everyone that Jordan had filled out his permit form in person at the park and indicated he'd stay at the Frosty campsite. Josie added that it showed one night, one person, and an orange tent. She'd heard there were off-trail camping areas farther up the trail that also held potential and needed to be checked.

"What if Jordan turned around because of the weather, went back to his car to wait and see if it cleared, then went up the Frosty trail after, say, 7:00 p.m.?" asked Sue, who was one of our video review volunteers. That, too, was possible—we had no information from hikers coming down the Frosty Mountain trail that late on October 10. And in this scenario, Jordan could have camped farther up the mountain than the Frosty campsite. Perhaps his tent slipped downhill and over a cliff because of the snow.

"Those cliff areas have been extensively searched," said Josie.

Mike B believed that Jordan had gone clockwise around the Frosty Mountain loop: up Windy Joe Mountain, then around to the Frosty campsite sometime on Sunday. This clockwise loop would be consistent with the 12:32 p.m. ping.

"Someone would have seen Jordan if he'd gone up the Frosty trail," he reasoned. "So if I'm wrong, and he went counter-clockwise, either he went off-trail as he climbed up Frosty, or the sighting by Ethan is not correct." He further suggested that more social media outreach should be done to find other people who had hiked in the area on that weekend.[14]

Our video conference lasted about three hours. New insights were gained into the likelihood of various scenarios, especially involving the Skyline trail. However, given the diversity of opinions regarding each scenario, we were unfortunately unable to narrow down priority search areas. As a result, we still kept all possible options open for consideration.

When I went out to the car, I found that the snow that had been falling earlier in the evening had become a blizzard. Whiteout conditions on my drive to Eastgate reduced visibility to about a metre and I could only crawl along the road. Halfway back, conditions were so bad that I couldn't decide if it would be safer to carry on or turn back. Is this what Jordan had felt when the snowstorm suddenly hit him last October? I, too, was alone but at least in the shelter of my car. He had been alone with no shelter except a tent in his pack.

Once again, I sent up a plea that Jordan had found someplace to shelter from the blizzard and throughout the coming winter months. I crept on toward the cabin, praying that Jordan had been able to do the same.

———

The team's determination in the video conference inspired us and renewed our energy. During our long discussion, several volunteers

———

14 Josie later followed up, connecting with additional hiking groups on social media. She also launched another poster outreach blitz to churches and retail stores in Princeton, Merritt, Hope, and Chilliwack—and extended her outreach to hospitals, including those in the United States. But still we were unable to find anyone who had hiked the path clockwise in its entirety on the Thanksgiving weekend.

had advocated strongly to prioritize Windy Joe Mountain, citing the many heatmap clues that had not yet been checked on the ground. When a new volunteer, Lauren, joined our team, I planned an off-trail search with her there.

On March 30, Lauren, Pascal, and I headed for the north side of Windy Joe Mountain. At the third switchback on our way up the trail, we dropped off and traversed east and west at constant elevation contours down the north-facing slope. It was, once again, steep terrain covered by still-deep snow and many layers of fallen trees.

We spaced ourselves ten to twenty metres apart and kept each other in sight as we descended. Despite the presence of the others, however, I felt a sense of solitude and vexation with the mountainous forest.

My son was taken, as you know, Tmxʷulaxʷ. I paused in frustration. *I deserve an answer as to what happened, or at least a sign of where to find him.*

All life, including humans, animals, water, and this forest, are intimately connected, came the familiar reply from Tmxʷulaxʷ. *If harm is done to one then it is done to all.*

But I fear my son is in danger. I'm seeking mercy so that I can bring him home to my family. Help me. Please.

How can I help? I am gentle, caring, flexible, but I cannot communicate in ways that you will understand.

You can, Tmxʷulaxʷ. You can guide my decision-making or use your power over the wind to show me signs in the forest.

I have strength to transform the wind and trees, but you will need to learn our way of communicating. We act in humility not in cruelty toward your son. Jordan needed water so go to the source toward the drainage.

At this I heard Pascal shouting our names and my conversation with Tmxʷulaxʷ evaporated. I realized I had drifted too far away. I shouted back and soon reconnected with the other two. We reached the edge of our search area, dropped down the hill, reversed course, and repeated the pattern toward a nearby drainage. After several more traverses, we reached the bottom. We had covered a lot of new ground but without finding any new clues.

————

In the evenings, alone in the cabin, I was often distressed by thoughts of our lives ahead without Jordan. Lynn and Stan, who owned the cabin, shared a book with me—*Lament for a Son* by Nicholas Wolterstorff—in which the author writes about losing his son in a mountain-climbing accident. They thought it might help me to read about someone else coping with a similar tragedy. I related strongly to Wolterstorff's words.

What *if* Jordan was never coming back? How would my family cope with such a loss? Each time I was out on the trails, I saw young men and women hiking and safely returning at day's end. Why not my son? All those people going out and back, none of them Jordan. Leaving me only with the silence of his absence.

I found it so hard to imagine the "nevers" that might lie ahead: never to embrace Jordan again, never to laugh together, never to watch pro sports or hike with him again. The list was endless and each one had its own meaning. Jordan would not be there to share Christmas dinners. He would not celebrate with us when his younger sisters, whom he adored, graduated from high school and university. He would not enjoy family events with us anymore. He would only exist in our memories. I resisted these thoughts with all my being, and as often as I could.

Losing a child is not the proper order of life, I felt. Children should bury their parents—that was the proper order. I had never before thought that my life, our lives, would do anything but follow a sequence: marry, have children, they marry, grandchildren appear, and eventually my death arrives. Jordan dying before me was never even considered.

That picture had splintered and broken. The death of a child is a horrible reminder that life brings wrong turns and defeats. Josie and I were worried, too, about the traumatic effect all of this was having on our daughters. We all needed a conclusion, irrespective of whether Jordan had survived. We all needed closure and a way to understand what happened, which would finally let us honour Jordan's memory and move forward in our lives.

So on March 31, I continued the journey to find closure. Trevor and I searched around the Three Falls trail in the Skyline trail area, at a lookout area over Nepopekum Falls, and off-trail to the north of the Skyline ridge. But still we found nothing.

I had, for a long while, counted the days and weeks that had passed since October 10, but on the cusp of April, that too, was becoming too difficult. I fought the sense of defeat and summoned optimism for the coming month. More snow would melt, revealing—surely—some clues, long hidden underneath.

Hang on, Jordan. We are still here. I will not go home again without you.

seven

APRIL WARNINGS TO GO HOME

In the mountains, you are sometimes invited,
sometimes tolerated, and sometimes told to go home.
—BECKEY, 1996

THE ALPINE LARCHES IN MANNING PARK ARE BELIEVED TO BE about 2,000 years old, among the oldest living trees in North America. Larch are deciduous conifers that typically reach heights between thirty-five and fifty metres. In the fall, as the temperature drops, they collect nutrients from their needles, which causes them to turn a golden yellow. Seeing the golden larches is a primary reason hikers come to Manning Park every fall.

The English word "larch" is derived from the Latin *Larigna*, which itself comes from the name of an ancient Roman settlement called Larignum in northern Italy. Julius Caesar once approached Larignum with plans to destroy it. He noticed a pile of wood outside the gates of the settlement and told his army to burn it. When they set a fire, it refused to catch and Caesar was amazed that the wood remained unburned. The townspeople, who had surrendered, were asked where the wood came from. They pointed to trees nearby—larch. Because of its toughness and resilience, the Roman architect and engineer, Vitruvius, during the first century, dreamed of a Rome made of larch.

So the larch trees that Jordan set out to see on Thanksgiving weekend 2020 set down their roots in Manning Park around the same time as those events in ancient times, and also the era when Christ lived. I felt a sense of solace that Jordan's desired destination of the Larches was connected to Christ through a beautiful and everlasting tree of life.

All these thoughts were in my mind as I set out on my first hike of the new month. It was Good Friday, April 2. Bob and I hiked up the Frosty Mountain trail to the fifth switchback and followed our climb with a grid search down the mountain to Lightning Lake. Before we set out, we subdivided the areas below the trail into rectangular blocks that could each be reasonably searched in a day. It gave me a sense of satisfaction to look at our progress and know that, slowly but surely, we were following a methodical plan to search every conceivable area of interest.

During our first grid search, Bob and I traversed down the mountain parallel to the Frosty Mountain trail along nearly constant elevation contours. Once again, the snowshoeing was exhausting because of unstable snow, the treefall beneath it, and the steepness of the terrain. As I crawled under and through tree downfall, I sank deeply into the snow and into unexpected sinkholes. My steps were laborious, yet my mind wandered. I felt another tense exchange with Tmxʷulaxʷ.

Why did Jordan climb this mountain, Tmxʷulaxʷ?

The beautiful larch trees higher up attract many people, came the response. *Jordan told his friends he wanted to see them.*

But why did he go alone? Could no one else have gone with him?

Yes. But he enjoyed the solitude. As you can see, many choose to hike solo here. It brings a sense of accomplishment and fulfillment.

*I partly understand, Tmx*ᵂ*ulax*ᵂ*. I know hiking alone comforted Jordan. I know he enjoyed his life in Vancouver and balanced its pace with the peace that time in the forest can bring.*

Any individual can appreciate me at a deeper level when they are alone.

*Tmx*ᵂ*ulax*ᵂ*, your power is mighty and you have my utmost respect. But I trust that you understand that, as a grieving father, I find your power has been cruel.*

My power would never willfully rise above any other form of life. The drainage here has a waterway, and that waterway finds the lowest path downward as a sign of my humility.

*You know my heart is broken, Tmx*ᵂ*ulax*ᵂ*, and needs solace. You speak words of wisdom but my basic questions need clear answers. Why would Jordan even try to climb this difficult mountain?*

There was no response.

I began again: *I understand how the serenity and beauty of this wilderness, especially the Larches, promised a spiritual experience that called Jordan to these mountains*—then a stumble over some fallen trees snapped me out of my meditation. Jarred back into the moment, I realized I'd lost a line of sight to Bob. I could hear him shouting my name from higher up the slope. I climbed farther up, shouting back. Reconnected, we continued our parallel traversing paths. I let Bob know that I would be taking a break at three o'clock.

Good Friday commemorates the crucifixion and death of Jesus. For Christians, of whom I am one, it is a day of mourning and sorrow. Christian tradition teaches that Christ died on the cross at three in the afternoon, on what would later come to be called Good Friday. As the hour when the Lord felt abandoned and forsaken on the cross drew nearer, I looked around to find an appropriate place to pray. I found a deep tree well and cleared away the snow nearby. It seemed appropriate to find the lowest place I could—searching for Jordan in these conditions had made me feel so small, as if I was caught down in a hole.

From my low, sunken position, I made my heartfelt prayer for Jordan. The Lord had mercy for the poor in spirit and showed compassion to those most in need and heartbroken. And so I added another supplication, that He might have mercy on me and my family by bringing us to Jordan.

After these solemn moments, I climbed out again and soon found Bob. We continued on down the difficult terrain. We eventually arrived back at the parking lot, but again with no new information to help us further narrow our future searches.

———

Up to this point in our searching, my interactions with the nature spirit had taken the form of imaginary or felt conversations while I was meditating or seeking signs and signals of Jordan in my subconscious mind. No interaction so far was strong enough to have any meaningful impact on our search process. That was about to change.

On April 3, I once again met John and Bob at the parking lot. Our intention was to start up the Frosty Mountain trail. Before setting out, we discussed specifically where we should search.

"My preference is to do a grid search off one of the switchbacks before the Frosty campsite," said Bob. "Other hikers have already looked there, but they didn't check the entire area with grid searches."

"I feel I have thoroughly searched those areas," said John. "I'd prefer to go past the Frosty camp and check areas to the west or east of the Larches, down into one of the drainage basins there. I think those areas below the cliffs are more crucial. They haven't been adequately checked by the SAR teams and previous volunteers."

"Both of your plans have good merit," I offered. "Here is my suggestion: Let's go up to the Larches as per John's idea, and on the way back, detour off the switchbacks down the mountain to pass through the areas suggested by Bob."

We agreed on the plan, although we all knew that combining both objectives implied a most strenuous day of snowshoeing. First we'd have to do a ten-kilometre climb—nearly all the way to the summit—and then descend the mountain in deep snow over steep treacherous terrain off-trail between the switchbacks.

The hike up the Frosty Mountain trail was, thankfully, uneventful. We stopped at the Frosty campsite. John relaxed with his usual practice during our break: holding out a handful of seeds and whistling for birds nearby. Within a few minutes, whisky jacks flew over and picked up the seeds from his outstretched palm. I did the same—it was a peaceful way to release the tension from continually searching and scanning among the trees.

After we passed the Frosty campsite, I experienced the Larches in the sub-alpine area for the first time. This section of the trail was on a plateau between two parts of the rising mountain. I felt an eerie and chilling sensation here because of how the sparsely treed area looked identical in all directions. It was frightening to see just how easily it was to become disoriented in the snow and lose the trail. I could turn 360 degrees and the forest looked almost exactly the same all around. There were no landmarks or markers to help me distinguish east from west, north from south, or up the mountain from down the mountain.

Even though the larch trees had long ago lost their fall foliage, it was still too difficult to see through them to properly orient myself. A few steps in the wrong direction could easily lead to disorientation. And in a snowstorm? Or when the path could not be detected? It was difficult to think about.

We finally reached an open area with a view out beyond the trees and I saw—for the first time close up—the Frosty Mountain summit and the adjacent box canyons. It was breathtaking. No mountain peak I had viewed ever before compared to seeing the Frosty Mountain summit from this vantage point. Its magnificence confirmed to me that Jordan's likely objective was the Larches, and possibly the first peak of Frosty Mountain.

The weather was clear and pleasant when we reached this subalpine area. We hiked farther, until we reached a ridge that divided the drainage basins on both sides of the Frosty Mountain trail (Frosty Creek drainage to the west and the interior drainages to the east). In this open area, we could see clearly to the summit and down into both massive drainage basins. I stopped to absorb the sight of these spectacular surroundings.

As I looked carefully down into the drainage basin east of the Frosty Mountain summit, I suddenly felt a powerful dark energy descend over my body, then I started to tremble. I looked to the sky, and the seemingly innocuous clouds suddenly became dark, the wind grew in force, and out of nowhere snow began to whip around us.

My heart jumped. A cold sweat covered my body and I was overcome by a dizziness that made me feel like my head was swirling in the punishing clouds overhead. Tears began to flow. And I had a deep sense that something very bad had happened nearby. Everything was sending me clear signs—the powerful mountain summit, the ominous clouds, the blistering wind and snow. Tmxʷulaxʷ was communicating in the strongest possible way.

Bob and John were well ahead of me by this time. John had crossed a valley to the west to check something unusual. Bob had continued straight ahead up the final rocky ascent before the summit. I followed him, but the overpowering feeling I received from the surroundings convinced me that it was time to turn around.

One of the key rules of safety when mountain climbing is that if one person feels uncomfortable or unsafe, then all should respect that and act accordingly. No hiker should override or dismiss the safety concerns of another—the group should take the preferred course of action of the person feeling unsafe, as long as that choice is a safe one.

After I reached them, for the first time, I expressed a reluctance to continue forward. I usually stuck to our intended route, irrespective of the difficulty of the terrain or snow cover. But on this day and in this place, Tmxʷulaxʷ sent me the loudest, clearest signal so far. It was time to get down off the mountain. As always, both John and Bob were supportive, so we turned around.

Passing back through the Larches, my sense of Jordan's presence was so strong that I could feel his suffering and anguish as he tried to orient himself among the trees. As I climbed across some tree downfall, I stretched to reach branches and twisted my body to fit through a small gap between the fallen trees. This brought a happier sense of Jordan, a memory of carrying him on my back while we played a childhood game. When he was a child, we had rubber tiles that fit together like a puzzle, each with a letter of the alphabet on it. We had to cover specific letters with a hand, foot, or knee. Jordan, from his perch, would keep encouraging me, contorted as I was, to cover one more letter.

When he was nine, we vacationed together in Slovenia to meet family. One of the most beautiful places we visited together was Bled, a small island on a lake encircled by mountains. Josie, Jordan, and I parked our rented car and walked around the lake. Halfway along, it began to rain. But we were so enjoying each other's company it didn't matter that we were soaking wet.

I also had flashbacks of a time of us canoeing together in Cape Broyle, Newfoundland. We rented a canoe and paddled with an instructor out the bay, up to where it reached the ocean. The instructor came along with a few other groups but allowed Jordan and I some free time to canoe independently. Jordan pointed out a cave on the other side of the bay. Adventurous and curious, he was confident we could canoe there together. So we paddled across to the remote area and right through the sea cave. Jordan was a risk taker, which may have played a role on that fateful Thanksgiving weekend.

I snapped out of these flashbacks as we got closer to the Frosty campsite. And I shared my mountaintop experience, then, with Bob and John. Although I didn't go into a lot of detail, I knew they both were aware something powerful had happened because of my emotional state. They embraced me, responding with compassion and comforting words. Normally we talked continuously throughout our searches together, but during times that felt more spiritual, we hiked quietly in honour to Jordan.

We did discuss, however, the possible scenarios of Jordan's disappearance given the chilling signals from Tmxʷulaxʷ. We went over various factors to consider before returning to search here again. First, the areas that I observed from the ridge down into the drainage basins were vast, steep, and still covered in deep snow, perhaps three metres or more, with continual wind drifts running down from the mountaintops. Given the limited hours of sunlight and the distance to be travelled to reach them and return before sunset, only a small area could be searched on any given day. Furthermore, and perhaps more importantly, the police SAR teams indicated that they had already thoroughly searched these drainage areas. Our focus had been to search new ground that had not yet been covered by others.

On the other hand, although we placed trust in what those earlier searchers said they had done, we nevertheless knew that clues could still have been missed. It was possible to walk through an area and miss something important just a few metres from your path, perhaps because it was concealed under trees, or you are temporarily distracted or not paying attention for a few critical moments. During my meditations with the nature spirit and when memories of Jordan came to mind, I knew I lost some focus. It was a concern to me—might I even have missed important clues while daydreaming?

On our return hike down the mountain, we reached a steep open hillside that seemed too difficult to snowshoe or even glissade down. John stopped, looked around, and thought for some time. He decided, after all, to sit and glissade. It was a long slide and it seemed like he almost lost control a few times. But despite swerving too far to one side of his desired path, he arrived safely at the bottom.

I was nervous about doing this slide. John shouted back and assured me it would be fine and not to worry. He promised to make sure that I got down to him safely. I didn't understand how he could make this assurance—if I lost control I could slide away from where he could help me. But I sat down, prepared my poles in the snow, lifted my snowshoes, and began to slide down.

The first half of the descent was fine. But then I started accelerating too fast and in the wrong direction. I pushed my poles into the snow but it wasn't enough compensation. So on I slid while losing control. Luckily, John was able to jump into my path, grab me, and slow me down—but not before I took him for another ride. We tumbled together in the snow but ultimately came to a stop with no damage done.

John had saved me, but it seemed like a dangerous move. When he jumped out, I could have directly hit his legs with my snowshoes at full speed. But he assured me it was not a problem because he would have rolled before any direct impact. He had worked out various scenarios in his mind and adjusted quickly as I diverted off his path. It was remarkable to me how well he understood the terrain and snow cover. He was able to predict how and where I might slide.

John was the truest of friends. He placed my safety and well-being above his own. Although he said the situation was always under control, I think he was prepared to do anything to keep me safe. Here was a person who had not known me before Jordan's disappearance, but now was so caring that he would hike anywhere and anytime to help me find my son.

Bob slid down safely after me and we continued along the trail until we reached the Frosty campsite. Then we diverted off-trail and searched areas between most of the switchbacks including between the first and fourth switchbacks. The sun shone all afternoon, softening and destabilizing the snow, which made each footstep down the mountain increasingly strenuous.

By the time we returned to the parking lot, I was so exhausted that I could hardly get myself into the car. It was a gruelling day. But some important new insights that pointed to possible places in the area around the Larches that Jordan may have become disoriented and lost the trail had been gained. This information would be useful for subsequent planning.

We had not planned to hike together on Easter Sunday, but Bob returned in the morning. He didn't want me to snowshoe alone on this holy and joyful day of Christianity.

The afternoon before, we had not thoroughly covered a plateau near the base of the mountain directly south of Lightning Lake. This became our day's plan: Do a grid search of this plateau.

Once we reached the plateau, Bob and I spaced ourselves apart and began covering the territory. As I walked, I had flashbacks of Jordan and previous Easter holidays together. When Jordan was a young boy, we had a family tradition: He dressed up as the Easter bunny and hid chocolate eggs in the backyard for our daughters and nieces to find. Every year, of course, his costume became larger. Jordan enjoyed dressing up and acting silly. He'd hide behind the girls and jump out while they hunted for eggs. We had many wonderful memories of this annual rite.

I heard Bob shouting my name. I looked toward his voice and realized we had lost visual contact. I adjusted my direction and we continued our parallel traversing of the area, back and forth in a grid pattern, until we had thoroughly searched the plateau. As on Good Friday, I made my Easter prayer in a tree well.

Nothing of significance was found that day. We were back at the car by sunset, where we solemnly wished each other good night.

Unfortunately, weird episodes and unreasonable characters continued to intrude on our lives. After I returned to the cabin on Easter Sunday night, a knock came on the cabin door. A woman whom I had never met burst inside. To my surprise, she started berating me angrily.

"Why are you still here?" she shouted. "Your son is dead. Accept the fact and go home! You should leave Eastgate."

I was so taken aback that I couldn't respond. Who was this person?

"Your presence here is upsetting," she went on. "Your son is gone and you need to accept the facts. Going out every day to search in the snow at Manning Park is crazy."

"My family and I need to find out what happened to Jordan," I finally managed to reply. "It is still possible to find clues that might lead us to him, even in the snow."

"You're unrealistic," she shouted. "He probably decided to leave his identity behind and impersonate someone else, so that nobody could find him." She continued for some time to scold and insult me.

I remained calm and did not argue back. I wanted to defuse the situation, since I couldn't let this conflict jeopardize my ability to stay in Eastgate and continue searching for Jordan. Eventually she calmed down.

"Have a Happy Easter," were her parting words. She dropped an Easter chocolate on a bench beside the door for me. "I'll leave now. I hope you find peace."

I threw away the chocolate bar after the door shut behind her.

I called Stan and Lynn to let them know what had happened and to see if they knew whether my presence was upsetting anyone else in the community. They assured me that the people they'd spoken with had only empathy and respect for my determination to find Jordan.

A few days later, the woman returned and apologized to me. She said that, although she felt very sure Jordan was dead, it was not appropriate for her to scold me for continuing to search for him. She said she was sorry and she wished that I could find peace. I accepted her apology.

Still, the whole episode planted self-doubt in my mind. Was she right that it was a waste of time continuing our search? Should I leave Eastgate because the search was upsetting for others? I consulted with Josie, Mike B, John, Trevor, and Bob. They all supported my desire to continue.

The incident also affected how I connected with others in the community. I reached out to another couple at a nearby cabin to keep them more frequently updated. And on days when I knew I'd arrive back later in the evening, I let them know in advance so they wouldn't worry about me.

———

On April 6, Pascal and I grid searched another area near Windy Joe Mountain. The idea in our minds was that Jordan could have been injured while trying to descend the mountain or cross Castle Creek over downed trees. If a person slips while traversing a fallen tree, it's possible to be impaled by an upward-pointing branch.

In this scenario, Jordan would have crossed the East Similkameen trail before reaching Castle Creek—but he wouldn't have known that it was an actual trail. Although the trail appears on hiking maps of Manning Park, most of it is not maintained by park staff.

Searching along the Castle Creek riverbed was precarious because of steep terrain and heavy tree blowdown. When we reached our turn-around time, we returned back off-trail. We soon realized, however, that we had miscalculated the time. By mid-afternoon we were still deep in the forest and surrounded by dense blowdown for many kilometres. We knew we could not afford to be caught off-trail after sunset, especially in this area. We tried to pick up our pace but could not move much more quickly because of the dense tree downfall.

We focused on finding a path of least resistance. Pascal carefully navigated through the downed trees—it required not only an assessment of what was directly in front of us but also of what lay beyond. An inexperienced hiker might have chosen a route that worked for the immediate vicinity but become trapped soon after—which would mean reversing course and trying a different direction.

With intense focus, we were able to choose pathways well enough to reach the parking lot before sunset. Though we had found no trace of Jordan, we had covered a significant amount of new ground. Given the difficulty of searching this area, we decided it would be more effective to search there again with a dog team.

On April 7, Trevor and I returned to the Skyline trail area and searched another plateau near the base of the north side of the Skyline ridge. Once again nothing was found. But I had memorable flashbacks of Jordan as a student at Memorial University.

As Dean of Engineering and Applied Science at Memorial University, I traditionally hooded the new graduates at convocation. Memorial's engineering programs and research are among the top tier in the country. Jordan earned his Bachelor of Engineering degree in 2018, in electrical engineering. He had insisted throughout his studies on getting no special treatment as the dean's son. But I hoped to embrace him on stage as he received his degree. I knew his preferences well enough to broach the possibility weeks in advance. Jordan was adamant: no special attention and no hug on the stage. Disappointed, I reluctantly agreed. Colleagues at the office wagered on whether or not "the hug" would happen on stage.

When the moment arrived, Jordan walked across the stage to me with a big smile on his face. I congratulated him and shook his hand, just as I'd done for every other graduate. He knelt, I hooded him, and I stepped back. He rose and appeared to begin to leave the stage. But then to my surprise, he turned around, stepped back, and embraced me. My heart thrilled with joy and the audience erupted in applause.

I keep a photo of that moment in my office. But even without the picture, I remember it clearly. And the image often appeared to me unbidden in the forest. It was one of the happiest and proudest moments of my life.

Jordan and I had many similarities, including our personalities. We both chose engineering. But the convocation showed some differences—I seemed to be more expressive about my emotions than Jordan.

After graduating, Jordan had several job offers from companies in Ottawa and St. John's. He also received offers to pursue a master's degree at McGill University and UBC. He chose UBC primarily because of an exciting industry-related research project in wireless communications with a world-renowned professor in the Department of Electrical and Computer Engineering, Dr. Lutz Lampe.

Jordan received a graduate scholarship from the Natural Sciences and Engineering Research Council (NSERC) of Canada in 2019 to complete his master's degree. This is a prestigious national award for students who demonstrate academic excellence, leadership ability, and outstanding volunteerism in their community. He completed his master's degree and research thesis ("Modular Spectrum Utilization for Next-Generation Fixed Transmission Networks") in August 2020. His research was presented as an invited paper, with the same title as his thesis, at the 2021 Biennial Symposium on Communications at the University of Saskatchewan on June 29, 2021. The article developed a new method for using additional parts of the radio spectrum to improve internet data transmission rates through wireless networks.

If only some of his developments in wireless communications could have given us a better understanding of the location of his cellphone pings on October 10.

When I searched off-trail in the forest, fear was often an unseen companion. I would occasionally find markings on trees or tracks in the snow that signified bears. I had heard several stories about these predators in Manning Park, but thankfully had not yet encountered one. I carried bear spray, but I nevertheless was constantly afraid of meeting one.

I was increasingly afraid of negative attitudes out of fear that a growing despair might turn away volunteers and leave me without anyone else to continue searching. As I searched among and below the fallen trees, I also feared suddenly discovering Jordan's remains. And I worried about being injured in a way that would end my ability to search for Jordan.

Some specific memories of Jordan helped me deal with this anxiety. He had enjoyed the stories of John Cheever, which included several pieces about fear and courage. And he shared lessons from those stories on a radio program at UBC. So, I would imagine conversations with him about fear and courage, as I did while hiking with John up Windy Joe Mountain.

Dad, I have a story of a fellow whose older brother comes to visit. The man lives in an apartment building. He learns that his brother is afraid of elevators—not heights, just elevators in general. Maybe the speed of going up to a certain height at a certain velocity scares him.

How does the brother overcome his fear?

The brother cannot explain it. They talk about him going to a therapist to be able to deal with this fear and how he has not been able to overcome it.

We should face our fears with courage. I connected this story with strategies for dealing with my own feelings.

It becomes a tragic story, though. The brother usually walks up the stairs. He lives on the twelfth floor. He is okay walking up to the twelfth floor. But then he gets a job in an office on the fifty-second floor.

If we avoid situations out of fear, we may lose opportunities or miss important tasks that need to be finished, I responded.

Exactly. But he couldn't take the job because he couldn't walk that many stairs every single day. He didn't want to embarrass himself by saying, "I'm afraid of elevators."

Jordan, if a person doesn't confront their fears, they will never attempt a situation to see if it's as hard as they thought. So they'll lose the opportunity to overcome their fears.

Recalling actual conversations with Jordan gave me strength and sometimes practical ideas that I could use in the forest. I could see how this memory was relevant to my actual situation and his words helped ease my anxieties.

John and I hiked toward the PCT campsite on April 10, and then on to the Frosty Mountain connector trail. We diverted westward off-trail into drainages that led north to the Similkameen River. We snowshoed through dense tree coverage for some time before the trees opened up and offered an extraordinary view of the entire drainage basin to the northeast of Frosty Mountain. The basin began near the summit and flowed down between several lower mountains contained within the Frosty Mountain trail loop. This basin took in the various tributaries that flow down and into the same primary drainage.

We could not see down to the base of the drainage because of the steep and heavily treed terrain on both of its sides. Farther down, the basin was flanked by steep cliffs.

John looked steadily and intently with binoculars right and left, up and down across this landscape but saw nothing unusual. He pointed to various hillsides that he had traversed during the initial search in October and November. I, too, took a long, careful look to see if any unusual structures or colours stood out among the trees or the snow. But I saw nothing.

We carried on off-trail through the meadows above the drainage. This area looked significant because Jordan could, realistically, have set up his tent here—then possibly encountered an animal or had some kind of accident. We searched thoroughly among the trees in this area, but again found nothing.

At the end of our day, we agreed that it was important to come back and search the area more thoroughly when the snow had melted and we could see clear ground.

Over the previous few weeks, volunteers examining aerial imagery had focused more on Ross Lake, at the southwestern edge of Manning Park and about thirty kilometres southwest of the Frosty Mountain trail. This effort was in response to the theory that Jordan could have changed his mind on the Frosty Mountain trail, reversed course, hiked the Skyline trail, and then lost his way, which ultimately could have taken him southwest to Ross Lake.

We felt a particular urgency about Ross Lake at this time because we had learned from Hope residents that there were abandoned cabins nearby. I was anxious to search there, but also afraid of what I might find. It was, as discussed in our Zoom meeting in March, also possible that Jordan had inadvertently crossed the border in that area.

Bob and I had strategized earlier about where to begin, which trail sections to cover, and how to connect with American authorities to increase awareness of Jordan's possible disappearance south of the border.

"It's a major challenge to reach Ross Lake at this time of year," Bob said. "It doesn't appear to be accessible from Manning Park until the summer."

"The summer trails are not used in the winter," I replied, agreeing with his observation. "It's too far to pack down a new trail ourselves. We'd need an overnight stop at Mowich Camp. But I've heard the snow is still deep there. And there's no easy water source."

The other option was to drive from Hope to Ross Lake. That wasn't a great option for us, either. To begin with, the road south from Hope to Ross Lake was about sixty kilometres and gravelled, in poor condition at the best of times, and filled with potholes. My vehicle certainly would not be able to make that road in winter.

"You know I'm skeptical about Jordan going to Ross Lake," Bob had said. "But I know you and Josie are anxious to search there. So we'll have to take my truck."

"I don't think that will work, Bob," I replied. "I've heard about a kilometre of the road is blocked by trees, about halfway along. It will be impassable until ground crews can open it up."

Logging had recently cleared large sections of forest at a few locations east of the road. This had exposed the edge of the forest to the wind and, facing a direct frontal exposure, large swaths of trees had collapsed.

Eventually we heard that the fallen trees had been cleared from the road and some grading had been done. So on April 12, Bob and I drove together to search around Ross Lake.

As we got closer, cabins began to appear. Some near the start of the gravel road looked abandoned. Were these the ones the local volunteers had mentioned? Had the cabins along the road been confused with cabins at Ross Lake? We carried on with these questions in our minds.

Ross Lake is at a much lower elevation than the Frosty Mountain trail and is much farther west. Spring had arrived earlier here and we found the ground snow-free. We parked the truck at a campground on the Canada-US border, then hiked through it and along riverbeds, looking inside any cabins we encountered.

"I don't see any private cabins here," said Bob. "Just ones for park rangers, on both sides of the border. And the ones at the campground look abandoned."

We could see a road beyond the trees, leading south toward the United States. The map showed the road ending, but possibly there were other campgrounds farther south on the lake.

"It appears the only way to access those campgrounds is from Highway 20 in the United States. From here, they'd be accessible only by boat," said Bob.

We continued to search thoroughly among the trees until we reached the border. Bob found a Missing Person poster on a display board: Alexander Pisch. US park rangers of the North Cascades National Park were searching for the thirty-five-year-old man, who had last been seen near Colonial Creek Campground (along Ross Lake) on Thursday, October 8, 2020. The poster said Alexander's white Toyota Corolla was parked on Highway 20, where he had set up an easel for painting.

Bob suggested that we contact the park rangers to inform them of Jordan's disappearance as well. Possibly they had searched areas for Alexander Pisch that might be helpful to us. We also felt we should share the areas that our team had searched for Jordan (and that we had not turned up any evidence of Alexander, that we knew of). Coordinating our efforts could be helpful.

I was intrigued to learn that Alexander had gone missing only a few days before Jordan—and in such close proximity. It seemed unlikely, but both might have been lost around Ross Lake. Could they have met and developed a plan for surviving together through the winter?

Josie contacted the PCT Association and park rangers in the Ross Lake area. All were willing to work together and share information. Some volunteers had previously mentioned they would connect with American authorities. But an official file on Jordan had never been opened in the United States due to insufficient evidence to indicate that he had crossed the border.

Because so many branch trails led off the primary PCT route near the international border, we tried to determine which areas had already been searched. We then could hire helicopters to fly over those that hadn't been.

Back in the truck, Bob and I drove to the exit point of the Skyline II trail and hiked eastward up it toward Manning Park. The route was mostly snow-free until we reached higher elevations. Periodically, looking westward, we could see the flood plain of Ross Lake. In October, when Jordan had first gone missing, that flood plain would have been covered by water. Water levels in the lake vary seasonally depending on hydroelectric supply and demand managed by the Ross Dam.

Imagining the flood plain as a lake suggested another scenario. If Jordan had become disoriented somewhere along the Skyline I to II ridges, and visibility was poor, he may have confused Ross Lake with Thunder, Flash, or Lightning Lakes. This may have led him to continue hiking west along the ridge toward Ross Lake. Alternatively, he may have become disoriented at the junction with the Hozomeen Ridge.

The number of possibilities was staggering.

There wasn't enough time on this day to search the Hozomeen Ridge, however. But we agreed that it was important to return later. The best plan at that time would be to stay overnight at Mowich Camp and then continue from there to Hozomeen Mountain, searching as much ground as possible.

After a long productive day, we hiked our way back down the Skyline II trail. My hopes, and Josie's, had been particularly high for finding abandoned cabins or other ways for Jordan to have been able to survive at Ross Lake. I'd imagined there might be an abandoned cabin in the wilderness there—maybe something built as a hunting camp. Instead, we'd found only holiday or government cabins. Bob and I had found no substantial evidence of Jordan ever having been there.

On the long drive back along the gravel road, Bob's truck suspension became damaged. He had continually swerved around the many potholes, but they were everywhere. We agreed that any future hikes to Ross Lake would be more productively reached from the Skyline II trail, rather than over this rough roadway.

———

April 13 took me in another direction entirely. Pascal and I hiked the Monument 78 trail to Winthrop Creek. Our main purpose was digiscoping the south side of Windy Joe Mountain. I recorded several good videos that afternoon.

Since GPS locations could not be identified in digiscope videos, I also took photos of the areas that I digiscoped. I recorded my own position on a map, too, in case volunteers reviewing the videos found anything that we should return to investigate.

As we hiked back to the parking lot, I again experienced flashbacks of Jordan.

Although a talented engineer, Jordan didn't limit himself to only technical pursuits. He challenged himself continually to learn new and creative skills, such as speaking Russian. He played piano at a high level, as well as the guitar and drums. He had joined a band with friends at UBC—and he could play all the instruments. He wrote his own songs and learned how to record his music and dub in all the instrumental tracks.[15]

Jordan also wrote poetry, which he wove into his song lyrics. His poetry was influenced by scholars such as William Roetzheim, an award-winning American poet. Jordan the poet was wise beyond his years. In his song-writing diary, he wrote, "Beauty without change is false and dies; true beauty is in change and surprise."

On the radio show he hosted at UBC called "Short Story Scores," he offered his opinions on a range of topics. He reviewed and discussed short fiction from well-known authors such as Amal El-Mohtar, Anton Chekhov, Neil Gaiman, and John Cheever.

I had known that Jordan wrote notes for his studies, of course, but not that he wrote poetry and sketched in those same notebooks. We talked about arts and cultural topics on various occasions. Jordan also reflected on self-improvement and strength of character in his diary. "Take a step forward to notice an imperfection; stumble forward pretending I didn't notice," he wrote. His poetry was thought-provoking and crafted with carefully chosen, meaningful words.

As we approached the bridge crossing Chuwanten Creek, Pascal and I passed a poster of Jordan. Anytime we passed one of these posters, I stopped, prayed, and reflected on how much Jordan was loved and missed. I hoped that his spiritual presence would send us a signal of his whereabouts.

---

15   Jordan's songs can be found on YouTube. Some of them include "Bone and Gristle," "CL Sincerity," "High Enough," "It's Pretty Clear," "Solitude from Sight," and "Wild Goose Chase" (an ironic title). His radio shows can be heard on Spotify.

At the end of the day, I thanked Pascal and expressed my positive feeling that our search was helpful, and that eventually we would find clues that would lead us to Jordan.

———

Trevor often mentioned Despair Pass, a junction point on the Skyline trail. Signage there was confusing and other hikers had accidentally made wrong turns at this spot. In Trevor's view, several possible scenarios could have occurred at Despair Pass. In one of them, if Jordan had lost the trail in the snow along the Skyline ridge, he might have taken a wrong turn here and wandered downhill into the valley.

On April 14, Trevor and I returned to the Skyline 1 trail, but this time we hiked as far as the Despair Pass valley—farther than we had hiked on any previous search. We snowshoed from Strawberry Flats up the mountain and approached the Skyline ridge. Although it was mid-April, the snow was still at least two metres deep on this north-facing side of the mountain.

Our goal was to reach the Despair Pass junction by the turnaround time. But as we got close to the ridge, the tracks we'd been following stopped and forced our pace to slow considerably. We were unable to reach the junction point by the turnaround time but did find a good lookout area over the entire Despair Pass valley. We paused there and looked carefully over the vast forested terrain below the ridge.

On our way back down, we once again turned off-trail at a place that seemed like it might be a route Jordan could have taken, had he lost the trail. Trevor and I spaced ourselves apart and headed down the mountain. My GPS unit suggested all potential paths downward would be over gently falling slopes initially, followed by much steeper slopes farther down. As we proceeded, we reached a point with a long line of sight through the trees. The terrain below us was very steep and covered in deep snow. I was reluctant, and frankly frightened, to head farther that way. As I stopped to reconsider, I retreated inward.

Tmxʷulaxʷ, I have reservations. Trevor is able to continue down this mountain here. He says it is safe. But it looks too steep for my abilities.

Courage under adversity is an important quality that you must build in order to survive in this wilderness. Courage is a characteristic that maintains our cycle of life.

Jordan is a brave young man with extraordinary courage.

Jordan carries courage like a bear. He has the strength to overcome the greatest enemy in this mountain wilderness—his own fear.

It is so difficult, Tmxʷulaxʷ, for me to imagine Jordan's suffering. You communicate here with me in a peaceful way. But I fear this mountain wilderness has caused great pain and suffering for my son.

Jordan found an inner strength to face his difficulties with courage and accept the reality of his situation. He was able to overcome his fears and show bravery, just like you, here on this mountain.

After lengthy reflection, I prepared myself, mentally and physically, for the path downhill ahead of me. I watched Trevor and found better ways to kick my heels into the snow diagonally, so I could move down the mountain slowly and safely. Snowshoeing down this steep slope over such a long distance was even more stressful because of how my body tensed and strained at each downward step. But eventually we arrived safely at the car.

Discussing what we had seen, we concluded that Jordan was not likely on the mountainside that we had just descended. If he had started down that way, he would not have stopped or camped on those slopes unless he was injured. They were too steep.

Snowshoeing through such a remote area had once again been helpful, even though no clues had been found. It gave us a more realistic perspective on probable scenarios because we had first-hand experience of the terrain.

As the artist Vincent van Gogh wrote, "The great doesn't happen through impulse alone and is a succession of little things that are brought together." Despite not finding any new clues for months, I felt confident that little things were coming together to soon bring us answers about Jordan.

eight

FIRST SIGNS OF SPRING

Their life is mysterious, it is like a forest; from far off it
seems a unity, it can be comprehended, described, but
closer it begins to separate, to break into light and shadow,
the density blinds one. Within there is no form, only
prodigious detail that reaches everywhere: exotic sounds,
spills of sunlight, foliage, fallen trees, small beasts that
flee at the sound of a twig-snap, insects, silence, flowers.
—SALTER, 1995

THERE WAS NO CLEAR TRANSITION FROM WINTER TO SPRING at Manning Park. Snow melted in some areas and temperatures warmed at lower elevations in April, but deep snow remained and it was still cold at higher elevations.

As the spring thaw approached, the snow became even less stable. It was another reason supporting the strategy to focus our searching on areas that would be snow-free first—south-facing slopes and areas of lower elevation—moving to new areas as they lost their snow cover. We would still carry our snowshoes, but now we would put them on and take them off as conditions dictated.

Although it was advantageous to search where we could see the ground, I felt it remained possible to find clues in the remaining snowy areas, as well. I believed that items of clothing, or a tent or backpack or other unusual signs, might be discernable—whether they had blown in or lay where they'd fallen. I had learned from experience that we could snowshoe safely in the mountains. Risks existed, of course, but thanks to excellent and experienced partners, we remained safe. So I was determined to keep going despite the snow.

I also had learned from life experience that sometimes people who work the hardest to accomplish a worthwhile goal attract the most criticism, particularly from those who contribute less themselves. I noticed this playing out when individuals criticized me, and from those who took aim at the dedicated volunteers who continued to search through drone videos or in person with me on the mountains. When a casual observer with little or no experience at Manning Park was skeptical (or worse) about our efforts and cited the apparent futility, I thought to myself: What would they do if it was their son who was missing?

Sometimes their comments reminded me of a speech made by former US President Theodore Roosevelt. In 1910, after completing his term in office and spending a year in central Africa, he toured Europe. He delivered a speech ("Citizenship in a Republic") in Paris about war, human rights, and the responsibilities of citizenship, which included these observations:

It is not the critic who counts; not the man who points out how the strong man stumbles, or where the doer of deeds could have done them better. The credit belongs to the man who is actually in the arena, whose face is marred by dust and sweat and blood; who strives valiantly; who errs, who comes short again and again, because there is no effort without error and shortcoming; but who does actually strive to do the deeds; who knows great enthusiasms, the great devotions; who spends himself in a worthy cause; who at the best knows in the end the triumph of high achievement, and who at the worst, if he fails, at least fails while daring greatly, so that his place shall never be with those cold and timid souls who neither know victory nor defeat.

For me, Roosevelt's words resonated with experiences I had faced while searching for Jordan.

I recognized that many of the people who felt we should stop until all the snow had melted were worried that harm could come to me or to those I was with. And that my family, particularly, would then have to deal with a second disappearance or added tragedy. But to me, holding off the search felt akin to giving up on Jordan. I believed, with the help I had, I would be safe and that it was better to keep looking through the winter—even if the result was finding Jordan's remains—than to not search until late summer. By that time those remains might be scattered to such an extent that we would never find him.

On April 17, John and I were joined by a new volunteer, Olga. The three of us set out on a more detailed search on Windy Joe Mountain. Our objective was to search areas where heatmap clues had been identified along and between major drainages on the south side of the mountain, which had lost a fair amount of snow by this time.

We hiked up Windy Joe Mountain and diverted off-trail close to the summit, heading south near the southernmost switchback. We stopped a few times on our descent and I droned over selected areas. Then we traversed eastward toward the heatmap points of interest.

Gradually the mountainside became steeper, and suddenly we reached rocky cliffs near the top of a drainage. We paused while John assessed the situation and determined a course of action. If we continued in the same direction, he said, our route would soon be impassable because of even steeper cliffs. Instead, we turned and descended straight down the mountain.

The ground on our descent was covered by steep and broken sections of rock, and the route led into a gulley. Safety was our priority. Due to the steepness, I turned and faced into the rocky hillside. John was below me. When I couldn't find proper footing, he held my legs in place and guided my feet onto secure, safe step-downs on bare ground.

These treacherous cliffs were not evident on the topographical map. Digiscoping this area from below also had not shown us the rocky cliffs along the drainages. If Jordan had somehow become lost on this side of the mountain, there were many places at the base of these cliffs where he could have been trapped, especially if he was injured or immobilized.

We made it through the cliff area, then reached another difficult spot—this time a field of boulders. Progress was slow, but we eventually reached Castle Creek at the base of the mountain, which was now flowing rapidly because of the snowmelt. We scanned the banks of the waterway for any telltale clues washed down from upstream but didn't spot any.

There were no ice bridges or other logs to cross over Castle Creek, so we continued to hike some distance upstream until we found an ice bridge that could support our weight.

We arrived back in the parking lot at eight o'clock, around sunset. It was a long, but productive day. We had managed to search a large area of new snow-free ground on Windy Joe Mountain and eliminate more potential search areas. Another special benefit occurred: Olga would become one of our most helpful volunteers in the coming months. She was particularly generous in donating summer hiking and camping gear to me.

As more areas on the south and east sides of Windy Joe Mountain became snow-free, these slopes became priority search areas—they had many unchecked heatmap clues. Pascal and I returned to the south side of Windy Joe Mountain on April 20. We, too, hiked nearly to the top, then diverted south near one of the last switchbacks. Pascal led the way, traversing across the mountain at a roughly constant elevation across alternating snow patches and clear ground. Donning and offing snowshoes slowed our progress. And once again we encountered terrain that was much steeper in places than the topographical map had led us to expect.

Consequently, we turned back before reaching our farthest search points. We reversed course and hiked back down the mountain. Even so, we fell further behind in our timing. As dusk approached, we diverted off-trail again and descended straight down between the switchbacks through snow.

I stumbled and fell several times. It was not the first time I'd become physically exhausted—when this happened, it was usually near the end of hikes and it often meant I fell a few times. Thankfully, these tumbles never kept me from hiking the next day. Even if I was achy, I always managed to find enough willpower to continue.

After a few hours and several tumbles, we reached the trail again. I slipped my hand into my pocket for my phone, so I could take a few photos. It wasn't there! Which meant it was somewhere off-trail, up the mountain.

It was too late to risk going back uphill to find it, as darkness was coming soon. I had to resign myself to rationalizing: a cellphone can be replaced—you have lost one day's photos but thankfully no more (I'd previously uploaded other search information onto the shared drive). Still, when we finally made it safely to the parking lot I was far from overjoyed. Not only had I lost my phone, we had found no trace of Jordan and I hurt from all the falling. Was the universe conspiring against me? Well, maybe—but I would not give it the satisfaction of showing my despair. I thanked Pascal for a productive search over new snow-free ground and headed for the cabin.

The next day, my priority was to buy a new cellphone. I was on the road for Princeton early in the morning. About halfway there, the car's engine temperature light came on. What was up with this cursed twenty-four hours?

With no cellphone, I couldn't call for a tow truck. So, jaw clenched, I pulled onto the shoulder, turned off the engine, got out, and opened the hood. After the engine had cooled, I restarted the car, drove to the top of the next hill, put the car in neutral, and turned off the engine while I coasted downhill.

I repeated the process and—after several hours—reached a mechanic shop at the edge of Princeton. Apparently, the car's coolant tank had cracked and the fluid had leaked out. The mechanic poured in water for a temporary fix and I drove on to Penticton (about seventy kilometres away), which had a Honda dealership. Leaving the car with them, I drove a loaner on to Kelowna, where I bought a new cellphone.

These were a difficult couple of days. John's words of wisdom—"one foot in front of the other"—were again helpful. And at least I found solutions for the car and the cellphone challenges before I reached home.

———

I spent April 22 strategizing at the cabin. Mike B and Stan, however, did a twenty-six-kilometre search of the Frosty Mountain trail. They started at the Windy Joe Mountain trailhead, still heavily snow-covered and with a lot of tree blowdown. About a kilometre and a half past the PCT campsite on the Frosty Mountain trail, Mike ventured off-trail northward into the bush for about five hundred metres.

Interestingly, Mike reported that he felt a strong connection in that area, similar to mine. We both sensed that something wrong had happened there but couldn't explain further (and we had limited witness reports from people in that area to corroborate this "feeling").

Mike discussed all this with Stan when he returned to the PCT campsite. He said it was an area that he definitely wanted to check again when the snow was gone. Though we didn't know it at the time, this area would become increasingly important in the coming months.

Early in the search, a group of psychics from a nearby community had contacted us. They believed that Jordan had fallen into one of the drainages to the west of the Frosty campsite and broken his neck there. Volunteers had partially checked some of the drainages in the area in October, but not all.

Psychics claim to have special perceptive abilities—telepathy and clairvoyance. As an engineer who relies on scientific evidence, I was not inclined to believe any psychic prediction. But I was trying to keep an open mind to all possibilities until evidence proved otherwise—including possibilities that I do not understand.

As my relationship evolved with Tmxʷulaxʷ, I was increasingly open to phenomena that are beyond the scope of normal scientific understanding. So on April 24, John and I searched off-trail in the drainages west of the Frosty campsite that the psychics had felt were important.

Shortly after we passed the campsite, we reached a forested plateau with few or no human or animal tracks in the snow. I followed John, not checking my GPS unit because he had often hiked in this area and I trusted that he knew where he was going. After about an hour of snowshoeing through the trees, we arrived at a location that looked familiar, but this time there were tracks in the snow—our own! During the previous hour, we had unknowingly hiked in a circle. Although I'd had little doubt before, this experience confirmed to me that even an expert mountaineer could get lost or disoriented in this terrain.

John and I diverted off-trail to the top of the first drainage. I could immediately see why these areas had not been thoroughly checked. The drainage descended gradually from the campsite down a gentle slope until suddenly dropping off a nearly vertical cliff. If Jordan had wandered off the trail in poor visibility near here, he could have slipped off the edge as the psychics had sensed.

It was clearly unsafe to descend directly into this drainage. Instead, we sidehilled, gradually dropping in elevation and crossing a sequence of drainages until we arrived at the Frosty campsite. We'd had a fairly good line of sight across these drainages but could not check most of the terrain in them. As I passed over the top of each one, I imagined various scenarios of what might have happened there. Filled with an intense love for Jordan, I was determined to check thoroughly under and around every tree, regardless of the difficulty of the terrain. My ankle, knee, and foot pain evaporated away.

Tmxʷulaxʷ, I'm pleading with you to guide me to find signs of Jordan. My love of Jordan is so deep that you know I will not end this search until he is found and brought home.

Love is the strongest force. It exceeds all others. Eagles here in the park symbolize love—they soar closer to the Creator than any other creature. They carry your prayers to the Creator.

I have tried to search this mountain like an eagle, using drones. But the trees have blocked sight of the ground. You have placed such challenging terrain here. It is extremely difficult to search thoroughly.

An injury on this mountainside would have directed Jordan downstream so watch carefully down the drainages. With your love and persistence, you will overcome these challenges of searching for Jordan.

Psychics have advised me that Jordan fell in this drainage below. The steep drop through the snow into the drainage appears too dangerous for me to search. It fills me with despair to imagine Jordan alone below, unable to call for help.

Although your emotional connection and love of Jordan have brought you sadness and despair, they will also help you find peace. Love brings a balance in life and an ability to reach peace with yourself.

I'm making every possible effort to search this park. Whatever happens at the end of this search, I want to have no doubts or regrets. My family and I have done everything possible to find Jordan. But how can our love help us find peace, without regrets, if we are unable to find our son alive?

No answer.

After stumbling over some fallen trees, I refocused on where I needed to be placing my snowshoes. I had to follow John's path ahead. I had no flashbacks of Jordan here; I was not able to feel his presence in this area. Still, there was a communion of sorts.

John and I finished this long, exhausting day disappointed, but with resolute determination. We agreed to come back to the same area when the snowpack receded.

When I wasn't remembering Jordan or looking for inspiration from Tmxʷulaxʷ during our searches, I often reflected on philosophical issues and questions—human suffering in the world, for example. I had seen others suffer, in my life, but my current circumstances were an entirely different experience. It is sad to watch others experience tragedy—I could commiserate, but I still felt disconnected. It was entirely different now that it was me and my family suffering.

The past seven months had given me a deeper understanding of suffering—and of all those around the world who were enduring it. I'd learned that although suffering is part of the human condition, every personal crisis can only be truly understood by the person going through it. I understood, now, that I could never fully comprehend the suffering of people caught in wars, of refugees, of parents who had lost a child to disease or violence. Even so, I knew my own feelings about the suffering of others had changed—their pain was more accessible and real to me. My empathy for others had been deeply renewed by my own family's loss and pain.

I thought about tragedies that had happened to colleagues and friends. One of my university colleagues had lost his son a few years before. I had expressed my condolences and talked with him at the time. But I now had a much clearer idea of his suffering.

I was also gaining a more heartfelt appreciation of other feelings and responses—helplessness, coping, fortitude. In today's society, when something unpleasant occurs, we don't just cope, we try to overcome or fix it. If the summer heat is too hot, we turn on the air conditioning. If we are sick, we take medication. So far, my family had made every effort to overcome our circumstances—but we had not succeeded.

I'd tried prayer, asking for signals or signs of Jordan. I'd looked to technology, but there didn't seem to be any piece of equipment or process that was leading us any closer to our son. We'd used every conceivable tool—drones, thermal imaging, GPS units, helicopters, online heatmaps, cell tower triangulation, social media, and hiking websites. None of them had provided any new information that led us any closer to Jordan.

Given my own knowledge of mechanical engineering, I was surprised at just how many limitations droning and imaging technology had when used for SAR missions. I learned that thermal imaging was not yet sophisticated enough to distinguish between smaller changes of temperature on the ground. I also learned just how much of a drone's line of sight is blocked by trees. So even if higher thermal resolution had been available, a drone using it would miss large sections of the ground because trees would block the line of sight.

One bonus was that thermal imaging could identify some anomalies in the dark—which might turn out to be an animal or small waterway. On a few occasions, my excitement had been raised when something unusual stood out. But when cross-examined with aerial imagery, each of these promising blips was explained by a natural feature.

I had also been astounded (and disappointed) to learn that no commercially available SAR software existed—specifically, something that would enable computers to identify human or unnatural objects in imagery taken by drones. One vendor did contact us to use a trial version of their program, but it was applicable only to images of open fields. With snow on the ground and a great deal of forest cover (which could partially obscure a human form), our situation was much more complicated.

However, we worked with all the tools the best that we could. I focused on droning in areas relatively near me and digiscoping locations that were farther away. Which is why, for example, on April 26 I hiked solo to a few locations near the Lone Duck Camp parking lot. From there, I had excellent views up the Frosty Creek drainage basin, from Lightning Lake toward the summit of Frosty Mountain. I connected my new cellphone to the telescope and scanned up and down the mountainsides near the summit, searching for any unusual signs among the trees. After taking several videos, I returned to the cabin and uploaded them onto the shared drive.

On April 27, I went back to Windy Joe Mountain with Pascal. This time, we tried to reach the west side of the mountain from the bottom. It wasn't long before we realized the extreme difficulty of the climb we had set for ourselves. Not only was it very steep but the amount of tree blowdown made the hillside impassable. By the time we'd reached a dead end, we had hiked too far from the Monument 78 trailhead to go back the way we'd come. Despite the difficulty, stress, and exhaustion of climbing over and around the fallen trees—two or three layers deep in some places—we had to persist onward and upward.

Pascal and I stayed ten to twenty metres apart to grid search the side of the mountain. Our thinking was, if Jordan had accidentally become lost or injured nearby, he might have moved down toward Castle Creek at the base of the mountain. Once again, in a trance-like state, I sought wisdom among the trees, trying to understand possible scenarios that may have occurred here with Jordan.

Tmxʷulaxʷ, I'm seeking your wisdom to understand how Jordan may have crossed over to this side of the mountain. If he lost the trail in the snowstorm, did he come back down the mountain toward Castle Creek? Did he see lights from the highway through the trees?

You ask for wisdom. Animals here in the forest use their gift of wisdom carefully for survival. This wisdom should not be confused with knowledge that you have gained so far.

I have incomplete knowledge. I don't know if circumstances brought Jordan to this side of the mountain. I need wisdom to align our limited information, to know where to focus our search efforts.

You have gained wisdom through your unwavering efforts to find your son in this forest. To nurture and devote your energy to seek new knowledge is to know wisdom.

I'm carefully observing all of the branches and signs of animals such as their tracks and game trails. But I have been unable to find any signs of Jordan, alone. Why won't you help by giving me signs of guidance from the trees, the wind, the waterways, Tmxʷulaxʷ?

You have found the ways to seek my wisdom. Continue to observe the signs of life around you. When you listen to my voice, it must be with a clear mind. Heatmap clues were found nearby so a vantage point ahead and down the mountain to the left will give you better guidance.

My meditation was suddenly disrupted by Pascal shouting that he'd found something interesting. It was a silver-lined object, possibly a small plastic bag but more likely a balloon. What was a balloon doing on the side of a mountain in the remote wilderness? Even though it seemed farfetched, I wondered aloud whether Jordan, lost, could have released a balloon as an emergency sign. We speculated briefly, but soon decided this bit of shiny plastic should be grouped with "things found that are not useful."

As the clock signalled our turnaround time, we headed down the mountain, this time along different paths at lower elevations, to cover as much new ground as possible. In the parking lot, Pascal reminded me that he would be returning to full-time work the following week and would only be able to come search one more time.

I was disappointed that I would be losing a hiking companion and felt even more loneliness at this news. I had already been preparing myself emotionally and mentally for the inevitability of losing volunteers. Still, I was so appreciative of the support Pascal had given us and I did recognize that people had to move on with their lives.

And I was determined to continue searching to the end, even if it meant that I would be doing it alone.

———

As April drew to a close, the creeks and drainage basins were more fully exposed. This meant that getting across some waterways became more challenging. There were a few permanent bridges in some areas, which allowed hikers on the major trails to cross easily. But when we were off-trail hiking, trying to access specific search areas in the mountains, creeks could often only be crossed by walking on fallen logs or going barefoot through the water.

Wading was risky, however. Before attempting it, I would assess the strength of the current, the water depth, the footing, and the distance to the other side. The force of the current could be deceptively strong, so channel obstructions downstream were also noted. I needed to consider whether, if I was swept downstream, I could be trapped among the fallen trees, unable to swim upstream against the force of the oncoming water.

The watercourses were generally fed by snowmelt, so the water temperature was freezing (and remained so, even in the early summer months). But there was little choice: If log crossings didn't exist or were too hazardous, we had to cross barefoot. It was a painful experience. My feet became very cold, turned red, and were numb. After reaching the other side, hiking hurt until the blood flow returned.

The water flow was typically lower in the morning and stronger in the afternoon, after the day's sunshine had melted more snow. This meant that a crossing that had been manageable by wading in the morning was usually much more difficult on our way back in the afternoon.

———

At the top of Windy Joe Mountain, hikers have an extraordinary panoramic view of Frosty Mountain (to the southwest), Mount Winthrop (to the southeast), Three Brothers Mountain (to the north), and Skyline Ridge (to the west). On the summit, which is a small, relatively flat, forested plateau, there's an old fire lookout tower. Nearby steep cliffs cannot be seen until you cross the plateau to the north or east. If Jordan had hiked close to the edge for a photo, could he have been caught off guard by poor visibility, wind gusts, or an animal, and fallen over the edge? If he had fallen off one of the cliffs near the summit, it would take experienced rock climbers to search for him.

On April 28, two new volunteers, Sean and Nick—both expert rock climbers—joined me to search around the summit of Windy Joe Mountain. They had kindly offered to check the most difficult cliffs. I hiked up the mountain with them and waited in the fire tower for several hours while they descended the nearby cliffs with ropes.

Operated by the province until 1965, the tower had been used as a location for monitoring for forest fires. Once it was decommissioned (replaced by aerial surveys), it was refurbished with information panels. A poster of Jordan was tacked to the door inside. It was warmer in the tower, and quiet except for the sound of the wind. I closed my eyes, imagined hugging Jordan again, visualized his smile, and embraced him in my thoughts.

As a young boy, Jordan was a role model for other children and an active volunteer in his school and community. He won a Community Youth Service Award when we lived in Whitby, Ontario. In elementary school, he coordinated the school milk program and tutored younger children. As he grew, we would talk about social, political, technological, and global issues. If our opinions differed, he would enthusiastically debate his side of a topic. I often changed my views because of Jordan's rationale. At other times, he switched his opinion. I was so proud of how he had matured as a principled and socially conscious young man of high moral character. He was especially mindful about those less fortunate in society.

I meditated and reflected on Jordan in the cabin for several hours, until Sean and Nick finally finished and returned. They explained to me how and where they had searched, reporting that they could not thoroughly check all areas because of the remaining significant snow cover. Their photos showed terrain with steep rocky cliffs with rocks at their bases and several caves. They had found no sign of Jordan in any of the places they searched.

We hiked back down Windy Joe Mountain. Sean and Nick were emotionally supportive of my efforts and encouraged me to stay strong and continue the search. They were convinced that we would soon find Jordan. They kindly offered to come back in a few weeks when the cliffs were entirely snow-free, to search again more thoroughly.

After a rest day, I solo hiked and droned from the highway along the Similkameen River and also digiscoped the north-facing slopes of Windy Joe Mountain. While doing so, I reflected on Jordan's integrity and humility. When I watched videos on the internet or downloaded files, he explained how and why I should be using paid services. Even if a free website could be found, he urged me to use a legitimate paid service, because he felt, rightly, that the originator of the content should be fairly compensated.

Tmxʷulaxʷ, you have knowledge of my son Jordan who has passed through this park. I would like you to know more about my son. He was a man of high moral character and integrity.

You can be very proud of Jordan. Honesty is among the highest of moral virtues. My desires are sincere to protect and promote the well-being of this forest and its waterways.

Please give me any type of sign of Jordan's location. I feel that I have spent too much time searching in the wrong places.

On many occasions, particularly at the resort parking lot, you have seen ravens. A raven shows honesty by understanding and accepting its role in nature.

I was unnerved by ravens. In Edgar Allen Poe's "The Raven," a raven carries the connotation of death.

I have seen ravens in the parking lot. It unsettles me that they come to my car as soon as I park. They often jump on the hood right in front of where I'm sitting. I get an ominous sense from those ravens.

Ravens are honest with themselves and how they use their abilities to survive. They do not seek the beauty, speed, or strength of other animals.

Ravens are scavengers. Some volunteers have found ravens hovering over dead animals. On our hikes, we watch for ravens, thinking they might lead us to new clues. I paused. Although I tried to resist thinking about it in this way, I understood that humans and animals are all connected in the cycle of life on this earth. *In our culture, ravens can be associated with death. I find their croaking calls chilling, especially when I think about Jordan's disappearance.*

I had, in fact, become resigned to the realization that ravens (and other signals from Tmxʷulaxʷ) were pointing toward Jordan's demise. It seemed more than coincidental that these birds grouped together on my car much more often than on others' vehicles.

In addition to honesty, ravens also represent insight and prophecy... I imagined Tmxʷulaxʷ responding.

That may be, but I was happy to leave this exchange behind.

After searching several hours by drone and digiscoping, I returned to the resort parking lot. Once again, a few ravens jumped onto my car when it parked. Their appearance and behaviour capped off another dreadful month. Still, they would not dampen my spirits or determination to continue placing one foot in front of the other.

nine

BURNING LOVE
IN MAY

*The forest did not tolerate frailty of body or
mind. Show your weakness, and it would
consume you without hesitation.*

—SHAH, 2005

A S ANOTHER NEW MONTH BEGAN, I RECONNECTED WITH
Bob and Olga to grid search three areas close to the parking lot
where Jordan's car was found. On May 3, we searched around
the Canyon Nature trail, the hillside north of the parking lot,
and a drainage basin west of the Lone Duck Camp.

These areas had been neglected because they were so close to the
resort. No one had imagined that Jordan could have disappeared so
near his car. Olga reminded us, however, of the possibility of foul play
at the parking lot. We hadn't considered that.

From Jordan's online searches of the trails at Manning Park, we
had learned in October that he was interested in the Canyon Nature

trail. Had he planned a quick hike there before starting the main Frosty Mountain trail? It seemed unlikely, but it was better to check and know for sure. About halfway around the Canyon Nature trail loop, we encountered a camping area, which I had earlier identified as a place to return to. We searched through the individual sites but found no trace of Jordan.

We went back, then, to the hill behind the parking lot, although to my mind that location seemed unlikely for several reasons—including that if foul play had occurred nearby, people would have noticed the animals and ravens attracted to the area after the fact. On the other hand, if scavengers had arrived from deeper in the woods or at night, they might not have been noticed.

The three of us spaced ourselves ten to twenty metres apart then grid searched the entire hillside. We stayed as uniformly parallel as we could, shouting out to each other if we went out of line. Although the area was at a low elevation and it was now early May, there was still deep snow on the hillside. Our search turned up nothing of any significance.

Next we drove together to the Strawberry Flats trailhead, to search at the base of the Skyline Mountain, on the north side. Again we separated and grid searched back and forth. Here, though, the terrain was a marshy strip of land about a hundred metres wide. It wasn't a quick search: The tree blowdown was dense and the area featured deep snow, sinkholes, and marsh. I became trapped in a thick network of fallen trees a few times, with my path seemingly blocked in all directions by dense trees, tree wells, or steep embankments. I'd have to reverse course, then I'd shout for Bob and Olga so they knew I'd had to backtrack.

Despite being the only people snowshoeing, the area was not quiet. Trees were swaying and their branches rustled in the wind. I could pick out the sluicing of water rushing down the mountain. And I could hear the humming, buzzing, croaking, and clicking of small animals and birds. I couldn't see any creatures, but I was certain they were nearby watching or listening to us. Sometimes I heard snaps or crackling noises from the forest—branches breaking or even movement linked to root action underground.[16] I listened carefully, trying to discern even the smallest sound that could be a subtle form of communication from Tmxʷulaxʷ.

Listening and learning more about trees had helped on our searches. It was important for volunteers to be able to recognize intertwined roots and stumps in areas of tree downfall when they scanned aerial imagery—as well as other phenomena associated with downed trees. Under the thick bark of a stump, for example, there is sometimes green tissue. Or new sprouts may poke out of the ground nearby. This is because living trees can sometimes keep a neighbouring stump alive until a new tree grows back from it.

Trees and branches sometimes grow in odd shapes and directions, in part because they compete for light and space. I have even seen branches of different trees growing into each other, reminding me of a friendship or partnership. It seemed trees have relationships, strong and weak, and some even grew together like a human couple. Through my experience of searching, I felt a growing sense of togetherness with Jordan through our common connection with the community of trees of Manning Park.

It took several hours to complete our searching on Skyline Mountain. When the three of us finally returned to the parking lot, we felt it had been a productive day. Areas that had never been checked before could now be crossed off our list.

---

16   I'd learned that tubes within tree roots draw water and nutrients from the ground, and from there the water and nutrients are forced up and out to the branches. Air bubbles can form in the tubes or block the water migration; they make a sound when they expand or break.

When I hiked with my most experienced and trusted partners—Bob, Trevor, John, and Pascal—it was more complicated to choose a good turnaround time. This was because we always headed into new terrain and returned on a different route than we'd taken going in. Trevor and John were completely familiar with Manning Park, Bob and Pascal less so. We would strategize together to choose the right time, and with enough forethought found that it was often so accurate that we arrived back at the resort within minutes of sunset.

On May 4, Pascal's final day of hiking with us, he and Bob joined me for another search on Windy Joe Mountain. The areas we targeted were the first to have snow-free ground and they still had many remaining unchecked heatmap clues.

We started from the Monument 78 trailhead and crossed Castle Creek over a fallen tree because the bridge had been washed out. We hiked off-trail up the mountain to our desired elevation, then began traversing, each at a constant elevation contour, around the mountain from the west-facing to the south-facing side.

Although the terrain was steep and littered with tree downfall, it was at least snow-free, so we could check thoroughly on the ground. Bob and Pascal both had more good fortune than I did—they found more game trails. Apparently cougar, bear, deer, and other animals also struggle to find their way through these woods; following their paths was always a bit easier than creating our own fresh tracks. Animals have a natural sense for finding the paths of least resistance. I sometimes deviated from the true grid in particularly difficult spots to follow another creature's route. Once through, I would shout to Bob and Pascal and realign myself with the grid.

At one point we reached an open boulder field. It was strewn with large rocks and bordered on the uphill side by steep, overhanging cliffs. Crossing it was particularly stressful and painful on my knees. There could be no flexion in my steps, as the rock surface constrained the angle of my knees.

When we reached our turnaround point, atop a precipice, we were rewarded with a striking view over the entire drainage basin above Castle Creek. I unpacked my drone and began scanning the terrain nearby, obtaining good video footage. That is, until the third video, when I lost both the signal and line of sight to the drone. It appeared to be far behind me on the other side of the mountain. I hit the Return to Home button, waited, but could not see or hear it. Had it crashed somewhere out of sight? I remained patient, waiting for several more minutes. Still nothing. Not only did I hope I had not lost this important piece of equipment—it was a little embarrassing having Bob and Pascal watch me do it.

Then we detected a faint sound. It was the drone, high above us. It arrived from an unexpected location, finding its way back to "home." I prayed it was a sign, a sign that Jordan, too, would find his way back home.

Bob and I spotted a black bear about a hundred metres away from us—that gave me a jolt. The bear sniffed the air and, noticing our presence, quickly fled. I knew that black bears generally have no interest in confrontations with humans. But in the spring, bears—especially mothers with young cubs—are hungry and would be interested in our food. Thankfully, this one promptly rushed out of sight.

We were always well prepared for a bear encounter. We carried bear spray, and I was ready to follow Trevor's advice: If you encounter a bear at close proximity, speak to it in a moderate but stern tone and back away. Don't raise your voice. Use a steady tone that is not irritating or suddenly changes. Also make sure your hiking poles are ready in case the bear charges. Then aim the poles at its eyes.

He assured me, however, that bears don't normally charge. The exceptions are if the bear is injured, or her cubs are threatened. I hoped not to encounter such a situation.

When we arrived back at the parking lot, I ended the day with special thanks to Pascal. He'd hiked with me every week over the past few months. I was disappointed to see him go but grateful for the time he spent with us.

―――

The snowpack melted quickly as May went on, which was encouraging. The longed-for spring conditions, however, also brought new challenges. Snow conditions on the ground changed more drastically from morning to night. The variations in conditions between outbound and return trips[17] had to be factored into our calculation of turnaround times. Also, in addition to the familiar issues posed by tree downfall, the deciduous vegetation was starting to spring back to full growth. Plants freshly budded and leafed reduced how far we could see into the forest— and alders grew thickly in open areas and along decommissioned trails.

Still, the early summer is the most effective time for ground searches. May and June gave us a short window of opportunity: maximum visibility between trees *and* the ground is clear of snow. This added new pressure to search as much new terrain as possible before the forest grew lush and visibility was obscured.

From February through April, deep snow and fallen trees over the Similkameen River tributaries had allowed us to take a shortcut to the Windy Joe junction. Going that route reduced hiking time to and from the junction by a few hours. But in the spring, snowmelt flooded the area. So on May 6, I set out to make new creek crossings by creating pathways over fallen trees spanning the creek.

While working, my thoughts once again turned to memories of Jordan and, despite my best efforts to believe he was alive, I also

―――――――――――――――

17 The overnight freeze was now not as deep, so snow was softer in the mornings. Where light could not penetrate the forest cover, the snowpack was more resistant to melting. This harder snowpack reduced the physical exertion required to hike uphill off-trail but made downhill snowshoeing more difficult.

considered the various scenarios of what might have happened to him. I recognized that his death was the most likely reality that would need to be accepted. Still, I clung to the fact that we didn't know *yet*, so there could still be hope. Most people, I knew, already assumed he could not have survived this long. So anything substantial that we discovered was likely going to lead to sadness for our loss, not the joy of reunion. It was our ongoing internal struggle: between hope and despair. These months were a powerful journey in dealing with mortality.

Death had been all around me in the forest—fallen trees, and the remains of animals. And in the wider world, many people had died in the pandemic—death rates from COVID-19 at that time were continuing to rise daily. My own grandparents, as well as other relatives, friends, and colleagues had also passed away in their own time. As I worked, I counted how the traces of death were everywhere. Only memories remained—everything becomes only a memory.

It seems normal to fear death, but civilizations such as the ancient Greeks believed it should not be feared. Plato and Socrates claimed that death motivates people to achieve goals and helps them to better appreciate loved ones. For these philosophers, death was a force that directed us in how to live our lives.

In this difficult period, I wanted death to remain in the background of my thoughts, not in the foreground—having it there would have been paralyzing and self-destructive. I was not yet among those who had suffered the loss of a loved one in my immediate family. My current situation was a depressing middle ground, as I continually switched between hope for life on the one hand, and the stark realization that Jordan's death was the most likely eventuality, on the other.

After a full day's work, I had created two safe new crossings through a flooded area. I cleared distinct paths through the dense undergrowth and across fallen trees over the creek. I marked the trees nearby with reflective tape, so other volunteers could find their way through the flooded area. And then I made my way back again to the cabin alone.

———

On May 8, John and I returned to the Lightning Lakes Chain trail. We searched off-trail around all four of the water bodies (Lightning, Flash, Strike, and Thunder lakes), including on the hillside around Thunder Lake and the areas at Strike Camp. We clocked about thirty kilometres.

The tracks as far as Flash Lake were well travelled, but we saw few or no paths in the snow thereafter. John broke a trail. The snow was still deep but in a few open areas the sun had reflected down through the surrounding mountains to leave snow-free ground. It became tiresome to repeatedly take our snowshoes off and put them back on again.

When we hiked together, John and I often talked—politics and our families were among our favourite topics. We shared experiences of our workplaces and discussed global issues, such as the pandemic and the economy. John always showed a positive upbeat attitude—the only time I recall him getting upset was when we found litter along the Manning Park trails.

He was surprised at the state of Thunder Lake when we got there. The water level was much lower than he'd seen it before. It was confusing as water flowed into the lake from the Frosty Creek drainage basin. There was no visible exit flow at the west end of the lake, yet the overall water level had gone down.

We found a massive buildup of fallen trees when we arrived at the drainage inlet. Had that restricted the inflow? John speculated that an avalanche or logjam might have changed the entire flow pattern in the lakes. We didn't have an answer. I wondered if any of these unusual phenomena were connected somehow to Jordan, either at the time of his disappearance or during the winter. Had an avalanche occurred nearby?

The day's route offered several spectacular views up into the mountains above us. It took us farther west than previous ground searchers had gone. John used his binoculars to scan the exposed mountainsides.

I shouted Jordan's name through a megaphone—the sound echoed a long way through the valleys and bounced off the mountains. If Jordan was out there and couldn't respond, he might at least have heard the sound and reoriented himself, or so I told myself.

I imagined how he could have survived. If I was able to find a way out of these places, he could have also. Could he have survived in the woods, staying put with a broken leg or other injury? He would have needed to find heat, water, food, and shelter. He could have found a cave or mine shaft and stored wood, twigs, bark, and leaves as a heat source. He could have known that dry wood rubbed together in a divot causes enough friction to create smoke and a spark—he didn't need matches. He could have found food sources in the forest through the fall (grouse, berries, mushrooms). Streams continued to flow even in the winter months. These scenarios, I knew, were all highly unlikely—but perhaps not impossible.

Our route took us by large stretches of new mountainous terrain, the sight of which allowed me to imagine a multitude of other scenarios that I had not previously considered along the nearby Skyline ridge—until Nicole had raised them at the Zoom meeting. As we moved farther away from the parking lot—Jordan's starting point—the possibilities grew in number. Just one of the drainage basins at Strike or Thunder lakes offered plenty of scenarios through which Jordan could have arrived there, then run into worse trouble through further disorientation.

When I speculated about the countless possibilities—which began to overwhelm me—John reminded me again: One step in front of the other. Focus on one hike at a time, one day at a time. Each individual hike was challenging enough without worrying about future possibilities.

We arrived back at the car shortly before sunset, after another long exhausting day. My entire body was in so much pain that I could barely open and close the car doors. When I fell asleep that night, images of trees, forests, and mountains filled my dreams.

On my drive back to Eastgate every evening, I usually stopped at a gas station where the cellphone signal was strong enough to upload the day's photos and video files to the shared drive. Once I got to the cabin, I knew, the signal would be too poor to transfer these files.

I'd call Josie when I got home, then clean up, but since the cell signal was often poor, we usually had only a short conversation that was sporadically cut off. Afterward, I'd answer emails and prepare for the next day. After a quick dinner, it was a time for quiet solitude. This usually included some time imagining Jordan emerging from the thick forest behind the cabin. I did this often, night and day.

My evenings also often included contacting new volunteers (who lived anywhere from Vancouver to Kelowna). They would all want to learn about the background and the searches completed so far. It was mentally exhausting to reiterate our story over and over again, especially the details of the areas already searched. I tried to keep it simple, responding to their emails by suggesting that we meet at the parking lot in the morning to discuss strategy and background then. This was, thankfully, sufficient for most volunteers. But a few wanted to speak to me—a challenge compounded because there was limited cellphone coverage at the cabin.

Typically, it was around eight o'clock by the time I reached the cabin. I tried to be in bed and falling asleep by ten o'clock—my mornings were early so I could make a 7:00 or 8:00 a.m. start time in the parking lot. During the winter, the start time was later, but I had to leave the house earlier so I could shovel the driveway. It didn't leave much time (or energy) in the evenings for phone calls.

One volunteer was particularly insistent, however, messaging Josie and me several times and wanting to speak in person. He said he was planning to travel to British Columbia from Alberta and camp for a few weeks at Manning Park to help search for Jordan. He asked me to join him. He seemed determined to help find our son. I agreed and we scheduled a day to meet.

When the day arrived, he didn't show up in the park and didn't contact me. The next day, still nothing. He messaged on the third day, explaining there had been delays at the Alberta-BC border, but that he would arrive the next day. Several more days passed with still no sign of him.

About a week later, he phoned around 10:30 p.m. He'd arrived in Manning Park, he said, and asked me where to go for a hike that evening! In retrospect, instead of waiting for him for several days and readjusting my schedule, I should have hiked with someone else.

This man was not the only volunteer searcher to behave bizarrely. On another occasion, a man claiming to be an experienced hiker in Manning Park contacted us, offering to thoroughly search Windy Joe Mountain. I hiked with other volunteers off-trail around the Frosty campsite the day he was there, while he searched on the other mountain. He texted me several times during the day suggesting we connect—which didn't make sense to me as we were hiking on opposite sides of the park. He should have known there was no possible way our routes would intersect.

He texted again around ten o'clock that night. He'd just arrived back to the parking lot, he said, and wondered if there were any taxis from Manning Park to Hope. This confused me. Any experienced hiker would have made travel arrangements. Why was he hiking in the dark, and without a ride afterward?

I didn't hear from him again.

Another evening, returning from a hike with John shortly after sunset, I noticed someone going into the forest—alone, in the dark, without a backpack, tent, or any hiking gear that I could see, and not wearing clothing appropriate for the weather conditions.

And I once found an empty duffle bag under a tree deep in the forest.

Were any of these strange observations or characters somehow connected to illegal activity or foul play involving Jordan?

Or did they just give us more unanswered questions?

Dense tree blowdown prevented solo hikers from accessing the East Similkameen trail area—it would not have been safe. The way for me, hiking alone, to access that area was via the Monument 78 trail, hiking to a point from which I could launch the drone across Castle Creek and over to the East Similkameen trail. This is what I set out to do on May 10.

Soon after I crossed the first bridge on the Monument 78 trail, I spotted a good lookout point—the junction of Chuwanten Creek, Castle Creek, and the Similkameen River. I settled at the location and unpacked my drone.

I had learned that the trees in this area of Manning Park were generally between thirty to forty-five metres tall. By this point in our searching, I had used the drone many times—but mostly flying it only as far as I could see it. I used a handheld controller to adjust its height, direction, and camera angle. This day, I held the drone stationary for some time after sending it aloft, then slowly guided it over nearby trees with plenty of clearance above the treetops. I looked around to identify the highest tree and then kept the drone well above that height.

The manufacturer's specs advise operators not to fly a drone in forests or any areas with trees. I had no choice but to disregard this guidance because my son was lost somewhere in the forest. The area I was deploying the drone that day was heavily treed—definitely not within manufacturer's guidelines.

I continued to fly the drone westward toward the East Similkameen River. It seemed entirely safe because I could see it was far above the height of the tallest tree. I checked from different vantage points and could see no higher trees anywhere nearby. So I continued to fly the drone past my line of sight, though I could still hear its buzzing.

It flew on for some time, capturing good video coverage of the ground. Then I stopped hearing the buzz and lost the video signal on my cellphone. The drone had hit a tree.

How could this be, when I was operating it far above the treeline? Was there an outlier tree of greater height?

I realized with a sinking heart that I'd failed to factor in the change in elevation. I had not adjusted enough for higher ground across the creek. It hadn't *looked* to be higher ground, but that was deceptive. An adjacent steep slope could make a gentle rise in elevation appear negligible. But that gentle increase had been enough to bring the drone closer and closer to the tops of the trees. I learned a good lesson the hard way.

I quickly pressed the Return to Home button, listened, and waited. Nothing. I crossed the nearby bridge and started to search the forest at the point of last contact with the drone. It should have beeped but I heard nothing.

So I started searching through the tree downfall. I must have checked under practically every fallen tree and peered up into the branches of every tree still standing. There were no signs of the drone anywhere. At the farthest limits of its flight, I grid searched practically every square metre. After several hours, I packed up and went back to the car without the drone.

It was a critical loss. The drone was a key tool in the search for Jordan. I urgently needed to obtain another unit. I had bought the last one online when I was a relative novice. Now, with practical experience, I knew much more about which drone capabilities I needed. That same day, I drove the few hours to Abbotsford to review what was in stock there. I returned to Eastgate with a best-selling (and more expensive) model and started testing it in an open field near the cabin right away.

I was instantly pleasantly surprised. The new drone was an improvement in many ways. Lifting off and returning home were simpler and more accurate manoeuvres. The initial calibration was also easier with only a button to press. The controller showed several views—including the camera view and a map of the location and the trajectory of the drone. I could now more easily track the drone's path and see how close it was to key landmarks, such as a creek or bridge.

It was also much more powerful. It had a longer range and battery capacity. It could capture better, longer videos. Plus the navigational controls linked more easily with my cellphone and the camera stabilization worked better in windy conditions. Not only that, it was smaller and lighter than the first drone, so I could pack it with me on long hikes (which I had not done with its heavier predecessor).

The drone crash that had brought my spirits low turned out to be a blessing in disguise. Even the timing was ideal: Drone capability had just recently become more critical because of the snow melt.

From this point on, the number of daily drone videos increased significantly. As my skill improved, the quality of the drone videos also improved. Volunteers searched the new videos and sometimes identified interesting clues. If they were sufficiently promising, I arranged hikes to the areas in question or asked other volunteers to check these spots.

Mike B was a great emotional support to Josie and me and helped us both through our grieving process. He and I had many conversations about Jordan during our hikes together. Mike found respectful ways to honour Jordan, too; whenever I stopped by a poster of Jordan, Mike paused with me.

I proudly told him about Jordan's impressive list of academic accomplishments—our son was talented in math and science. Yet he was also modest; Jordan wanted no special attention for his awards or achievements.

As Dean of Engineering and Applied Science at Memorial University, I always welcomed the first-year students in the fall semester. The year Jordan enrolled he was sitting in the second row when I spoke to the incoming class. There were probably some students who knew that

Jordan was my son. I would glance over to him as I spoke and our eyes locked. His said: Do not mention it. Jordan wanted to find his own way and make us proud of the accomplishments he achieved on his own, without any special consideration as the dean's son.

On May 12, I met Mike B at the resort to discuss strategies for upcoming searches. Then we drove over to the Monument 78 trailhead to search the trail as far as possible toward the border. As we headed out, I again meditated and reflected on my son. That day, I could sense a closeness in spirit with him.

Tmxᵂulaxᵂ, you have my son. He is like no one else who has passed through your space. He is an intelligent young man but humble in his demeanour.

Our life and animals here in the forest carry humility. To survive in the wilderness, an animal sets aside its own interest when it becomes part of a family pack. Its life is lived for the pack.

Jordan is considerate and unselfish toward others. Even his earliest teachers said: Not only is he a good student, he shows a kind-hearted nature toward other students.

Jordan understood humility. Your son was a sacred part of this world.

In university, Jordan was named several times to the Dean's List. I was extremely proud of him when I handed him this award.

Jordan was unselfish and respected by his teachers and friends. Your pride in his accomplishments is evident.

Tmxᵂulaxᵂ, you should not speak about Jordan in the past tense. I speak of him in the present in hopes that he may still be alive somehow and somewhere. I speak of his youthful times using the past tense, but please understand—while he is still here in your place, we should use the present tense.

In an animal pack, each member understands its limitations.

This response turned my thoughts to bears. *Did Jordan encounter one of your animals here in the forest?*

No answer.

By mid-afternoon, Mike B and I had not quite reached the international border, but we were more than ten kilometres from the trailhead. We turned around, reaching our starting point just before sunset.

In mid-May, the park and trails were open to the general public, but there was still significant tree downfall on most of the pathways. Several sections of the Monument 78 trail were densely covered, for example. Anyone trying to hike these trails needed to be experienced in navigating through a thick network of slippery fallen trees.

On May 14, I hiked the Monument 78 trail and drone searched areas around Castle Creek and the western slopes of Windy Joe Mountain. About four kilometres from the trailhead, I gathered several good drone and digiscope videos. Then, on a section of trail heavily covered by tree downfall, I came to a particularly difficult spot.

Interwoven branches prevented me from going over the tangle, and I couldn't see how to go around the tree in any direction. There was, however, a small gap below the trunk. So I got down low and assessed the gap. It needed to be large enough for both me and my backpack to fit— since I knew I would not be able to toss the pack over and I didn't want to push it through ahead of me. I had to be able to see where I was going.

I started to crawl and was past the halfway point before something on the top of my pack snagged. With little room to manoeuvre, I couldn't reach around to unhook it. I readjusted my position and pushed forward. Still not enough. I tried several more positions and directions. None were able to unfasten me from a small branch locked into my backpack.

More force was required. So I tried again, harder, and was free! But when I stood up on the other side, I was quickly engulfed by a vapour cloud. I scooted out of the cloud, hoping it was from my water bottle.

I felt my upper back—my shoulder and upper arm were wet. Then, slowly, I started to feel a terrible burning. It felt like my back was on fire. I had accidentally released the bear spray from the canister at the side of my backpack!

The burning quickly became painful around my back, shoulder, and arm.

What to do? I couldn't search online—I had no cell signal. So my priority was to get back to the parking lot as fast as possible and maybe head for the hospital. Fortunately, I had only a few kilometres to cover.

I ran as best as I could, trying various strategies to relieve the pain. I waved my arms around to increase air circulation, running like a large bird flapping its wings in a desperate bid to take off. The flapping only briefly helped.

I considered the creek—no, still freezing cold.

As soon as I reached the parking lot, I hauled out my cellphone and searched. I was relieved to see that the bear spray was not lethal. And that the pain would ease within a few hours. The website suggested increasing the air circulation and washing the affected area with water. I quickly drove back to the cabin and followed these instructions.

Over the next few weeks, despite soaking my shirts several times, they continued to create a burning sensation when I put them on. It confirmed to me the long-lasting and powerful strength of the bear spray. I now understood how a direct spray in a bear's face would convince the animal to retreat.

I never did figure out how the canister could have accidentally fired, however. Two mechanisms have to be activated to trigger the spray. I didn't think branches could do both, especially pulling the trigger. Regardless, I had learned a good lesson—and I never again put the bear spray where it could possibly become ensnared.

On May 15, John and I hiked up the Frosty Mountain trail, returning to search off-trail areas around the Larches and into the drainages nearby. John believed these were priority locations.

To my surprise, there was still at least two metres of snow on the Frosty Mountain trail beyond the fourth switchback. I was so anxious for this snow to disappear, so we could search bare ground. But I had to accept that weather conditions were beyond my control. I diverted my energy to factors that I could influence—such as strategies about where to search and how to bolster my own physical endurance so I could continue.

Around the sixth switchback, the terrain transitioned from a steep uphill climb to a plateau with forested meadows. We found tracks in various directions in the snow here, and false spur trails that ended abruptly. I reflected on our hike in April, when John and I had become disoriented and hiked in a circle in this area before realizing we were "lost" off-trail.

Given how easily confusion could arise, we decided to search the terrain on a route parallel to the trail. As we snowshoed toward the Larches and the Frosty Mountain summit, we passed the Frosty camp-site. I felt an eerie chill, considering how Jordan might have struggled in the disorienting terrain here. Certain places, especially this one, sent shivers up my spine when I imagined what Jordan may have experienced nearby. The forest felt menacing and forbidding to me here. As I had noted in the deeper winter, the landscape still appeared identical in all directions, the trees without any distinguishing characteristics. My heartbeat was unusually elevated as we pushed through the snow.

As I followed behind John, I reflected on Jordan. It was distressing that I could only remember him, not experience him. Memories came from the past. We were not creating any new experiences together here in Manning Park. Still, I could console myself with pleasant memories—like Jordan's enjoyment of and ability in music. He'd studied piano to Grade 8 and often played at home. I enjoyed listening, even to his practising.

I remembered, too, a vacation in Florida in 2010, when we'd gone to an NFL game together in Miami. I'm a Pittsburgh Steelers fan, as was Jordan, although to a lesser extent—but his favourite running back, Ricky Williams, played for Miami. We made our way discreetly through the tailgating parties in the parking lot, reluctant to show ourselves as Pittsburgh black and gold fans in a sea of Dolphins blue and orange. The game was exciting and close. A swarming Pittsburgh defence allowed the reigning Super Bowl champs to defeat Miami 30 to 24. Jordan and I both enjoyed the game, but mostly we enjoyed spending time together. I saw the photo of us at the game in my mind's eye as we hiked along.

John and I continued off-trail until we reached a few open areas from which we could see above the trees west of us and into a large drainage basin. This area was critical to check more thoroughly, with grid searches. But the snow was at least two metres deep still. We committed to returning as soon as the snowpack receded.

We had travelled past the Frosty campsite by that point, gradually climbing. I had not realized, however, how far we were below the actual trail. It told me something new about how easily a hiker could become disoriented up there.

We moved on until we reached a box canyon below the Frosty Mountain summit. Here, the steep mountainsides surrounded us. It was overwhelming to suddenly see this enormous wall of mountain directly in front of us. I had flashbacks of Jordan in a similar predicament. I could feel a strong presence nearby. Images of my son moved through my mind like a photo album full of memories. After stumbling over some rocks, I refocused on the path ahead.

John and I continued forward, though I was snowshoeing some distance behind him. We needed to head back to the trail—and he had decided the safest approach was straight up the mountain. I knew I had to really focus.

Our gruelling ascent was up a steep slope by a series of short switchbacks. When that became too difficult, we snowshoed up diagonally, alternating back and forth every ten or fifteen metres.

Once we reached the trail, we turned and headed back down the mountain. We kept to the path until we reached the lowest switchback, then diverted off-trail again to cover as much new ground as possible.

Although we found no new clues, I felt our work off-trail near the Frosty campsite—and the unusually strong feelings of Jordan's presence I'd felt there—confirmed we should prioritize that area as soon as the snow melted.

ten

GRANOLA BAR
WITH A PHOTO

She grew into a forest, she could not be found.
—OKA, 2017

O
N MAY 17, I SET OUT ON MY FIRST OVERNIGHT TREK. IN
March and April, Bob and I had discussed searching areas that
were much farther away so that overnight camping would be
necessary. It would require a much larger backpack, carrying
more food, a tent, and a canister stove. The larger backpack weighed
about twenty-two kilograms, which would definitely slow me down.
Olga had kindly given me some gear I'd need and I bought my own
single tent rather than share a larger, heavier one.

Bob and I planned so we could search around Monument 78,
leaving the option open for one or two nights of camping. We'd
take a path southward up Windy Joe Mountain then head down

the PCT toward Monument 78 and go north until we finished at the Monument 78 trailhead.

As we started to climb, I needed more frequent water breaks. It was soon clear to me, too, that a larger, heavier pack made stopping for a break more complicated. Bob suggested sitting on a fallen tree when removing and putting on the pack—sitting made manoeuvring easier. After a few hours, too, my body adjusted to the physical demands. I was able to pick up the pace so I was almost as fast as when I wore my lighter pack.

We reached the PCT campsite before noon, setting up our tents and putting our food in a metal storage locker to avoid attracting bears, before heading off to search (wearing our lighter packs). We concentrated on the south side of Windy Joe Mountain, investigating heat-map clues. I carefully checked our previous hikes in my GPS unit to make sure that we covered new ground—snow-covered areas that had been previously checked we would not examine again until they became snow-free.

Although our grid search did not produce meaningful new results, I did find new vantage points for droning. We stopped several times to collect videos.

We turned for the campsite in the late afternoon, but we had seriously underestimated how long it would take us to get back. The forest was dense with tree downfall—three or four layers thick in all directions. When I shouted Bob's name, I did not hear his answering call. I was frightened, but continued moving, although slowed to a snail's pace.

As I made my way over each tree, I searched ahead for the path of least resistance and toward a line of sight that could help me escape the brutal network of fallen trees. It seemed endless. If Jordan had somehow come into this area, there would be many ways he could have been hurt. I refocused on searching carefully below each tree.

Tmxʷulaxʷ, how do I find a way out of this maze?

Look ahead more steps in advance and try new ideas if your plan isn't working. Consider a thirsty bird that finds a container of water but can't reach the water with its beak when perched at the top.

The bird should keep trying.

It keeps trying but eventually gives up—

I will not give up until Jordan is found.

—then the bird finds a new idea. It drops pebbles into the container. Eventually, the water level rises to the top. Then the bird can drink.

I have another idea—rather than sidehilling toward the campsite, I'll descend and sidehill. It should be lower than this elevation.

"Greg!" Bob's shout came from an unexpected direction. Still trapped in the fallen trees, the sound of his voice calmed me. I found a way to adjust my path until I found another passable route.

We finally reconnected at the campsite and began preparing dinner together, then turned in around nine o'clock. Unaccustomed to sleeping alone in a small tent, I tossed and turned before finally getting a few hours of sleep.

To my surprise, when I opened the tent flaps the next morning there were several centimetres of new snow on what had been bare ground—unexpected this late in May. Heating our breakfast and packing up the tent was more challenging in the snow. And the new conditions caused us to adjust our plans. We decided to move down the PCT to search around the Canada-US border.

Before leaving, we stopped to admire the view. The PCT campsite is beside a clearing in the forest. It gives remarkable sightlines down a valley and across several mountain ranges. The view of the sunset the night before and the sunrise that morning—at a horizon line of mountain peaks—had both been spectacular. I marvelled at the daily cycle of light that gives life to everything on Earth.

That morning's trek was my first time hiking this section of the PCT. We searched westward up toward Frosty Mountain and eastward down to Castle Creek. The sections of trail at the major drainages were heavily covered in tree downfall. We had previously posited that Jordan might have tried taking shortcuts from the Frosty–Windy Joe Mountain connector trail down to the PCT. Our eyes soon told us that this scenario was unlikely.

Around noon, we reached the Canada-US border and the Monument 78 campsite. A strip of land several metres wide had been cleared of trees to mark the line of the international boundary. We noted another metal food storage container; inside, I found a granola bar on top of a photo of Jordan. It reduced me to tears. I lowered my head in honour and memory of my son.

The bar had probably been there since October—few people would have been snowshoeing this deep in the forest in the winter. Undoubtedly, other people had opened and closed the container through the fall. But nobody removed the granola bar. Whoever had left it knew Jordan would be hungry. It was a beautiful gesture by a caring soul.

I stood there for a long time, my hand on Jordan's photo, imagining holding his actual face not just an image of it. The photo showed Jordan in his graduation gown. I remembered how proudly we had held Jordan on his graduation day at Memorial University.

The moment had to end, however. Bob and I turned north along the Monument 78 trail. I stopped to digiscope several areas on the side of the mountain from the Frosty Mountain connector trail down to Castle Creek. Eventually we arrived at the trailhead. We had hiked about twenty-five kilometres on this second day, wearing heavy backpacks. I was beyond exhausted when we arrived at the parking lot.

That hike brought me to such a point of physical and mental fatigue that I needed more than one day to recover. My knees and ankles were in unbearable pain. It was clear that if I didn't take better care of myself, I wouldn't be able to do any more long hikes in coming weeks. And I wanted—needed—to be well prepared to search the more distant and remote areas that remained: Hozomeen Mountain, Despair Pass, and the south side of Frosty Mountain down the Princess Creek drainage. So I rested for three days and then did a solo hike on May 22 to drone areas off-trail on Windy Joe Mountain.[18]

The days were now longer than when I'd arrived. I could cover much more ground, starting earlier in the morning and returning later in the evening. I always began shortly after sunrise and got back to the cabin around sunset, sometimes shortly thereafter. I remained mindful that others in the community were aware of my daily searches. I kept in close contact with a few community members and let them know anytime I camped overnight.

On my solo hike up Windy Joe Mountain on May 22, I reflected on ways to connect more deeply with Tmxʷulaxʷ. I whispered into the wind and opened my heart and mind, so that I might hear signals from the forest. I hoped Tmxʷulaxʷ would guide me in the right direction.

Looking carefully around and below fallen trees, I peered into the shadows to see if anything was hidden within them. To see beyond the shadows, I needed to look closer. It always seemed like a trade-off: The longer I stared in one direction, the less time was available to search farther along a trail. I was continually making this difficult decision, whether to search longer in one area or move on to another.

Some clues flagged on heatmaps were shrouded in "camouflage." I would step closer, to try and distinguish between something that was meaningful and something that was deceiving. Some clues were hidden by false trails or covered by rocks, fallen trees, and snow. But searching

---

18 I was not the only person to make solo hikes. On days that I rested, Trevor also searched by himself. We'd discuss strategies and priority areas together and he'd make his plans. On May 29, for example, he searched off-trail along the Monument 83 trail. He reported that tree blowdown was very difficult between the seven- and ten-kilometre marks.

long enough would eventually reveal what had spurred viewer interest when volunteers were scanning photos and drone videos.

As the last remaining signs of snow disappeared in this area of the park, I reflected on the change of seasons. I, too, needed to change tactics for the coming months. A new plan required more drone activity that strategically searched the ground in selected areas—now visible— that could inform our subsequent hikes.

After completing my droning around the last switchback on Windy Joe Mountain, I decided to turn back. The trail beyond was still covered in snow. I collected further drone videos on my return hike, including off-trail in the interior drainage basin. As usual, when I got back to the gas station in Eastgate, I uploaded the videos. On this day, soon after I did so, came a rush of excitement—volunteers had identified a piece of coloured fabric!

I quickly found the video and traced the path of the drone. When I looked closer, the fabric seemed familiar. The drone had hovered near one of the switchbacks. The object, partially covered by tree branches, nevertheless reflected sunlight. I remembered the area: It was close to the trail and a cliff that dropped abruptly from the switchback.

I sat at the computer, staring at the image. My backpack, on the floor where I'd dropped it, was just visible in my peripheral vision. I groaned, realizing that I might just have droned over the place where I had set my backpack on the ground.

Embarrassed, I shared this news with the volunteers.

It was, however, another lesson learned. From that day forward, I carefully placed my pack—and myself—out of the drone's field of view, or I'd stand beside it when I droned so that we both were clearly identified.

———

As I developed more and better skills with the drone, the amount of new ground I could search each day grew rapidly. I learned how to control the drone's altitude more accurately and fly it as low as possible—without hitting trees—so it could scan the ground more carefully. My ability to search more quickly and critically meant I could focus on key features in the surroundings, ones that could indicate human activity.

On May 23, I did another solo hike, droning along Castle Creek. I wanted to find new lookout points, so I could get footage from across the creek and over to the East Similkameen trail. That area was still largely unchecked and difficult to access on the ground.

Each time I passed by the Monument 78 trailhead, I paused at the poster of Jordan. I gazed into his eyes and asked him to give me a clue. I loved and missed him and the time we spent together so much. Jordan, like me, would have shown tears in tragic circumstances. I wished that I could wipe away the tears he had shed, as he had struggled through the forest wilderness.

Once again, I had to move on. Instead of following the usual trail direction on this day, I diverted off-trail immediately. Our tracking maps had indicated this was a direction and an area not yet searched on the ground. It was densely covered with shorter trees. I reached a waterway flowing into the Similkameen River. Near a large tree that had fallen across the river, I stopped to assess the area for droning.

As I rested, I reflected on the sensations I felt in the moment. I took a deep breath and focused on my feelings, thoughts, and what I sensed from the environment. The crisp air of the forest was refreshing and relaxing. Despite the tremendous stress of the past eight months, I knew I needed to stay calm. My mind ran to other thoughts, but I returned to focus on my breathing and to practising mindfulness: inhaling and exhaling, one breath after another.

In the solitude of the forest, I connected with the presence of Jordan. Whenever other thoughts or feelings distracted me, I refocused back on him. As Tmxʷulaxʷ had communicated, I could not change my situation, but I could change my outlook and my attitude about the circumstances.

I watched the river currents move downstream, and imagined they were feelings and emotions. There were strong turbulent currents and calmer waters. Similarly, extreme anxiety passed through my body, but then these emotions passed by and settled down. I needed the turbulent emotions to be temporary, so they would not paralyze me.

I collected several drone videos that day of new ground in the East Similkameen area. After they were uploaded to the shared drive, volunteers again reviewed them. Alas, no clues of significance were seen.

On May 24, I returned to drone areas near the summit of Windy Joe Mountain that had not been previously searched on snow-free ground. The snow was completely gone on the trail up to the summit but several of the north and northeast faces of the mountain still had snow cover off-trail. So I hiked to vantage points from which mostly clear ground could be seen.

As the snowpack receded and more ground became visible, I felt that winter's hidden secrets would soon be exposed. There would be no further concealing of the truth. It was not a matter of *if* but *when* we would be together again with Jordan. As the snow receded, I also sensed Jordan's presence ever closer. In my thoughts and prayers, we formed a connection and shared our thoughts.

Jordan enjoyed rankings, so we had sometimes discussed our top fives—best sports teams, for example, or best meals. *Jordan, you are greatly missed and loved,* I silently communicated to him. *Remember how we enjoyed strategy games and debating about the best musical bands or art?*

I wonder why people use ratings for music or art? Although, ratings can save time—we can't experience every work of art. There's only so much available time.

Ratings can help us make decisions, by giving us more information. But any ranking is subjective. Opinions vary.

Other people's opinions can impact your experience.

I agree, Jordan. My impression of an artwork may be different if I've heard an opinion or explanation before I see it. There might be a personal connection or some other reason that I otherwise wouldn't have factored into my ranking.

A number alone can cheapen an analysis, though. What makes a 10? What is perfect art? There are qualitative and quantitative factors, as well as subjective and objective measures.

Jordan, you have wisdom beyond your age. Please son, send me any signal or sign, to find you and bring you home.

And so it went on. I spent nearly the entire day meditating about Jordan. I felt him close to me through those hours, but I was unable to find any new clues. Still, I collected many drone videos where we could examine snow-free ground. Our volunteers reviewed the videos promptly. But they, too, found no new clues.

On May 26, I set out to hike alone to the Monument 78 campsite and search along Castle Creek near the international border. This would be one of my longest solo hikes, well over thirty kilometres, and would include several drone searches along the south side of Frosty Mountain.

I started out around 7:30 a.m. and hiked until 7:00 p.m.—a long day, but the hours passed quickly. My thoughts were focused on the seriousness of reaching my destination and droning the southeast drainages behind the summit of Frosty Mountain.

When I reached the border, I hiked a short distance off-trail northward and found an excellent lookout point for droning. It offered a full view of the southeast face of Frosty Mountain. I was overwhelmed to see how steep this flank of the mountain was, and the enormous size of its drainages.

By this point, I had learned to navigate the drone much farther (up to a few kilometres away) and relatively close to the treetops. It was still tricky, however, to manually fly the drone along a mountain face because I had to account for the rising elevation. My method was to fly the drone in a grid pattern, moving the drone controllers while watching its path on a topographic map on my cellphone. I would use key waypoints and edges of the desired grid search, then fly the drone in equally spaced paths back and forth, to thoroughly cover a search area.

In earlier months, I had needed flat ground and a fairly wide-open area to launch and land the drone—so it was often not possible to use the drone when I was on steep terrain or in dense forest. Over time I learned to launch from my left hand while I worked the controller with my right. Gradually I became accurate enough in flying the drone that I could land it on my outstretched hand as well.

I collected several drone videos across the southeast face of Frosty Mountain on May 26. These focused especially on areas that were distinct possibilities for Jordan to have fallen in as he hiked along the ridge connecting Frosty with Windy Joe Mountain. I had been unsettled from the very beginning of our searching by the fact that a major drainage to the west of the connector trail, about halfway between the two summits, had not been adequately checked on the ground. We identified this drainage and surrounding areas as priorities to be searched once the snow thawed.

Consequently, when Mike M—who had joined us in our search in October—and his partner, Stephanie, indicated they'd be available to camp overnight from May 28 through 30, we targeted the forests around the connector trail, and nearby off-trail areas as our destination. As we started out, I struggled again to adjust to the heavier weight of the camping backpack. But I soon settled into a steady pace up the mountain trail.

We hiked at a good pace and reached the PCT campsite before lunchtime, unloading our packs and setting up before going on to the connector trail. To my surprise and frustration, there was still deep snow off-trail in the areas where I wanted to search. We chose a point to divert off-trail at a spot that I estimated would lead to a snow-free area farther on. We were without snowshoes, having assumed the snow would be gone. Our off-trail pace was thus quite slow—we sank into the snow with each step. Nevertheless, we separated onto three parallel paths and continued through the forest in the hope that the snowpack would recede by the edge of the forest plateau. Our plan was to search down the mountain into one of the interior drainage basins, if snow there had sufficiently melted away.

I tuned into the frequency and sound of crunching as I punched my feet through the snow—and the sloshing of slushy water underneath. Sensing Jordan's presence, I turned my thoughts to him, forging conversations from ideas he'd spoken of in the past.

Jordan, I'm sensing that something happened nearby. But I can't find any snow-free ground to search thoroughly. It has been a nightmare since we learned of your disappearance in October.

I have a story about nightmares, I felt him reply. *It's about what happens to nightmares when they end. You just wake up and you're back to normal.*

I feel like I haven't woken up yet. I'm still in a nightmare. I only wish that I could leave this nightmare.

I love you, Dad. Think about what happens if you don't wake up and you get stuck in a nightmare. "Oh my gosh," you think, "this is what happens." And you know it could be a bit frightening.

It is indeed frightening. So I'm just focusing on the goal of finding you and bringing you home.

There are three rules of nightmares. The first rule is that you can't change the setting. The lighting is what controls the mood. Lighting has to be able to, you know, bring your mood up and down, but you can't control that unfortunately.

Jordan, I have imagined the darkness of your loss in nightmares. But I try to avoid going there as the despair becomes paralyzing.

The second rule is that you can control whether your nightmare hurts you or not. I think that is pretty important. I can't let things hurt me unless I let them—that's a pretty nice rule.

Jordan, I've had nightmares about you suffering and that I was unable to do anything to help you. Fear has been one of the feelings that hurts most during a nightmare, as well as confusion and sadness.

The third rule is about speaking—you can skip the not interesting parts in your nightmare. So if you're going through a nightmare, and you're like, "This part's not a dream," or "this part is kind of boring, I don't really want to take part in it," then you can just skip it.

Jordan, I wasn't aware of your knowledge of the psychology of dreams. You have learned a lot more than just electrical engineering. I didn't know about these features of dreams.

After hiking a fair distance through the forest, the snowpack had not changed. Mike, Stephanie, and I reconvened to discuss modifying our plan. We decided it would be more efficient to search ground that *was* snow-free. So, with some time remaining before sunset, we shifted to grid searching an unchecked area on the southeast-facing flank of Windy Joe Mountain.

We separated and set our parallel paths across the mountainside to an area I hadn't noticed before—at a slightly higher elevation than the official "summit" at the top of the trail. This vantage point had a stunning view of the entire valley below. I pulled out my drone and sent it a few kilometres down into the valley, farther than ever before. I stopped it at carefully designated points and rotated it 360 degrees. Then I turned the camera lens toward me and rotated the gimbal so the lens faced directly inward toward the mountainside, rather than normally downward to the ground. This careful periodic rotation was a powerful way to more thoroughly search the ground from different angles and directions.

Finally, it was time to fly the drone back up the mountain, which was a bit difficult because I'd dropped its elevation significantly. It was critical to keep raising the elevation as the drone returned to the Home location (I wanted to sweep the ground between the trees for a last time, as it came back, not just lift the drone vertically and then fly it in to me).

Suddenly I lost the video signal on the camera. Then it came on, sending scattered imagery of tree branches. Then it was gone again. I pressed the Return to Home button and tried other steps. No success.

More lost footage. More embarrassment in front of my hiking friends.

Mike offered to search for the drone—maybe it had fallen right to the forest floor? I pulled up its last recorded GPS position on the screen. We looked in that direction and saw a steep drop-off down the mountainside and difficult rocky terrain. I was concerned it was too rough to attempt getting the drone back. Mike, an experienced mountain climber, believed it was safe. He set off to search among the trees.

Stephanie and I soon lost sight of him. We waited nervously as the minutes ticked on. After about half an hour, we heard his voice from below.

"Found it!"

Soon he returned safely with the drone. I was amazed he'd been able to locate it—among massive trees on the rocky edges of a steep mountainside. What a great contributor to our team.

Upon examination, it seemed the drone's gimbal mechanism had been damaged by the crash. A secondary point, since my first concern had been Mike's safety. But he confirmed that he was fine.

Mike explained that he'd been able to find it because it was beeping, and because it had fallen all the way to the ground. Adding to our good fortune, the pieces could be reassembled well enough for its continued use on our trek (I would later have a permanent repair done by a shop in Vancouver). Meanwhile, I'd learned another lesson: Be more careful when returning a drone up the side of a mountain. I figured I should have either rotated the gimbal forward periodically to assess the height of oncoming trees or raised the elevation faster and higher.

We worked our way slowly back to camp through another difficult section of tree blowdown, labouring in a grid search that sometimes crossed seemingly endless layers of downfall. When we finally could sit down and rest at our campsite, Stephanie said it was the most difficult hike she'd ever done.

We had planned for two nights of camping so we could search a lot of ground in the interior drainages—assuming they'd be snow-free. But we changed this plan, too, based on what we'd found. So after just one night, we packed up and hiked back down Windy Joe Mountain to search the East Similkameen area on May 29.

Unfortunately, the East Similkameen trail was another terrible mess of tree downfall. Despite its label, the "trail" was not maintained and was mainly one massive pile of fallen trees after another. I had recommended this area to Mike and Stephanie because it was mostly snow-free and definitely not an area that I could search on my own.

During a water break, as we sat resting on a pile of trees, a colourful grouse crawled from beneath some branches and walked over to Stephanie. It no doubt had plenty of predators in the forest, yet it still calmly walked right up to us. We were surprised and delighted when it was playful with Mike and Stephanie.

As I watched, I could only think about how Jordan might have been able to survive with grouse as food. It would have been very easy to pick up a rock and hit this grouse, and I knew grouse were plentiful in Manning Park. This small bird, walking around in front of me like a little chicken, gave me a glimmer of hope that somehow survival was possible. Despite how unlikely I knew it was by now.

We completed our search as far as we could, then returned to the resort before dark. I thanked Mike and Stephanie, expressing my hope that we could meet again soon to search another area of Manning Park.

––––––

During the previous few weeks, Josie and Mike B had connected with a local hiking group to coordinate dozens of volunteers who were willing to help our search efforts on the ground, now that the snow was disappearing. This was an important opportunity to make the best use of new resources, so I carefully analyzed how and where they should search and how to organize this larger effort.

The volunteers offered their own advice, too, on how to coordinate grid searches in the coming weeks. One idea was to subdivide the park into blocks of two or three hundred square metres, colour code them by difficulty level, and assign a different block to each volunteer. It was an interesting idea, but it had time-consuming administrative challenges. We needed someone to use software to categorize blocks into levels of difficulty and update blocks after hikers had searched an area. One volunteer expressed interest in doing this, but then when I asked for help they didn't follow up. I didn't have time to do it myself, so I moved on to another approach.

Josie and Mike also planned a separate major search by contacting an organization called Bring Me Home, which used the canine teams of the Canadian Canine Search Corps (CCSC). They were set to search Manning Park in mid-June. I also received several calls and emails from individual volunteers looking for advice and suggestions of where to prioritize their own search efforts.

Josie and Mike worked with BC Parks to make the necessary preparations for the two larger groups. We were all concerned about the lack of fallen tree clearance on the trails. Unless these routes were cleared soon, the volunteers would have to spend too much time and energy navigating fallen trees, which would mean less area searched each day.

To assist the canine teams, BC Parks agreed to cut paths on the weekend of June 5 and 6, including along the Frosty Mountain and Skyline trails from the Lightning Lake sides, the Windy Joe Mountain and Monument 83 trails to the snow line, and the initial parts of the Monument 78 trail. Penticton staff and other volunteers also came out to help. This was a great relief to us all.

Josie and Mike also passed along information and recommendations to the volunteers coming to search with Bring Me Home. It was difficult to know their experience level, so Mike provided them with some basic guidelines, which included:

- Anyone searching off-trail needs to have Class 2-3 terrain experience (experience with moderate scrambling on steep, rocky terrain that requires handholds for climbing and safety);
- Sturdy backpacks and light mountaineering boots are required;
- Trekking poles and work gloves[19] are recommended; and
- Be prepared for weather conditions to change rapidly at higher elevations.

The North Cascades are known for large convection cells from which storms can quickly form, delivering rain, hail, or snow throughout the year. And the areas of interest for the coming searches varied in elevation between 1,200 and 2,400 metres. Even in June, there would still be snow-covered areas, especially on north-facing sides of mountains and within areas of thick forest cover. Some areas even had permanent snowfields, where hikers would want to wear micro-spikes.

At this time, as well, bears were going to be out and active. Although black bears are most common in the North Cascades, the occasional grizzly may be encountered. Hikers were asked to always carry bear spray, which is also effective against other potentially dangerous animals in the park, such as coyotes, wolves, cougars, and moose. One new volunteer, Tony, had reported that he'd encountered an aggressive bear on a Windy Joe Mountain–PCT search he had done on May 31. It was something to flag for other volunteers, especially as that area had been identified as one to be searched when the ground was free of snow.

Finally, it was also conveyed to the volunteers that cellphone coverage in the park was non-existent outside the main resort area. To communicate with others, FRS/GMRS radios were recommended; their range was one to two kilometres.

---

19 Devil's Club grows in the park. It can reach three metres in height, and has crooked stems covered with hard yellow spines that can cause infection (hence the necessity for gloves). Its bright red fruit is poisonous.

As May drew to a close, we still had found no substantial evidence to suggest what had happened to Jordan. With the summer thaw accelerating, however, I felt it was now only a matter of weeks until our questions would be answered.

It had to be so—my own leave of absence from Memorial University ended in August. And although I'd avoided bringing it up, Josie had mentioned it in one of our phone calls at the end of May. There was no avoiding it: The stress and pressure would be intense in the coming weeks.

It was unbearable to think about returning to St. John's without Jordan. He could not remain a missing person. We needed resolution.

All hands were on deck for June.

eleven

JUNE THAW

Never go into the deep parts of the forest,
for there are many dangers there, both dark
and bright, and they will ensnare your soul.
—BEATTY, 2015

S JUNE ARRIVED, I SENSED A RENEWED ENERGY AMONG THE
volunteers. Not only was more and more ground being
exposed, John had recently turned up one of the most promising clues yet.

When I had been on my overnight trek with Mike M and Stephanie,
John had searched on his own around the Frosty Mountain summit.
He had spent considerable time using binoculars to scan the drainage
basins to the west and east of the Larches. He had found a vantage
point near the Frosty Mountain summit with a wide view of the Frosty
Creek drainage basin where he could search the slopes on either side of
Frosty Creek. Volunteers had covered the ground on the east side, but
very little had been done on the west side.

At one point, in some treetops on the west side of the mountain, a few kilometers down from the summit, he noticed an unusual bit of red-orange. He stared at the coloured patch for more than an hour, trying to discern what it was. Discolouration from fallen trees? Something natural catching the light in an unusual way? Nothing he could come up with seemed to fit, because the coloured patch seemed to blow around like a tent tarp. He concluded it could be a piece of coloured fabric, blown and then caught on the treetops.

When we reported John's new clue, excited volunteers immediately wanted to search the area. They found that two other clues had already been identified as possible tents at the same location—definitely worth further investigation. Because of the steep terrain, we presumed a tent had not been set up nearby. If it was tent material, it would have blown in from somewhere else in the basin.

When I picked up Trevor on the morning of June 1, we discussed John's new clue. We knew John would not have reported it unless he felt it was substantial. Was it possible, I asked Trevor, to reach that remote area and return on the same day? In addition to its distance, it was in steep, hazardous terrain. Trevor suggested hiking the Lighting Lake trail to the west side of the Frosty Creek drainage, finding the path of least resistance up the mountain toward the ridge, then side-hilling through the forest in the direction of the Frosty Mountain summit. That became our day's plan.

After about six hours of hiking, we reached the location. We grid searched up and down the mountainside in the area (as identified by the marker on my GPS unit) but found nothing out of the ordinary. I hiked higher, to drone around the location of the clue. The footage showed us a section of fallen trees with exposed trunks that were unusually discoloured, and an opening in the tree cover that may have fit with John's line of sight from the Frosty Mountain summit. But fallen trees couldn't explain the movement of the coloured patch that John had reported seeing. Maybe the varying intensity of sunlight, as nearby trees swayed in the wind, had given John the impression of a moving tarp?

I had high expectations that something would be found here, but the location revealed no new information about Jordan. To my dismay and disappointment, even the most promising of clues had not brought us closer to Jordan.

Trevor and I descended through the Frosty Creek drainage, high enough above the creek to avoid the steeper banks flanking the waterway. It was a long and still precipitous route through dense tree downfall and periodic patches of deep snow. Once safely down, I asked Trevor how he rated the difficulty of the hike on a scale from one to ten. He gave it a ten, naming it among the top most difficult hikes in his life. My exhaustion and soreness could readily confirm this rating—especially the pain in my ankles and knees—as I could barely get myself into the car.

The forest along the East Similkameen trail was at a relatively constant elevation, but the trail through it was difficult due to large patches of dense tree downfall. Droning, though helpful here, was also challenging because the flatness of the terrain meant the drone soon flew beyond our sight.

On June 2, I launched one of the drones[20] in the forest in the East Similkameen area while hiking with Trevor. I sent it aloft well above the maximum height of trees in the area, but after about ten minutes I lost the video signal. To my embarrassment, while "teaching" careful drone use to Trevor, the drone had crashed into a tree on the far side of the Similkameen River. I pressed the Return to Home button and tried to relaunch, but neither worked. The drone was tangled in branches.

---

20   I had bought additional drones so Trevor could also use one, especially when he hiked alone. I shared what I'd learned about flying a drone with him, so he could maybe avoid making the same mistakes I had.

Trevor and I crossed the river to search for it, using the device's last GPS coordinates. Eventually we found it—but with damaged gimbal and camera mechanisms. It was unclear whether it could be repaired. So, one more lesson learned about the importance of maintaining a line of sight to the drone. The ground had appeared relatively flat, but there must have been some elevation change that prevented the drone from having enough clearance above the trees.

This time, however, the mishap did not end the day's efforts. Fortunately, we had a second drone with us. So we continued to search among the fallen trees, but we found no clues.

On June 3, Trevor and I hiked the Lightning Lakes Chain trail, collecting drone videos over the plateau near Rainbow Bridge, the marsh between Flash and Strike lakes, and areas around Strike Camp. We also did a grid search off-trail behind the Rainbow Bridge plateau and ground searches around Strike Camp.

As I droned over Flash Lake, two women passed us on the trail. One of them stopped to angrily rebuke me for flying a drone. She scolded me about how it was inappropriate—this area was an undisturbed forest wilderness and the sound of the drone was unnatural and intrusive.

I explained that I had approval from BC Parks and that I was using the drone to search for my lost son. This news appeared to embarrass both women. The second woman said she had heard of Jordan as a missing person. She expressed sympathy while the first held her head down and walked on.

Later, Trevor and I paused for lunch at Strike Lake. When I walked to the shore to fill my water bottle, I noticed the women nearby, also lunching. The second woman came over and again conveyed her sympathies. She gave me some money to help with the search and a small card with a prayer to the Virgin Mary. She told me that she had followed our search for Jordan and although she couldn't hike with us, she hoped a financial contribution would help our efforts to find him.

She expressed admiration for our determination to find our son and said she would do the same if she had lost her own child.

When I looked over at the first woman, she expressed her regrets from a distance and appeared to apologize for her earlier remarks. She hadn't known that I was searching for my lost son. I accepted her apology.

The encounters with the two women, so different in nature, reminded me how we know so little about what others are dealing with in their own personal lives—and how hurtful it can be to act quickly on our assumptions. When we meet people casually, they may show no sign that they are living in a crisis. It was a reminder that we should always begin with kindness. People can be too quick to judge others and then act based on what they see, before they understand the full situation.

After lunch, Trevor and I grid searched separate areas of the forest behind Strike Camp. We were about twenty metres apart and could see each other through the trees. Snow still covered the ground here. When I stretched over one fallen tree, I was alarmed to see fresh bear tracks. My thoughts turned to Jordan and whether he'd had an encounter with a bear.

Jordan, bears are nearby, I'm terrified of the thought of you facing a bear attack. I know you were prepared with bear spray.

Dad, I love you, don't be afraid. I have a story of a bear who deceived a hiker in the forest by misrepresenting itself as a person.

Is this a story that explains what happened to you? Did someone or something deceive you into making a bad decision?

There was a bear that could turn into a man. A woman flirted with the bear, in the man's form. They ended up getting married and they were happy for some time. Then the bear grew jealous. He thought, she only likes me when I'm in a human form, not my bear form. "You don't like me for who I am," he accused her. When the bear turned into a human, he took off his fur. The woman set out to burn the fur and break the curse. But when she set it on fire, the man cried out that it hurts.

The woman is trying to stop the bear from deceiving her. Jordan, I can feel that you were deceived among false spur trails that led you in the wrong direction.

I sensed from this meditation that Jordan felt he was under pressure to do or see something particular in the park—or perhaps it was pressure from Tmxʷulaxʷ, regarding an incoming storm or darkness at sunset—which led to a wrong decision.

I returned to the car in the late afternoon while Trevor continued on to Thunder Lake. Its water level had risen because of snow melt, making it more difficult to reach the west end. The water forced him higher on the embankments, through dense patches of vegetation on steep scree slopes. He camped overnight at Strike Camp, making off-trail passes the next day over all flat areas adjacent to the trail.

He slept out again that night, and on June 4 searched beyond Thunder Lake. His route led toward the border, an area that had not been checked by the SAR team.

"I hiked beyond the proper end of the Thunder Lake trail," he reported to me later. "The trail rapidly deteriorated along the lake and ultimately joined a sprawling network of animal trails. I searched along one of the higher ones and got a good view toward the valley beyond Thunder Lake. I also bushwhacked down to a creek bed."

Trevor had ventured into terrain that I hadn't seen. He had crossed a dried-up creek and gone on to a place where he had a full view of Hozomeen Mountain. I asked him if he felt Jordan could possibly have descended into that valley from the Skyline trail.

"It's possible. But I didn't notice any sign of a human presence in the areas I searched."

Still, we thought it would be worth checking deeper into the wilderness later in the summer, from a campsite closer to Hozomeen Mountain.

On June 5, John and I hiked with two new volunteers to the spot where John had seen the red-orange colour in the treetops. Trevor and I had not found anything promising on our ground search there, but John was still convinced it was fabric that he'd seen. So this time we would search for it from a different direction: up the Frosty Mountain trail first, then down the steep edge of the mountain west of the Larches. It would also allow us to search more new ground, which was good.

John and I were both surprised when one of the volunteers arrived wearing shorts, running shoes, and a T-shirt. Although it was warm in the parking lot, John explained, there was still deep snow and likely freezing temperatures at higher elevations. Warmer clothes, and proper hiking boots were needed. But the volunteer replied that he was an experienced professional and didn't need John's advice.

I was troubled by the situation and his attitude—the young man was dangerously unprepared, in our opinion, and that put all of us at risk. If he became frostbitten or fell into deep snow or a tree well, we'd all be at risk trying to rescue him. Despite our reservations, he insisted that he knew better and was experienced with mountain conditions and Manning Park.

John took me aside and said that when he guided tours elsewhere in British Columbia, Alaska, and other mountain ranges, if any member of the group was unprepared, the tour would not proceed. It made good sense and I considered calling off the day's hike. But when John added that he had extra clothing in his backpack, he felt we could proceed. Reluctantly, John agreed. It seemed clear to me, though, that he remained agitated by this volunteer and his attitude. I was also disturbed but attempted to keep the peace by engaging everyone in productive discussion.

We set off, finding the ground clear of snow for the first few kilometres. As we approached the Frosty campsite, the first patches of snow appeared. We kept on ahead, across the plateau. I asked the volunteer several times if everything was okay and offered one of my jackets. I could see him trembling from the cold. He replied that everything was fine and he didn't need a jacket. He obviously was not fine—but seemed too proud to admit that John had been right.

When we reached the Larches, John searched for a good location to traverse down into the Frosty Creek drainage basin. He pointed out the spot on the far side where he'd seen the coloured fabric. From our vantage point, it wasn't detectable with binoculars—John said we'd have to be higher up, near the Frosty Mountain summit, to see it.

We started down a steep hillside where most of the ground, fortunately, was snow-free. As we approached a plateau near the waterway, the snowpack became deep and the wind was strong and cold. John guided us to the other side of the water and on to the location of the clue. After looking about carefully, we still found nothing, to John's surprise. Once again we concluded that what he'd seen—from several kilometres away and through binoculars—was likely discoloured fallen trees.

By this point it was past lunchtime and we were far from the Frosty campsite. We had planned to leave by going down through the Frosty Creek drainage, but massive tree downfall and steep banks along the creek would have slowed our return until well past sunset. John suggested we instead climb to the Larches and connect with the trail along the ridge.

Looking up at John's proposed route, I was frightened—it was a very steep climb up over a few kilometers. This was one of the few times that I felt seriously incapable of the effort it would take. John knew my abilities well by now, however, and he gave me the confidence to begin. He reassured me that I was capable and reminded me: one step in front of the other. He did, however, climb behind me, ready to help if I slipped or felt I couldn't go on.

It was extremely difficult, and long. But John was right—I eventually managed to reach the top. Remarkably, our companion in the running shoes was also able to do it without mishap.

We stopped for a water break close to the place where, on April 3, I'd been overwhelmed with strong feelings of Jordan's presence. As we sat down, a terrible dark energy descended over my body again. This was the second time that this had happened in the park. I trembled in anguish and sensed that something horrifically wrong had happened nearby. And once again, the sky was suddenly darkened by clouds, the wind picked up, and snow began to fall. It was astonishing to me how quickly the weather could take a turn for the worse at this location. My heart raced and I wept bitterly, dropping my head so the others could not see.

But there was no disguising my tears. The volunteer with running shoes came over to console me. He rubbed my back and shoulders. He knew what was happening. There was no need for words. And from that moment on, I no longer considered that young man foolish.

John had his own unique empathetic way of consoling me as well. Looking at him gave me the strength to pick myself up again. He was my rock—strong, solid, and unwavering in his support. I knew I could always rely on him to help and support me.

But I could not explain how or why this location and the feelings it brought on affected me so profoundly. Mystified, I wondered if I was perceiving events in the past, beyond what my normal senses were picking up. Inexplicable as it was, I knew that something important had happened to Jordan somewhere nearby. The sense of déjà vu was unlike any sensation I'd ever felt before—as if I'd entered a parallel universe for an instant in time and shared the pain of my son. I couldn't identify what happened or whether he'd suffered an injury, animal attack, or had become lost in the forest. But I sensed it was his agony that I was feeling and that whatever it was he'd experienced had happened nearby.

I also felt that Tmxʷulaxʷ was sending a clear message that I was unwelcome here. Winds were pushing me to leave. The dark clouds seemed to frown at me, wanting me gone as soon as possible. Even the peaks of the nearby mountaintops seemed to be urging me to leave. I stood and we quickly made our way back to the trail.

As we returned through the Larches, I continued to feel Jordan's presence. I stayed behind the other three, slowing to meditate on my son.

Jordan, my dear boy, I have an unusually strong sense of your presence here and feel something terrible may have happened to you. You have been a focus of my dreams. I'm wondering if you're sending messages through images in my mind while I'm daydreaming here.

Dad, everyone interprets dreams differently. So, when something happens in your dream, you might take one meaning from it, but another person might see something completely different.

Son, I had images in my dreams of you meeting up with someone at the resort before your hike, who later deceived and hurt you. The dreams ended before I could see what happened.

Dad, you can say that about a lot of things that happen in dreams.

When I'm meditating about you, Jordan, here in the forests and mountains, I'm hoping to see signals or signs that point to you. But I do wonder if the images that come into my mind are simply influenced by my own emotions.

I think dreams are just stories your brain is telling you to help you to get through.

Son, I am afraid of what may have happened to you somewhere nearby. For the sake of our family, who love and miss you so much, I can't fall apart here. Please give me strength to continue.

Dad, I love you, Mom, and my sisters so dearly. You are so strong, Dad, so don't give up.

At that point, I realized that my meditation had caused me to fall far behind the other three hikers. We were still in the Larches, with three of us wearing snowshoes, as the snow was still at least a metre deep. I was stunned at how the volunteer in running shoes had been able to manage over such long distances in the snow without snowshoes.

Eventually, I was able to catch up with the other hikers. When we got to an open area too steep for snowshoeing, John sat down and glissaded. I was next in line but was nervous about it. I went over some of the worst-case scenarios in my head. Losing control and veering into a tree. Tumbling and rolling off-trail into a pile of snow. John shouted encouragement and broke up my doomsday analysis, as if he could read my mind.

"Just stay calm and dig in your poles, Greg! I'll grab you if you veer off."

So I sat and started sliding.

All went fine until about twenty metres from the bottom, when I lost control and began moving off John's tracks. I readjusted my poles but I had too much momentum to steer. And I was heading straight for a large tree.

John jumped toward my path, keeping one hand on a tree. He was high enough to reach over me as I slid by but still get enough grasp on me to slow me down. When I stopped, my clothes were full of snow but neither John nor I were hurt. I hugged him and expressed my heartfelt gratitude. Once again he had placed his own body at risk to keep me safe.

"No worries, Greg," he said, as calm as usual. But we both knew how he had placed my safety above all.

After I recovered, John and I looked back up the slope to watch what the volunteer in shorts and running shoes would do, glancing at each other and shaking our heads. John shouted some suggestions and offers to help. I was astounded to see him glissade down, his bare legs tilted up in the air, with no poles to control his slide. He dug his bare elbow into the snow to control his direction and speed! I was very glad when he reached the bottom safely.

We made it back to the parking lot shortly following sunset, after another long day. For the first time in several weeks, I felt we had gained important signals about where Jordan was lost. They weren't tangible and couldn't be marked with any specific clue, but they were very real to me. Off-trail around the Larches and down into one of the adjacent drainage basins would be the priority search areas as soon as the snowpacks receded.

———

While we were searching near the Larches on June 5, another skilled volunteer, Tim, had gone off-trail into the interior drainage basins near the Frosty campsite—areas that we were hoping to prioritize once the snow was gone.

"The south-facing side of the drainage was mostly clear of snow," Tim reported to me later, "but the north-facing side is still about 80 per cent covered. I think it will be another couple of weeks before that side is worth venturing into again. It was even snowing half of the time I was up there, though it doesn't look like it will stay around."

News of this amount of snow cover *and* new snow was disappointing. It suggested that it might be well into July before the ground was completely clear.

"I didn't find any clues," Tim went on, "but I did see several yellow flag markers about ten metres apart, running parallel to one of the creeks. Each flag had 'FO' on it. I don't know what it means—possibly BC Parks will know?"

"There have been search teams in the area. It's likely from one of those groups," I replied.

"Yes. So I was thinking—if they were there last fall, and Jordan had become lost nearby, he might have followed them farther down the drainage."

It was worth considering. I asked Tim if he'd seen anything unusual when he'd descended lower, but steepness had prevented him from venturing farther. "I think it would be worth investigating further with drones," he added, "especially now that the snow has mostly melted on that side and the undergrowth hasn't really come in yet."

Tim's report on ground conditions was helpful in preparing future search plans. We prioritized these interior drainages. Having someone report on the actual snow conditions helped us pinpoint the ideal time to redirect our efforts there.

June 6 was my 56th birthday. Several people encouraged me to take the day off—relax, drive into the city, go see a movie, or go to a good restaurant, they urged. But I wanted to be close to Jordan on my birthday. And, since the last reported sighting of him—Ethan Morf's—was somewhere near the second switchback of the Frosty Mountain trail, I decided to head there and spend my birthday in meditation.

As I headed up the Frosty Mountain trail, I noticed there were enough openings in the treetops where I could launch a drone. So I collected a few videos, then moved on and released the drone again. Despite taking care—in trees, on the mountainside—I suddenly lost the video signal.

Another drone crash, and this one on my birthday. Why today?

I had only lost my line of sight to the drone for a second or two, but it had been enough that it flew into a tree. I jammed my thumb on the Return to Home button, but it was too late. I could hear the drone falling through branches and hitting the ground. It was still beeping, however, and the GPS point on the screen was close enough that I decided to look for it myself.

As I removed my backpack to prepare, I was passed on the trail by another hiker, a volunteer who had come to search for Jordan farther up the trail. We talked and I introduced myself as Jordan's father. I was too embarrassed to say that I'd just crashed my drone nearby. After she went on, I started down the side of the mountain.

I climbed over, around, and under the expected expanse of fallen trees. The beeping led me right to the drone, but I could see that the crash had damaged the gimbal mechanism. Another trip to the drone repair shop would hopefully fix it. By this time, I had bought a few extra drones, so that I could continue droning if—when—one was damaged.

Once I'd regained the trail, I climbed a short distance to the second switchback, where I stopped and rested. I concentrated on Jordan and prayed that he would watch over me and our family, guide me by revealing a clue, and give me strength to continue. I recalled some of our favourite times together, visualizing who was there and the time of day.

I could hear Jordan's voice in these memories. I focused on it, repeating his name, asking him questions. Many were simple, requiring only a yes or no: Had he hiked in this direction? Had foul play occurred? Had Ethan really spoken to him near here? Had he camped overnight? Had he ever reached the Frosty Mountain summit?

I listened for answers, waiting for an image or signal from the forest. I felt I received answers to some questions but wondered whether I was just making up what I wanted to hear. Sometimes, however, I felt a response before I had even formed a question, so it seemed like I had established a connection. I decided I would trust what had come to me—whether I *knew* it to be real or not—and use it to guide our future searches.

After a lengthy time of reflection, I took the trail down and went back to the cabin. With a lost son, another damaged drone, missing the rest of my family, and knowing my unhappy wife and two daughters were far away in St. John's, it was the worst birthday of my life.

About halfway along the Frosty–Windy Joe Mountain connector trail, a critical waterway flows northwest into a major interior drainage parallel to the trail. The initial VPD SAR team reported they had searched those drainages. But Trevor, John, and I continued to pursue efforts there because the area had greatly troubled me since October. I'd gotten relatively close a few times with searchers, including with Mike M, Stephanie, and Bob. But we had always been unable to investigate the area thoroughly because of lingering snow cover (and it was too far from any starting point to reach and search on a day hike).

Trevor and I made a plan to thoroughly search and drone those areas on June 8 and 9, by camping overnight at the PCT campsite. Once we reached that destination on the 8th and set up our campsite, we continued on to the connector trail. Near a waterway of primary interest, we diverted off-trail and grid searched and droned from a good vantage point overlooking a couple of drainage basins. As we walked, I gazed over the valley below, sensing Jordan's presence in an unusually strong way. It was my first direct view over this long set of interconnected drainage basins. I was sorry to see that the snow was still deep in the forest below, making it difficult to pick out any new clues. I imagined what scenarios might have put Jordan down into that terrain below me, chilling images that frightened and distressed me.

Jordan, I'm sensing images in my mind here, and sometimes I have nightmares at night, as I can see you suffering in one of these drainages. Help me decide which direction I should go, from here.

I would probably take the right path, I felt him reply. Because if you follow the right rule, every single time you'll be able to get out of the maze. You can also follow the left path, but the right path is the default.

I imagined what this might mean. We were hiking along the connector trail toward the Frosty Mountain summit. In this direction, there was a key decision point: go right off the trail into the interior drainages or left to connect with the PCT and head toward Monument 78.

I sensed the right-hand path was the better choice. This course of action also matched my feeling about that particular drainage west of the connector trail that had been neglected in past searches.

Trevor and I soon reached an open area at the edge of the forested plateau and began droning over the interior drainage basins. We attempted to move into the drainage halfway along the connector trail, but our progress was limited again by snow cover. We searched extensively through the forest but found nothing.

The next day, we again hiked to the connector trail but this time continued as far as daylight permitted toward the Frosty Mountain summit. If Jordan had set out on a clockwise loop (as the cellphone pings suggested), he would have taken this path and hiked in this direction. Trevor and I passed through occasional open areas that gave us spectacular views over the large interior drainage basins below. Many of these open areas had likely been created by fires started by lightning strikes, Trevor explained.

When we reached the basin that was parallel to (and west of) the trail, I gazed down, once again transfixed, while Trevor sent the drone over the terrain below us. The view gave me a strong sense of awe—and that this area was important. I sensed somehow this was a special drainage.

I suddenly realized what it was: I was overlooking the same drainage basin (but from a different angle) that had generated such strong feelings in me on April 3 and June 5, when I had been searching with John and Bob. On those days, I had been looking down into it from the *west*, from the ridge leading to the Frosty Mountain summit. Now, for the first time, I was looking into it from the east, from the Frosty-Windy Joe Mountain connector trail. When I had hiked the connector trail previously with Mike M and Stephanie, we had not seen the interior drainage, because we had turned back before reaching a lookout point due to snow cover.

Interestingly, this area didn't chase me away as it had during my two earlier experiences in the Larches. But it nevertheless sent chills up my spine. Why were bad feelings stronger from the other side looking down into the same drainage? Could this be a clue about Jordan's direction of travel—counter-clockwise around the Frosty Mountain trail loop, instead of clockwise from Windy Joe Mountain?

Over our two days of hiking on this high ground, Trevor and I collected nineteen videos. I was hoping to learn that volunteers would find something positive in this area that I was growing ever more certain held some answers.

On June 11 and 12, Trevor searched on his own along both embankments of Castle Creek. Some of these areas had been searched in the fall, and later when the ground was covered by snow, but not all of them.

"At the spot where a log crossing would normally put a hiker onto the Monument 78 trail, I stayed on the west side of the Creek and bushwhacked upstream," Trevor reported to me. It was an area where Jordan could have wandered into if he had attempted a shortcut off the PCT or taken a wrong turn from the top of Windy Joe Mountain.

We discussed whether Trevor had spotted any clues that would benefit from closer droning or a grid search of the area. He'd seen no signs of human activity on the west side of the creek but did detect animal activity in several places, especially bear activity. Although this effort had yielded no new signs of Jordan, it had been over snow-free ground and allowed us to remove more possible scenarios from our list.

Bob, meanwhile, had searched one of the lower plateaus off the Frosty Mountain trail on June 11 and turned up...a golf ball.

"Was Jordan a golfer?"

It wasn't something we'd done together. "It's possible he took it up in Vancouver," I offered. We discussed whether the golf ball meant anything and how it might have gotten there, but soon switched to more important questions.

"Were you able to grid search the entire plateau?" I asked.

Snow had prevented that, but Trevor suggested it was worth doing soon. I agreed that off-trail areas around the Frosty campsite, including drainages nearby, were the best areas to prioritize.

By this time, Josie and I felt that we had basically mobilized all possible forms of assistance and technological help except for one: dogs (which I strongly felt should have been used more in October). So I had a renewed sense of hope when, through Josie and Mike B's efforts, the CCSC agreed to help us. Based in Calgary, the group does SAR work, looking for missing persons and human remains with specially trained teams of dogs.[21]

---

21 The Canadian Canine Search Corps (CCSC) is a not-for-profit organization that provides services on a minimal cost recovery basis. The group offsets...

The dogs the CCSC uses have a remarkable sense of smell. They can detect bodies at a distance of several hundred metres. They are trained to locate human remains even long after they have been exposed to the elements, scattered by scavengers, or buried. They are also capable of detecting remains under water.

The CCSC team arrived on June 11 with six search dogs certified in the detection of human remains. Their plan was to do intensive searching over three or four days. I had the pleasure of greeting some of the dogs on the team, including Koda, Scarlet, and Copper. I gained a new level of admiration for dogs and appreciated their intensity in finding my son over the coming days.

On the morning of the first day, Mike A brought welcoming remarks and prayers on behalf of the local Indigenous community. I stood behind the CCSC volunteers and their dogs, with tears streaming down my face, as Mike spoke about Jordan in a respectful and dignified way. He explained how the land, water, forests, mountains, and humans were all living entities connected as one. They deserved our utmost respect, he said, and would share signs of Jordan if we listened carefully.

Mike suggested that during our ground searches, we should periodically gather water in our hands from creeks we passed and blow its water vapour into the forest. Water was the source of life in the forest, he explained, so all living beings in the woods recognized and responded to it. Water was the most important liquid for all plants, insects, and animals. If we did this practice, it would bring us into a closer and more intimate connection with living beings in the forest, and ultimately lead us to Jordan.

...expenses through fundraising and public donations. CCSC relies on the generosity of the public and people to operate. All monies donated to CCSC go directly toward helping to find and recover the lost and missing to bring closure to their loved ones. You can learn more at www.caninesearchcorps.com. Please consider making a donation to CCSC.

My communications with Tmxʷulaxʷ over the past few weeks made Mike's words on this day especially meaningful to me. My meditations had been limited to carefully observing what my senses were telling me about my surroundings. But this new advice gave me a more active way to share the source of life—water—with Tmxʷulaxʷ.

The dog teams began by focusing on the lower slopes of Frosty Mountain and off-trail on Windy Joe Mountain. Each team was assigned a path so the maximum area could be covered. The weather was changing, so some areas were searched multiple times. In order not to bias their strategizing with our own opinions of higher priority areas, we simply provided all the factual information to CCSC. They then analyzed it and drew their own conclusions.

The dog teams were deployed for three full days. At the end of the day on June 13, nothing conclusive had been found in any of the search areas. In their opinion, CCSC said, Jordan was not to be found anywhere on the lower slopes within three or four kilometres of the Frosty Mountain trailhead.

Snow coverage and other factors had prevented some areas from being searched completely, including the slopes off-trail between the second and fourth switchbacks on the Frosty Mountain trail. CCSC concluded that it was unlikely that Jordan would be found there. I agreed with this assessment; ground crews had searched there in October and November with no luck.

Three dog teams searched on Windy Joe Mountain over two of the days. Their work had been difficult because of the many steep cliffs, sharp drop-offs, and other challenges. Our drone footage was helpful in reducing exposure to hazards for the ground teams.

Three dog teams also searched along the Skyline and Lightning Lake trails over two of the days, and in a few drainages below the north-facing slope of Frosty Mountain.

The remaining snow cover, however, had been an issue. CCSC recommended searching three areas once the snow melted fully. First,

222 · GREG F. NATERER

the upper plateau around the Frosty campsite—my own first priority when the ground was snow-free. CCSC believed that Jordan may have stepped off the trail at one of the lookout points (which would explain why the hiker Vincent had not seen him), continued along the plateau, and set up his tent off-trail at some distance from the campsite. Their second priority was farther along the Skyline trail. And their third priority were the two major drainages below the Frosty Mountain summit.

Mike B helped the dog teams with logistical support during their three days in the park. He was a great facilitator and organizer. With his military background, he pointed out all pertinent details so everyone would remain safe—such as ground conditions and difficulty levels—and he efficiently guided the teams to their desired search areas. On June 13, Mike and I hiked to a washed-out bridge along Castle Creek to help a dog team get back to the parking lot from Windy Joe Mountain.

At the end of each day, I drove to the Hampton Campground, where the CCSC volunteers had set up. My hopes were high—then dashed—each time. Still, I tried to convey our sense of determination to the volunteers, and I thanked them sincerely for their efforts. Their work conclusively determined that certain areas could be confidently excluded from future searches.

On the final evening, after signing out with the CCSC team, Mike B and I debriefed, then joined other campers who had kindly invited us for dinner. They were aware of our search for Jordan and conveyed their sympathies. One woman then shared her recent dream: that Jordan was lost in Manning Park and trapped behind a wall of ice. He was trying to escape but couldn't break through the wall.

I trembled as she spoke. She meant no harm, but I had to struggle to hold myself together. Mike quickly intervened and turned the conversation to another topic.

At first, I wished the woman had not told me of her dream. But on reflection, I felt it had some deeper meaning. It was not just a random assembly of images, and the wall she'd seen had some significance. What it was, I could not fully grasp. But I soon would.

Shortly after the ccsc searches concluded, we received a major new clue: A hiker who had been out on Thanksgiving weekend had taken photos of footprints in the snow near the Frosty campsite—and their tread matched those of Jordan's boots. Josie had determined this through his banking records by contacting the store and asking about the pair of boots we knew that Jordan had bought.

It was surprising that this clue had not come to our attention earlier. But some witnesses had not carefully examined their photos for footprints nor were even aware that our search had been ongoing through the winter.

It was possible, of course, that another hiker had been wearing the same brand of boots. But given the timing and location of the footprints in the snow, they appeared to support the theory that Jordan had lost his way in the vicinity of the Frosty campsite on Saturday evening. The photo also suggested that Jordan was much farther up the Frosty Mountain trail than several of us had previously assumed, well past the second switchback mentioned in Ethan Morf's account. But it raised a puzzling question: Why had hikers coming down the trail that day not passed Jordan on his way up?

The clue placed Jordan near the Larches, which raised the possibility that he'd become lost and gone into one of the three drainage basins west of the Frosty campsite. I had heard of a staff member at Manning Park becoming lost there about a decade earlier. The staff member had crossed all three drainage basins before being eventually found at the far end of Thunder Lake. We had initially thought this was a very unlikely scenario—why would Jordan climb down and up through three basins? The second and third basins west of the Frosty Creek drainage basin had been largely neglected so far in our own searches.

We had forgotten that, if you are lost and you can't see the long view through the forest, you don't *know* that one drainage basin will be followed by another and another. So you might keep on going, hoping you were heading in the right direction. Maybe, this had been Jordan's experience. So—the second and third basins west of the Frosty Creek drainage basin went higher on our list of places to search.

I spent the next few days analyzing our drone videos. I had not given up on finding software tools that used machine learning or artificial intelligence to identify a specific colour or unusual object in the imagery. Many volunteers had been reviewing our new drone videos the day they were uploaded. They scrutinized them closely and were able to find unusual features much better than I could. I wondered if a software tool could provide even closer scrutiny, perhaps for clues too small or difficult for the human eye to pick up.

I discussed this at length with Pascal, who had expertise about software. We even considered using satellite data—but the resolution of satellite imagery was too low for a detailed comparison with the drone video.

I also reached out to potential vendors of object detection software, including Amazon. But their algorithms suffered from a lack of data to "train" the software (sample data of colourful objects in forests, for example). There was little or no training data for object detection in a mountain wilderness, especially with snow and objects partially obscured by treetops.

Pascal also suggested trying a redness threshold: running a moving window across still images from the drone videos to see if one pixel was redder than its neighbours. But it seemed that obvious red objects were not always correctly identified by the machine learning algorithms.

We concluded that our human approach could outperform all the current machine learning alternatives. Our volunteer crew of video reviewers, thankfully, remained on duty.

twelve

ANOTHER SIDE
OF THE MENACE

It does not matter how slowly you go
so long as you do not stop.
—CONFUCIUS, 551–479 BCE

THE SOUTH SIDE OF FROSTY MOUNTAIN WAS THE MOST MEN-
acing and inaccessible of the areas we had searched because of
its remoteness, high elevation, and treacherous rocky slopes. In
October, I had viewed this area from the SAR helicopter. The SAR
team had not done ground searches on the southern face because they
felt a tent or backpack would have been visible from the helicopter
surveys. I was not convinced, however, because I had seen that there
were shallow caves and trees on that side of the mountain, which I felt
may have obscured clues.

My brother Marko and his friend Ed arrived from Ontario on June
13. Together along with Trevor, we spent five days and nights camping
and searching these remote slopes and around the international border.

Marko, Ed, and other friends had also come in October, searching extensively around the north and east sides of Windy Joe Mountain.

We set out from the Monument 78 trailhead at sunrise on June 14. Our backpacks were quite heavy, since we carried five days of supplies. We reached Monument 78 at around ten o'clock. By 10:30, Trevor had also arrived—a remarkable feat since he'd stayed the previous night at the resort. With an extra five kilometres to cover, he'd set out at around 5:00 a.m. and run much of the way to join us. Seventeen kilometres with a heavy pack on his back! But there was no resting. We all hiked at least another dozen or more kilometres in steep rocky terrain south of the Frosty Mountain summit that day, which made Trevor's total coverage around thirty kilometres. His endurance and stamina were extraordinary.

As we were setting up camp, I went to the food cache to store our supplies safely away from bears. Jordan's poster was still inside, and the same oatmeal bar still anchored it to the top shelf. Once again I was touched emotionally that no one had disturbed the granola bar offering. I stayed a while longer, to hold Jordan's graduation photo.

Our goal for the day was to search the Princess Creek drainage south of the Frosty Mountain summit. It was a complicated challenge. Not only did it span the international border, our elevation (1,300 metres) was much lower than where the drainage started (2,300 metres). It would be a very steep climb to reach the upper edge.

We began climbing through open and more gently rising terrain along a drainage southeast of the summit. Then we sidehilled across to the Princess Creek drainage. Marko and Ed had not brought snowshoes, it being mid-June. But once we reached 1,800 metres elevation, we ran into snow-covered ground. It became increasingly deep as we went on. Wearing boots, and not snowshoes, made our sidehilling much more difficult.

Trevor and I stopped several times to collect drone videos. We scanned a vast area of remote wilderness on the south side of the Frosty Mountain summit that had not been previously searched.

In a remote area, we crossed the international border unknow-ingly—recognizing it only after the fact. It was barely distinguishable from the tree growth on either side. If Jordan had been lost in the for-est somewhere south of the Frosty Mountain summit, it seemed clear to me that he could also have unintentionally crossed into the United States—something others had earlier discounted.

They claimed the clear-cut line at the border would be visible. Maybe in theory—but they hadn't seen what I now observed. Jordan could have crossed the border line without realizing it, especially in a snowstorm, darkness, or poor visibility.

We traversed northward at a nearly constant elevation toward the Princess Creek drainage, but soon recognized we had a time problem: We would not reach the top of the drainage in time to allow us to get back to the campsite before sunset. The realization brought dismay; the purpose of this day's hike had been to search the drainage. We were so close to reaching our objective but were running out of time. However, Trevor assured us that, if we picked up the pace, we could reach the drainage by 2:30 p.m.—and that would leave us enough time to return to camp by sunset.

As it turned out, Trevor was once again right on the mark, as he had been in every other situation where we faced time pressure. Once we reached the drainage, we were able to search down along both embankments. Then we found our way back to the campsite in time to watch the sun set.

As we prepared dinner by the campfire, we were joined by the unbear-able company of mosquitoes. Ed kindly gave me his mesh face mask and jacket. These clouds of pests had not been a problem during the day because we were continually moving. But when we stopped, they were intolerable. Wearing mosquito nets was the only way to endure them.

The mornings that followed all started early. On each day we tack-led a different search area near the border, adjacent drainages, and Castle Creek —all areas too far away to be accessed on a regular day hike. With four of us, our grid searches could cover a fair amount of new ground.

As we hiked farther south of the Frosty Mountain summit, I was amazed by the striking features of the terrain—especially the massive canyon at the top of the Princess Creek drainage. Several areas had massive tree blowdown. Once, in the depth of the forest far from any trail, we noticed an unusual shape. As we moved closer, I could make it out clearly—an abandoned trapper's cabin! My heart skipped a beat. A cabin meant a possible shelter for a lost hiker. It was a shocking discovery so deep in the forest. There were kilometres of dense forest all around, and it was built of wood that would have been brought in. The logs did not look to be made of the same wood as the surrounding trees.

The cabin was about ten square metres in size with no windows. It seemed structurally sound. Given the number of massive trees that had fallen throughout the forest in the park, it was astounding that none had crushed it. Inside there was no sign of any recent human activity. The year 1941 was marked on one wall, along with a few names. I wished the cabin could reveal any clues if my son had passed nearby.

On the following day, when we found ourselves on the west side of Castle Creek, we needed to locate a safe place to cross the waterway and return to camp. At one spot, the tree trunks spanning the river had thick branches. Over the past few months, I had gained more and more confidence with these difficult log crossings. But this log was several metres above the water. Marko and Ed went across first. They were experienced hunters and had no problems crossing. I had to focus much more carefully, but made it safely as well.

After several more hours of bushwhacking through dense forest, we reached another opening near the border. Trevor stopped suddenly, then Marko and Ed became motionless. A large moose was grazing in the undergrowth directly in front of us. It was majestic and massive, and must have weighed at least 450 kilograms. We all stood quietly watching—and it looked back, its big round eyes fixed on ours, for all the world behaving as if it had no reason to fear us. After about five minutes of staring at us, it went back to grazing and ignored us.

We had to pass that spot, however, to reach the campsite. Marko and Ed advised we veer off-trail to go behind and around the moose. Their hunting experience gave them insights into moose behaviour and we followed their suggestion.

We had a productive week together, though we found no new clues. I learned more about the terrain and the PCT near the border, including that there were dozens of trails that Jordan could have followed if he'd accidentally crossed into the United States. The PCT goes through the North Cascades National Park and extends far to the south. Josie contacted American authorities, asking them to place flyers and posters at various trailheads and campgrounds. We hoped to make more hikers south of the border aware of Jordan's disappearance, and that they would pass on any relevant information to authorities.

I drove Marko and Ed to the airport and promised to keep them updated on the search.

A new volunteer, Danny, initiated another major search effort, by coordinating a team of several BC hiking organizations. His idea was to engage dozens of skilled volunteers to search selected areas in early July, including camping overnight far from the Manning Park Resort. Josie and Mike B were also involved in organizing the hiking organizations' logistical details so that the weekend they arrived would be as productive as possible.

A strategic plan was needed to effectively search the highest priority areas and make the best use of the time and skills of this diverse group of volunteers. The areas off-trail around the Frosty campsite and the Larches, including the interior drainages, remained the highest priority.

As mentioned, I had found the meadows before and after the Frosty campsite to be the most confusing areas on the Frosty Mountain trail. This was where it was most difficult to stay on the "official" trail (especially with snow cover, as Jordan would have experienced). I sketched maps showing the priority areas, which were divided into banded regions and parallel paths so that each zone could be grid searched. They were all areas that had been relatively unchecked on the ground. For experienced volunteers who were willing to go off-trail, I identified a number of parallel one-day hikes: up Frosty Mountain, east into the interior drainages, and down and out via the Windy Joe Mountain trail. If at any time anyone felt unsafe in the drainages, they would be able to reverse direction and return down the Frosty Mountain trail.

We urged them to use technology so we (and they) could track the areas they were covering. For example, individual searchers could record their path then send us their KML file.[22] Another volunteer would then be able to hike on an adjacent and parallel route (also tracking their path), and so on, until eventually a full band was covered. Or, if it was too difficult to move parallel to someone else's track, volunteers could use GPS points as markers, taking note of any times they had to deviate from their intended route.

If a large group was able to set out together, they could space themselves twenty metres or so apart and cover a full band much quicker.

Not surprisingly, I soon found there were challenges getting volunteers to send files. And if file-sharing was delayed, then others might end up repeating the same paths. I had to keep track and send out reminders. But with all I was already doing, it was clear that we needed organizers to collect and coordinate the data.

In addition, sometimes volunteers searched along tracks that were not sufficiently precise. They overlapped routes hiked by other

---

22 A Keyhole Markup Language (KML) file is in a format that allows hiking programs to display the path travelled on an electronic map.

volunteers and so the integrity of covering the ground in a true grid was compromised. It led to gap areas or tracks repeated by multiple volunteers.

Marko suggested a better idea: map out the specific grid line we wanted each volunteer to follow and assign it to them, instead of asking them to hike and then send in their KML tracks.

So that's what we did. We mapped out paths designed to thoroughly cover an entire selected region, including some key GPS points to give a little flexibility and guide hikers back to their route if they had to divert. We made ourselves available at the starting point of the hikes to explain how to download their designated KML file into their handheld GPS units. Fortunately, many volunteers came asking where to search—and we had routes ready for them.

Volunteers were continually contacting me. I kept track of each path they hiked (with an assigned track number) on a master map. Josie or I would give the adjacent track number to the volunteer next in the queue (with some leeway for their comfort and the difficulty of the terrain). We conveyed details about the expected trail conditions and hiking difficulty to each volunteer. They could then decide if they were comfortable or not with an off-trail route.

Using this structured approach, with so many volunteers once again available to us, I was confident it would now be only a matter of time until we found Jordan.

On June 19, Trevor returned to the Despair Pass valley, hiking solo off the Skyline 1 trail. As noted earlier, he felt that one of the most confusing trail junctions in Manning Park was the three-way crossing of paths to and from Ross Lake, Strawberry Flats, and Lightning Lake. Trevor had become aware of several hikers who had been turned around at this point—and anyone lost at this junction could easily have veered off-trail into the Despair Pass valley.

He shared what he'd found when he returned: a lot of snow still on the ground in the forest and north-facing basin, and a lot of flooded bogs. He'd collected some drone footage, however, and added that with the number of drainages in this valley, it would be useful to return and search further. But he had not found any significant clues.

On June 21, with the snow levels finally receding past the Frosty campsite, I solo hiked up the Frosty Mountain trail to the Larches. Once again, I found the scenery and the panoramic views breathtaking. I am certain they are what attracted Jordan to Manning Park.

I spent hours droning over the nearby drainages both west and east of the trail. It was my first time alone in the location that had twice generated overwhelming emotions and a strong sense of Jordan's presence. On this day, however, Tmxʷulaxʷ did not drive me away. I found it interesting that the strong messages to leave had only occurred when I was with others. Now, on my own, I felt welcomed. Was there some deeper meaning? I again felt a subconscious connection to Jordan's presence, though I could not pinpoint his location.

Jordan, while I search here from the Larches into the drainages, I have a recurring fear of what happened to you.

Dad, don't be afraid. You have determination and will find answers and peace. Let me share a story about fear with you. It's about a mother who is afraid of planes. At the airport, her son notices her tensing up as they approach the gate.

How does the son help his mother deal with this fear?

He tries to get her to ignore it, so he doesn't make her feel uncomfortable. But he recognizes that she is uncomfortable. So he suggests that they cancel the flight and travel another way.

One of the ways I have tried to overcome my fear is to identify it as a challenge. A fear to be overcome.

The man and his mother discuss her terrifying fear. To avoid admitting her fear, she says she's bored and doesn't like being stuck with a lot of people and breathing the same air.

She had not genuinely confronted her fears. As I gain understanding of my own fears, I hope to feel empowered enough to confront them, not give disingenuous excuses.

This exchange and Jordan's story strengthened my determination to overcome my fears of how this searching might end.

I collected many drone videos of the drainage basins below the Larches that day, but I could see that at least half of the ground was still covered in snow. More waiting was required. But we would return once the snowpack was gone.

As I was spending my day in the Larches, Trevor was also solo hiking. He had gone hiking off-trail on Windy Joe Mountain and into the interior drainages—an area also still waiting to be thoroughly searched when the snowpack disappeared. He had more luck with finding clear ground, however, reporting that, "At first, where the drainage was gentle, there was still some snowpack, but as soon as the terrain steepened, the snow quickly receded."

He indicated that he was not able to do a thorough grid search, staying close to the waterway, and had not turned up any clues. We planned to return to the area within a few weeks and search it from a base camp.

On June 23, Trevor and I hiked the Skyline trail together. We ascended from the east near the Rainbow Bridge instead of from the north at Strawberry Flats as we had previously done. We found most of the terrain to now be snow-free.

After three major switchbacks, we reached the eastern section of the Skyline ridge, with its stunning views. All of the highlights of Manning Park's geography could be seen to the south, including the Frosty Mountain summit, drainage basins on all sides, and the mountain ranges of the North Cascades, Windy Joe Mountain, Hozomeen Mountain, Mount Winthrop, and Chuwanten Mountain. It was no mystery why it was called the Skyline trail.

Our goal for this hike was to drone over as much ground as possible on the south-facing side of the Skyline ridge and across the Lightning Lake valley into the Frosty Creek drainage basin.

Trevor and I alternated our drone flights. We had packed about seven extra drone batteries, which we were able to recharge en route with portable chargers. I would fly the drone, looking down at my cellphone, while Trevor kept it in sight and warned me of hazards. With several drone crashes to my name, I no longer tried flying the machine out of view. By this time, Trevor had also been flying a drone by himself for over a month and he had become more proficient at droning beyond a visual line of sight. He used only a marker on the map showing the drone's location.

It was remarkable to me how Trevor carefully navigated the drone up to four kilometres away, deep into the drainage basins. He managed to keep it high enough above the treetops to avoid any crashes. As with our own hikes out and back, he had also developed a good sense of knowing precisely how long it would take to return a drone on low battery. He would monitor the battery level and masterfully calculate a turnaround point that never lost the drone signal.

We collected hours of good drone video imagery over several open areas on that day. But we were only able to cover a fraction of the entire Skyline ridge and Frosty Creek drainage basin. So we returned the following day.

This time we hiked from Strawberry Flats to the western part of the Skyline trail. From here, we were able to drone across Flash and Strike lakes into the drainage basins farther west, covering the Middle and Passage Creek drainage basins. And, when we got there, I discovered for myself just how confusing the Despair Pass junction was. Arrows pointed in the wrong directions and there were fewer arrows than possible choices. One arrow pointed down to the Skyline II ridge, which a hiker would intuitively think would be uphill, toward the ridge. In poor visibility, darkness, or snowfall, it would have been easy for Jordan—for anyone—to turn in the wrong direction.

To get a better sense of what could have happened, we continued down one of the paths that *seemed* wrong. After a few switchbacks, we arrived at a massive tree downfall that barred our way. Not only did it entirely block the trail, it intruded into possible switchbacks nearby. We climbed over some of the fallen trees but couldn't see the continuation of the actual trail in any direction. This, too, could have easily confused Jordan.

Fortunately, Trevor was experienced with the terrain and pitfalls of accidentally diverting off-trail in the wrong direction. We reversed course and found our way back to the clearly identifiable trail. We continued to scan nearby areas by droning and ground searching. There were long moments of quiet while we hiked, which gave me time to reflect on what I had been reading and thinking about ... the meaning of life.

Douglas Giles is a philosopher and psychologist, and one of several authors I had read the work of during this time. I took inspiration from his work and from other philosophers writing about personal identity, mindfulness, and human suffering. These thoughts led me to focus on signals and signs that the forest might send to help our search.

Tmx^{w}ulax^w, the scale and size of this wilderness seems endless. The problem of finding Jordan feels unsolvable.

To understand a problem, we need to first understand its underlying nature and function. All events have an end or purpose toward which they move.

Some people say everything that happens in life has a reason. But what could possibly be a reason for losing my son Jordan?

This spruce tree has grown from a small seed because the purpose of the seed was to grow into a large tree. All life forms in the forest fulfill a purpose, not as a result of their impulse or preference, but because it is inherent in their nature.

My understanding of the natural laws of the forest is limited. The forces of nature are powerful but beyond my comprehension.

By observing living beings in this forest, you are learning more about the laws and principles of the natural world. Your sensory experiences will give you a better understanding of universal truths about nature.

I'm continually seeking answers, Tmxʷulaxʷ, but haven't received clear signs pointing me in the right direction. I'm so exhausted, mentally and physically, from searching. Why is this happening?

This forest is purposeful and orderly. Turning back from the ridge would have been out of character for Jordan so the better path is straight ahead.

These feelings seemed to come from somewhere else and were not my own thoughts. And they only occurred while hiking in more remote areas of the wilderness.

John and I hiked back up the Frosty Mountain trail on June 26, after I'd taken a rest day. In the meadows near the campsite, we diverted west off-trail and zig-zagged down the mountain to the bottom of the Frosty Creek drainage basin, then returned along the embankments of the drainage.

By this time in late June, temperatures had soared to the mid- and high 30s in the parking lot. Much more snow had melted. But as we bushwhacked off-trail from the Frosty campsite, there were still, remarkably, areas of deep snow on the mountainside. I had to occasionally pull out the extra fleece jacket I kept in my backpack.

John and I searched specific areas he believed had not yet been checked. I now had much more stamina and could generally maintain his fast pace, but the terrain down the Frosty Creek drainage was gruelling. The embankments were steep and dense tree blowdown made it difficult to keep up.

Not only could John move quite quickly over fallen trees, he also searched thoroughly on all sides. I needed to put more attention on the ground to ensure each of my footsteps was safe. I would also stop for a few moments to take a photograph or check my GPS location. When I looked up he was gone. He moved so quickly that I could lose him in a few seconds. I would then shout his name and reorient myself when I heard his reply.

This day's sidehilling on the steep embankments was another very difficult trek. There were large patches of loose dirt and only a few bushes to grab—plus steep drop-offs. I kicked into the dirt on every step to gain traction. Several times I slid down over fair distances. The temperatures reached the high 30s, the forest was thick, and there were swarms of mosquitoes. Physically, it was a whole new kind of demanding experience from earlier snowshoeing treks. I sometimes felt as if I would collapse from exhaustion.

John could sense when I was close to a breaking point and would pause for me to catch my breath. I chewed gum and ate candy to give myself a sugar boost and to divert my attention long enough to get back up on my feet. Then John would say some encouraging words and we'd continue on our way down the drainage.

One of our conundrums was to decide how closely to follow the waterway. Jordan would most likely have gone to the water to set up camp, so it was critical to check the ground on both sides of the drainage. On the other hand, the embankments were steeper and more V-shaped near the water (and collected downed trees), all of which limited movement. We hiked by the waterway as much as we could and climbed farther up when the terrain became impassable. We searched as much of the drainage as possible, leaving the inaccessible sections.

In the late afternoon, we reached a section of flat ground near the bottom of the drainage, where the water flowed into Lightning Lake. John was again well ahead of me. I could see him in the distance with a coloured object. I couldn't tell what it was, but clearly John had found something significant.

I got to him as quickly as I could. He held up a slightly torn green backpack. My heart sank. Jordan's backpack was light green. A frisbee, pop can, plastic bag, and a few other torn items were scattered on the ground nearby—all in dense forest at least a few kilometres from any trail. There was no campsite nearby or any viable location to pitch a tent. Had an animal carried these things so deep into the forest? We retrieved and carried them out with us, although the items were likely not Jordan's.

As we arrived back near sunset, I could see children playing and families swimming and boating in Lightning Lake. It was a hot sunny afternoon and vacationers were enjoying the weather. The contrast of their happy family time with my own family's situation was crushing. Would there be any closure to this endless searching?

The following week, an unprecedented heat wave oppressed central British Columbia. Lytton, a small town about two hours from Manning Park, broke the record for the hottest temperature ever recorded in Canada for three consecutive days—over 50 degrees Celsius, with some locations in Lytton normally a few degrees hotter than the weather station. When we ventured out, we had to make sure to take adequate water—especially as the snow was fast disappearing and would no longer be a ready source. We drank a lot and needed to know exactly where our next refill would be found.

Hiking with a heavy backpack in this intense heat meant sweat continuously poured off my body. I had to be careful not to lose too much salt. Hyponatremia is a dangerous condition that occurs when sodium in the blood becomes too low. Although I significantly increased my water intake, I still found I could not keep up with how much I lost. I carefully planned each sip between water sources—I could not afford to miscalculate the distance and be without it. I found it best to carry two to three litres and I used a water filter to replenish from natural waterways.

On longer hikes with John, I mistakenly miscalculated my water supply on a few occasions. When I ran out, my lips quickly became dry. I was embarrassed to ask John for some of his—I should have known better. But I didn't need to ask; he knew the problem and offered me some of the extra he had packed "just in case." John always found a way to anticipate what I might need and take care of me under any circumstances.

Another consequence of hiking in these intense weather conditions was that, for the first time in my life, my legs would severely cramp in bed at night. They locked so tightly I couldn't initially figure out how to move them. These painful charley horses grew more severe as the hot days wore on.

Their cause, I discovered, is often dehydration. Although I had significantly increased how much water I drank, it was not enough. I changed my approach and began drastically increasing my water intake before I set out in the morning—much as camels do. It made a big difference and eventually the charley horse problem went away.

In late June, a social media posting alerted us to an unusual sighting on the highway west of Manning Park. The witness described a man wearing a red coat wandering along Highway 3 around Cayuse Flats a few weeks earlier, and the details matched Jordan's height and jacket colour.

On the one hand, this was uplifting news. On the other, it seemed highly unlikely that Jordan could have gotten so far from his initial starting point, even after this much time. Yet there were a few scenarios in which Jordan could have arrived there. If he had become lost in the Despair Pass valley and continued northwest, or reached Ross Lake and hiked north along the Centennial trail, he could have reached Cayuse Flats.

The witness reported that "there was no vehicle anywhere nearby... the man was running in the ditch along the highway and then disappeared into the woods." Could Jordan have suffered a mental breakdown or brain injury?

We had to know, so our focus shifted to Cayuse Flats. On June 28, I went off to investigate with a new volunteer, Linsay. The heat wave was pushing temperatures into the mid-40s where we planned to hike. We had plenty of water and hiked to creek locations where we could replenish our stores as needed. But the heat was so intense that droning was difficult—my cellphone continually overheated and shut itself off.

I had learned the warning signs of heat exhaustion: muscle cramps, dizziness, nausea, and vomiting. When I felt dizzy or my pulse raced, we'd find a shady area. We'd planned our path so we could regularly rest in shade and cool down. Noting a set of marked paths off-trail on our GPS units, we decided to look for them instead of retracing our route into the woods. The alders and undergrowth were quite dense, however, and slowed our pace substantially. We hiked fairly close to each other toward those other trails, but it was difficult to keep a visual line of sight.

As we came out into the open, I went to have a look at the area where the witness had seen the man running. All I found nearby was a pile of tires, cans, and plastic off the roadside down a hill. As odd as this appeared, in such a remote area, it didn't really seem to be connected to Jordan. We concluded that the Cayuse Flats sighting was unusual, but not something that we had to look into any further.

Linsay and I met again on June 29, however, and hiked to the summit of Windy Joe Mountain. My objective was to thoroughly drone all the steep slopes around the circumference of the plateau at the summit. Water management was again a major issue. The many waterways I'd seen flowing down the mountain in previous months had now disappeared. And we could not afford to be stranded without water.

I collected several drone videos. Once again, as I guided the drone several kilometres down a valley, I lost its signal when it was out of my line of sight. A warning message appeared that my cellphone was overheated. I switched approaches and tried to bring the drone back with the handheld controls. This was more difficult because I couldn't see the drone's location or GPS coordinates on the map. So I hit the Return to Home button and was soon relieved to make out the drone's buzz, and I was able to return it back safely.

My cellphone overheating, however, meant the drone now refused to lift off. It was another extremely hot day with temperatures in the 40s. As Linsay and I hiked around the top of the mountain, the heat became a concern for our own functioning, as well; our water supplies were low and there were no creeks nearby. Thankfully, at this elevation, there was still snow in the shade of some trees.

We packed our bottles with cold snow, but a container full of snow produces only a little water. As we hiked back down the mountain, my supply once again grew low and I became very thirsty. I knew the next water source was at least five kilometres away, possibly farther. I tried to pace myself, taking just a little sip every kilometre and diverting my attention to signals from the forest.

Tmxʷulaxʷ, I still cannot comprehend why this accident happened to my son.

Why something happened or whether a course of action is good or not is explained by objective rational reasons. Humans can choose which ends to pursue.

Jordan was well prepared for an overnight hike in the cold. Josie and I hold onto hope as it motivates us to continue searching, despite the long odds.

Every event occurs because of a higher purpose toward which the events were directed, to achieve certain ends. Like humans, other beings here in the forest have their own ends and purposes for existence.

Could foul play or something sinister have happened here?

To free yourself from feeling hostility in this park, learn to become more harmonious with the natural world. As I've mentioned before, strive to better understand the natural laws of this forest. What may appear as evil is an interpretation that arises out of ignorance and fear.

I am trying to overcome my fear and anger.

To achieve your goal, act in a way that is more productive. Then your thoughts and actions will lead to a useful outcome.

When I surround myself with individuals that have a positive outlook, they help find new ideas and alternatives.

Yes, thoughts and actions that focus on a positive approach will provide strength to continue forward.

How do I continue holding a positive outlook in such hopeless circumstances?

Just like a masonry worker who uses tools to form bricks and stones, you will use ritual behaviours to remain level-headed in the face of adversity. Every methodical step forward brings you closer to your goal.

These thoughtful reflections helped me to pass time and reach the waterway with no ill effects. I anxiously refilled my water bottles. Back at the car, I thanked Linsay for searching with me despite the scorching and trying conditions.

That was my last hike in June. Another important month was drawing to a close without a conclusion. The clock was ticking closer toward my August deadline. With only one more month left, the sense of urgency was palpable. We could not endure another month without a resolution. It was time for all of the pieces of this dreadful mystery to come together.

thirteen
ANGEL OF JULY

*Look deep into nature, and then you will
understand everything better.*
—ALBERT EINSTEIN

BEGAN THE NEW MONTH OF JULY HIKING WITH TREVOR. WE
trekked into the interior drainage east of the Frosty campsite—to
the area where I had felt Jordan's presence most strongly. It was our
top priority area to search once the snow had disappeared. And the
snow was finally now almost entirely gone.

We hiked up the Frosty Mountain trail and veered east off-trail into
the forest before the Frosty campsite. Volunteers had searched this
area on the ground in October, but this time we went farther down
into the drainage. We droned over many areas. The terrain was steep
with major tree blowdown and dense undergrowth.

As I climbed over and around the fallen trees, I again felt anxiety and
fear of suddenly finding Jordan's remains. On the one hand, I fervently

hoped to find clues. On the other, I also feared what they might reveal. As I fought my fear, I felt Jordan's consoling presence.

Son, you enjoyed short stories by authors like Cheever. You shared them on your weekly radio show at UBC.

Dad, there is a story of a man who drives across a bridge and starts losing control. He doesn't drive off the bridge but has a very difficult time breathing to get across.

He had a fear of bridges.

He does get across the first bridge but recognizes that it is a concern. He is thinking—I have to be really concerned about this because I live in San Francisco with the Golden Gate Bridge. He'll eventually have to drive over the bridge and be in situations where he will have to confront his fear.

Fear can be useful when it makes us alert to dangerous situations. But an exaggerated fear is...overplayed. What happens next in the story?

What happens is that he finds a hitchhiker who awkwardly pressures him into feeling a bit more comfortable getting across the bridge. The hitchhiker does this by singing odd tunes to distract him. His mind is so occupied by this angel of the bridge that he's able to cross it.

Jordan, an angel helped him conquer his fear—I have felt your presence watching over me like a guardian angel, keeping me safe, and taking care of my physical and emotional well-being.

The man doesn't even realize that he gets across the bridge. He thinks, oh my gosh, I just conquered that fear. "Where have you been all my life?" he asks this hitchhiker. Then the hitchhiker gets out and disappears.

Jordan, I hope there is a guardian angel watching over you and taking care of you. Your presence has given me strength to better deal with my fears in the forest.

People can overcome their fears in different ways. The way this man overcame his fear of bridges was to have a hitchhiker sing a song. Maybe there is a way to conquer your fears in this forest—not by a distraction, but by some other way.

Suddenly I realized Trevor was out of sight, but I could hear him shouting my name. I was quickly able to locate him and we continued on to approach a ridge from which we started to descend. Very soon the terrain became too steep. I stalled, unable to see how to go any farther.

We reversed course and climbed back up. Using our GPS units, we followed a path northeastward along the ridge, which ran between the drainage and the north face of the mountain. Although on the map its elevation contours showed it was safer to descend, the route itself was encumbered by severe tree downfall. There was no observable path of least resistance down the mountainside.

We had a long, slow, physically exhausting descent. Trevor led the way out and we arrived back at the parking lot by sunset. Once again, this area had given me a clear sense of Jordan nearby, but we were unable to find any trace of him on the ground.

———

July 2, however, brought us a major new clue. Near the Larches, a hiker on the Frosty Mountain trail had looked over the ridge into the box canyon immediately north of the summit and seen a sleeping bag at the snowline—hidden for months beneath the snow. We quickly assembled a team to thoroughly search the area the next day. It was seen at the top of the drainage closest to the summit, which flowed north into adjacent drainages. Several volunteers joined me on July 3, including Lutz and his wife, Britt; Max and Dean, two volunteers who had searched extensively in October; Barb and Jordy, two other new volunteers; and a member of the CCSC team with a search dog.

The eight of us started promptly at sunrise and hiked quickly up the Frosty Mountain trail, headed for the ridge that overlooked the drainage basin. I had snowshoed near there with John before, and Trevor and I had both droned the basin—separately and together. I was extremely anxious and nervous about what we might find.

Max and Dean, who were in excellent shape, arrived at the ridge first. By the time I got there, Max had descended into the drainage and was searching the ground, while Dean was searching among shallow caves on the side of the mountain. I was amazed at how easily Dean climbed around the rocky cliffs, into and out of the hollows.

Max found the edge of the sleeping bag at the snowline and freed it. It was red.

Jordan's sleeping bag was light green.

Our shared sense of defeat was huge. We had all been so convinced that this discovery would end our search. My own feelings were a little mixed—every day that Jordan was not found left me only shreds of hope for his survival. I was not looking forward to a signal of death. But still, it was time for the searching to be over.

I offered to join the searchers below but the others advised otherwise. The drop down the cliffs from the ridge was too treacherous. As I sat beneath a tree and looked down into the drainage basin, I felt despair and terror as I imagined what might have occurred down there on the 2020 Thanksgiving weekend. At the same time, I felt Jordan's presence consoling me.

As we waited for the volunteers below to finish their survey, the dog searched among the trees and along the nearby waterway. Nothing was detected. Max soon returned with the sleeping bag. We examined it and confirmed it was not Jordan's. Whose it was we did not know—it could have blown down there in heavy wind or even belonged to another lost hiker.

As we returned down the Frosty Mountain trail, we crossed paths with Bob and his friend Kevin P, from Calgary. Bob had often spoken about Kevin and his unique talents, suggesting he could offer unique help in our search. It was a pleasure to finally meet Kevin.

Bob pulled out a map and asked me for suggestions of where he and Kevin should search over the next few days. They planned to stay overnight at the Frosty campsite. I pointed to areas within the interior drainage basins that had not yet been checked. We reviewed the areas previously searched and the remaining gaps, not knowing at the time that my guidance to Bob and Kevin at this moment would prove to be unforgettable and life-changing. They continued up the trail while I returned with our team to the parking lot.

Our disappointment was now tempered with encouragement: More items were being found as the snow melted. Something helpful, we were sure, would soon turn up.

———

Trevor and I set out on a long-planned trek on July 4. Our idea was to camp beyond the Frosty Mountain summit, search the south side of the mountain along the border, as well as the Princess Creek drainage from the top, and by the small lakes on a plateau below the mountaintop.

I'd now been in the park for almost five months. Finally, for the first time, I climbed to the summit of Frosty Mountain, at an elevation of 2,426 metres. I reached the summit in the early afternoon. The view in all directions was spectacular. There is not much room on the peak, but I was not frightened. I did, however, feel humbled by the breath-taking panorama all around me.

Looking south toward the United States, I had a partial view of two ponds in the forest and the Princess Creek drainage. They didn't appear far away, but they were much lower than my perch. The south side of Frosty Mountain was very steep and mostly covered in boulders.

Trevor and I made our way slowly toward the first pond. I used my hiking poles to balance myself and stabilize my footing. Eventually the hiking became exceedingly painful for my knees and ankles. I had gained enough endurance to manage about an hour hiking through a boulder field—but not several hours and down such a steep surface.

I was, of course, wearing the heavier camping backpack, which could easily cause me to lose my balance when stepping across boulders. I readjusted the weight on my back often and that, in turn, stressed my shoulders. Altogether it meant I had to take more frequent breaks than ever before.

Finally we neared the pond. The surrounding terrain was densely forested and featured sharp cliffs—it was a beautiful, but windy, scene. We found a few flat areas near the water and set up our camp, banging our anchor pegs into rocky ground. Once all was secure and we'd eaten, I crawled inside the tent to rest and recover from the day's hike. In the silence, I heard a sound like rainfall—but it wasn't rain, it was mosquitoes! The moist, warm air was saturated with dense clouds of the flying insects. Wearing a face net was the only way to function outside, and I spent a lot of time swatting mosquitoes inside the tent before I could sleep.

Thoughts of Jordan filled my mind as I tried to nod off. The air and surroundings were peaceful, but my mind was racing and unsettled. I was restless all through the night.

We arose early on July 5, ate, and refilled our water supplies. We had unloaded much of our stuff into the tent so we could move faster and more easily. The day's objective was to search thoroughly down the Princess Creek drainage. The terrain we crossed was again steep and treacherous. I was physically exhausted before the sun hit noon.

Then my exhaustion was pierced by an emergency message from Josie on my GPS unit.

Bob and Kevin found Jordan's backpack.

I understood the implication and it crushed me. In that moment, I knew, finally and without doubt, that my beloved son had been ripped from my life.

Trevor was ahead of me. I shouted the news and fell to the ground in tears. Trevor came back immediately and embraced me.

"Where?"

"Near where the sleeping bag was found."

I needed to speak with Josie, but I couldn't. The GPS unit could only send and receive short text messages by satellite communication.

There was no cellphone signal on this side of the mountain. So I wrote Josie that I would try to get back into cell range as soon as possible. It would have to be somewhere higher on the mountain, on the Frosty Mountain ridge.

Josie felt so far away. I so wanted her to be with me.

After I pulled myself together, our day's plan immediately changed. We got back to our camp and packed up as quickly as we could. Then we headed back up and over the mountain. Running back up a steep boulder field with heavy camping gear in the scorching heat required an unreal effort. The situation was so stressful and exhausting that I fell, hard, several times, only narrowly escaping serious injury.

Still, it took us several hours to reach the Frosty Mountain ridge— the only possible location where a narrow line of sight to one of the cell towers might give me a cellphone signal.

It was enough. I called Josie and learned that Bob and Kevin had spotted Jordan's backpack in a drainage east of the Frosty Mountain trail, relatively close to the summit. It was in the same drainage basin as the sleeping bag from a few days earlier, but along another waterway, and not in view from the locations searched earlier.

We had been looking in this area several times. It was relatively close to the Frosty campsite, but the ground had been snow-covered for months. It was quite far from the opposite side of the ridge, the area where the psychics had been sure of. But it was exactly in the vicinity where I had felt Jordan's presence most strongly on both April 3 with John and Bob, and on June 5 with John and the two other volunteers.

I learned that Bob had sent Josie a photo he'd been able to take of the backpack (and the GPS location) on the evening of July 4. He, too, was in a remote place and unable to use his cellphone. Josie called Mike B after getting Bob's satellite message. Mike consulted with a police friend, then immediately called 911. They transferred him to the Princeton RCMP who set in motion the process to reactivate the search the next morning.

When John received the news, he quickly made his way to the park so he, too, could search the area. Josie bought a plane ticket and would arrive the next day.

I wanted to search the drainage basin myself. Both Bob and John advised against it. They were more experienced hikers and, knowing my limitations and abilities, they believed it was too dangerous, especially in my emotional state. They would search thoroughly themselves and keep me informed. I never doubted or questioned any advice from Bob or John.

Trevor and I arrived at the Larches by mid-afternoon on July 5. We made our way to the edge of the drainage basin and looked down. We were unable to see any unusual colour that might be Jordan's backpack—we assumed it was hidden in the trees. The SAR team had already arrived and were moving down the drainage to search for Jordan's resting place. We could not see them.

Trevor and I had to decide whether to go down the mountain or set up a campsite nearby. If we were leaving the mountainside, we had to do it soon so we would be down before sunset. I could not think clearly and just followed Trevor's advice. My body was on autopilot. We could not communicate with Bob and John and wanted updates from them. So, we decided to leave.

I returned to the cabin and phoned Bob and John. They confirmed they had found Jordan's backpack where Josie had told me. They had searched nearby and found no further evidence but suspected that Jordan had moved farther down the drainage. They would be back tomorrow to continue searching there.

———

On July 6, Bob, Kevin P, and John ascended Frosty Mountain to continue the search. Dean joined as well, connecting with Bob and Kevin in the drainage basin. A dedicated volunteer, Dean was skilled in searching the most difficult terrain, where few others were willing to go.

Josie arrived in the early afternoon. Our friends, Tom and Keira, drove her to the park. Josie and I returned to the cabin and awaited the day's outcome. I was a mess—I couldn't eat and I was in shock—but I was relieved to be able to hold Josie and share our grief together.

Shortly after dinner, Bob and Kevin arrived at the cabin. I welcomed them inside and introduced them to Josie.

"We're so sorry to come and share our news tonight," Bob began.

I knew immediately they had found Jordan.

"Do you know what happened to him?" I asked.

"Jordan was well prepared for the hike. It seems, though, that he was caught off guard by the snowstorm and lost the trail," Bob said. "It could have happened easily to any hiker. And those snow conditions were completely unexpected."

"We're not sure why he dropped his backpack," Bob continued, "but I suspect it was related to hypothermia. We think he tried to find his way back by going down the drainage. He was headed in the right direction—back to the parking lot—but he likely didn't know that drainage would become so treacherous."

"The SAR team told us they'd searched that drainage thoroughly in October," I said.

Bob didn't respond to that but continued to describe what they had discovered.

"We got as far as the section where the drainage branches to the northwest. The terrain becomes extremely difficult after that." He paused and, becoming emotional himself, he asked me to sit down. "But Dean was able to go on. And he found evidence of Jordan's resting place."

We all paused then, and bowed our heads.

After a few minutes, we talked about what all this meant and where Jordan had hiked on his last day. Bob felt, and John later agreed, that he had gone up the Frosty Mountain trail in a counter-clockwise loop. He had probably lost his way somewhere in the Larches past the fourth, fifth, or sixth switchback, after the storm hit. He continued toward or past the campsite, parallel to the trail, but not rising enough in elevation. When he came out of the forest, he was at the base of the box canyon beside the summit. Or else he tried to backtrack but was disoriented. An animal attack was possible.

Bob also shared with us how crucial Kevin had been in finding Jordan. He said that Kevin had seen mental images and had premonitions about Jordan over the few weeks before he came to British Columbia.

"He told me about these premonitions," said Bob, "but I didn't share them with you because I thought you would be doubtful or skeptical."

Kevin said that, after Josie and I had told him specific details about Jordan's character and life, he had begun to feel a connection to Jordan's spirit. He followed the sensations and images he'd "seen" in his mind to the areas where first the backpack, and later Jordan's remains, were found.

"When Bob and I hiked off-trail by the Frosty campsite, and before we even started that hike, I sensed images of a treetop with a specific shape, and that it was the key turning point," he said. "It was a crucial junction. Once I found it and turned, it correctly pointed us in the direction of Jordan's backpack."

"Were you and Bob searching together?" I asked.

"We lost each other for some time," Kevin replied. "But when I turned at the tree I recognized from my premonition and moved in that direction through the forest, then suddenly Bob appeared in front of me. Soon after, we found the backpack."

I expressed our sincere thanks for his precious help to our family. But Kevin wasn't finished.

"I need to share with you my visions and dreams of Jordan during the past few weeks since Bob contacted me," he said. Josie, Bob, and I listened intently.

"Jordan wanted me to tell you how much he loved you both, his sisters, family, and relatives. And that he is in a better place now."

In his dreams, Kevin had sensed his other deceased relatives. Jordan hid behind them, as if he did not want to be exposed up front. But once Kevin identified him in the group, then Jordan came forward.

"Do you know why he didn't want to reveal himself?" I asked.

"He knew his mother was still hopeful of finding him alive and he didn't want to take away her hope," Kevin replied. "Now, with the summer arriving, he felt it was time to reveal himself."

"Why did he let me and others suffer so long, searching this forest day after day, week after week, through so much pain?"

"He knew you were strong and would not give up, but he couldn't bear to take away his mother's hope."

Although I was initially doubtful of Kevin's premonitions, his accurate directions to Jordan's backpack and some remarkable revelations about Jordan's character were compelling. He revealed information that only Josie and I could have known as Jordan's parents. I felt somehow Kevin had a subconscious line to my son and would know the answer to my burning questions.

"Did he hear my prayers?" I asked.

"He was walking with you on every hike and heard all of your prayers," Kevin said. "He was always beside you. He stayed with you to keep you and the volunteers safe. There were many times when something could have gone seriously wrong, but you always found your way out safely."

"Why, then, was it you, Bob, Dean, and John that found Jordan, instead of me?" I asked.

"Jordan didn't want you or his mother to find him in the condition he was in, at his resting place," Kevin answered. "He wanted you to remember him as the vibrant young man of whom you were so proud."

I had an image, then, of another dream—the woman I had spoken to a few weeks earlier at the Hampton Campground. She'd seen Jordan trapped behind an ice wall. I felt it, too, explained something important. I was on the opposite side of Frosty Mountain—an icy mountain—when Bob, Kevin, and John had found Jordan's backpack. The mountain was the wall of ice separating Jordan from me. Jordan had not wanted me to find his backpack and resting place, to preserve our memories of him as a vigorous, strong young man.

These men were a gift. And so was the fact that I was not alone when Jordan's backpack was discovered. My dear friend, Trevor, who was about the same age as Jordan, was at my side.

Finally, I could also identify who ultimately deserved the most credit for finding Jordan: my wife, Josie. She had continued to find more volunteers during the winter. Throughout the depth of our despair, she persisted. She found Bob through a recruitment effort in March.

Bob hadn't known us. He was inspired by Josie to join our search efforts. Bob then brought Kevin to Manning Park. Kevin pointed Dean in the right direction, down that drainage to Jordan's resting place.

From Josie to Bob to Kevin to Dean to Jordan—the chain of events began with Josie.

Bob and John believed that Jordan was probably hypothermic by the time he dropped his backpack. This happens after prolonged exposure to freezing temperatures. Eventually the brain becomes colder and stops functioning properly. Dizziness and disorientation set in as the body starts losing heat faster than it is generated. As the body temperature drops, heat flows back to the core from the extremities, to keep the heart functioning properly. This can lead to feelings of overheating—people with hypothermia been known to remove jackets and sweaters. Eventually, however, this cannot maintain the core temperature. Heat is released from the core and death soon follows.

When Jordan emerged out of the forest at the top of the drainage basin, he faced the enormous box canyon and summit of Frosty Mountain. He would have assessed his options: retrace his steps back along the same path, where he had already likely lost his trail in the snow, or work his way down the gently descending valley into the interior drainage basin. Without knowing what lies ahead, it would have made sense to follow a waterway out to lower ground.

But this drainage basin was a deadly trap. Its rolling slopes and meadows, sweeping away to the north (toward the highway and resort) initially appear to be easy to hike down. Gradually, though, its V-shaped walls steepen. Eventually, following the valley floor becomes extremely difficult. If this had happened on the Saturday night, further complications were darkness, snowfall, and downed trees. As I now knew only too well, it consumes increasingly more energy to climb over, around, and through a network of tree downfall.

When Bob, Kevin P, John, and Dean hiked down the drainage from the backpack to Jordan's resting place, which they said was more than five kilometres farther on, they were astonished by how far he'd travelled and the difficulty of the terrain he'd navigated. They judged that Jordan had made a superhuman effort to stay alive amid worsening odds. He bravely pushed on in the face of life-threatening adversity, showing fierce determination to survive, and courage.

I thought about other people I'd met in the past nine months who had been lost in Manning Park. Blessed by good fortune, they had been able to find their way out of the forest. But the snowstorm had tipped the scales away from Jordan.

One soldier perishes in a war, while another survives, not because one is stronger or braver than the other. Much depends on the complexity of the circumstances—many aspects of which are beyond their control—and many are often inexplicable. Jordan faced a set of circumstances beyond his control and which, to me, remain inexplicable.

———

The next evening, Mike A paid a visit to our cabin. He wanted to tell us that he had continually prayed and thought about Jordan and our family since the search initially began in October. We expressed gratitude that Mike had honoured Jordan and his struggle to survive in the wilderness, and had made important contributions to our efforts.

"In our Indigenous beliefs, it is an honour that Jordan was called by Mother Earth and given back to Tmxʷulaxʷ," said Mike.

When he said these words, I was initially unsettled by the explanation. I wondered why my son was taken, among all of the other hikers who climbed the trails of Manning Park on that fateful weekend in October 2020. But Mike's words of wisdom gave us comfort to know that Jordan's untimely death had a deeper meaning in Indigenous beliefs.

Earlier, Tmxʷulaxʷ had advised that my sensory experiences would allow me to better understand universal truths about nature. Through Mike's explanation, I had learned that Tmxʷulaxʷ was right.

Mike B played a key role in quickly reactivating the search through the Princeton RCMP. He camped at Manning Park for several nights after Jordan's remains were found. He reported some dreams related to Jordan. When he hiked around the Canyon Nature trail loop in the afternoon of July 8, suddenly a thunder and lightning storm appeared. Mike saw a bolt of lightning strike the ground near the junction of the Frosty–Windy Joe Mountain connector trail—the location of Jordan's resting place.

Mike called Josie in tears. Josie offered to go and pick him up, but he reassured her it was a flow of emotion from Mother Earth releasing Jordan.

In the next few days and coming weeks, what had actually happened to Jordan would continue to be discussed. Not everyone agreed with the way Bob and John saw it.

Dean and Max, for example, remained convinced that the 12:32 p.m. cellphone ping was correct, and that Jordan had hiked in a clockwise direction, climbing Windy Joe Mountain first. As he approached the

Frosty Mountain summit from the northeast, the storm caused him to lose the trail and go down into the interior drainage too early, before reaching the Frosty Mountain trail.

And so it remained inconclusive whether Ethan Morf had actually seen Jordan or not on October 10, 2020. Neither our searches near Ethan's reported encounter nor Jordan's final resting place revealed conclusively which route Jordan had taken. Several dog teams had searched the lower slopes a few kilometres around the trailhead of Frosty Mountain and not found anything in that area. It was consistent with the eventual outcome—Jordan's resting place was many kilometres away from the trailhead.

What was confirmed, however, was that the times when I had felt an intense emotional connection with Jordan, near the Larches east of the Frosty campsite, happened because Jordan *had been* nearby. They were episodes of extrasensory connection between me and Jordan, as real as if we were sharing the same journey on that Thanksgiving weekend in 2020.

The Princeton RCMP also kindly offered to take Josie and me up to the Larches by helicopter. On July 14, the pilot dropped us along the ridge overlooking the drainage basin in which Jordan's backpack had been found. We spent solemn and dignified moments of silence. I had brought flowers from the backyard of Eastgate neighbours. Josie tossed them into the drainage basin.

The days in which Jordan's remains were recovered were extremely emotional. On July 18, the CCSC team returned with a canine team. With Mike B, Tom, Kiera, and Trevor, they searched around the area of Jordan's resting place to ensure nothing was left behind. John searched separately and found Jordan's parking pass. At the end of another long day, Josie and I invited the searchers to the resort restaurant to give our thanks to all.

Throughout the search process, I prayed and hoped to be able to carry Jordan out from Manning Park. So, after returning from the

Valley View Funeral Home in Surrey, Josie and I went back to the park, near the Windy Joe Mountain trailhead, with Jordan's urn. I found a location in an open field with a direct line of sight to a section of mountain closest to Jordan. We placed the urn on a tree trunk there and reflected on his life well lived. I then carried Jordan out from Manning Park.

———

A Celebration of Life in honour of Jordan was organized for July 26 at Green College at UBC. Many of Jordan's friends and the search volunteers were there. His master's degree parchment in electrical engineering was given to Josie and me by UBC's Associate Dean of Applied Science.

Jordan's friends spoke highly of his character, his kind-heartedness and personality, his good sense of humour and brilliant mind. They shared solemn memories but also told stories about funny times they'd had together. People who had volunteered to help us told stories about the search that comforted us. Many said they had been inspired by our love and determination to find Jordan. Mike B said the reason why he and others had kept coming back to Manning Park or searching imagery online was because of our determination as parents. This fortitude energized them. He added that if we had given up, so too would have the volunteers.

We took a group photo afterward with our core volunteers. These individuals were truly "salt of the earth"—a term that is defined as "representative of the best or noblest elements of society," people who are considered "to be of great worth and reliability" and are "solid, dependable, unpretentious, honest." Our volunteers were all this, and more.

———

Josie and I returned to St. John's soon after the Celebration of Life and made arrangements for a funeral at the Basilica Cathedral of St. John the Baptist. It was held on August 3, 2021. These are words from the obituary published in the local newspapers.

Born in 1995 in Fredericton, New Brunswick, Jordan Philip Naterer was called by Mother Earth on October 11, 2020, in E.C. Manning Park, BC. After accidentally losing the hiking trail in unexpected snow conditions at Frosty Mountain, Jordan fought a courageous battle to escape out of treacherous terrain. His remarkable distance travelled through steep drainages under the worst imaginable blizzard conditions was a testament to his super-human effort to survive.

Jordan was a graduate of Memorial University's engineering program in 2018. He was an NSERC Graduate Scholarship holder and finished his master's degree in electrical and computer engineering at the University of British Columbia in 2020.

Jordan was a brilliant young man with many diverse talents in engineering, music, poetry, cooking, among others. He was exceptionally warm hearted and wrote "all I do is try to be kind" in his personal diary for song-writing notes.

Father Critch hosted the funeral and gave a beautiful, solemn, and dignified sermon. Among the most difficult tasks of my life, I spoke words of remembrance of Jordan near the end of the service.

───────

As I write this book, Jordan has been gone for more than three years. When I see young men now, I am always struck by Jordan's absence. In all the gatherings to come, the rooms to enter, the trails to follow, he will not be there. Josie and I still have three children, but one will always be absent.

I wish the clock could be turned back to the day before Thanksgiving weekend 2020. Maybe a different sequence of events could have prevented Jordan's accident. If he'd left his apartment an hour earlier or later, he might have avoided whatever circumstances caused him to lose the trail. But I can't stop or turn back the clock. It keeps going forward, unforgiving.

Despite the difficult circumstances and terrain, my family showed great determination to find Jordan. Together with hiking partners from February onwards, I searched about 1,600 kilometres on- and off-trail throughout Manning Park.

If we had found Jordan earlier or there had been another cause of death, would it have eased our pain? I doubt it. During one of my hikes up the Frosty Mountain trail, I passed a father walking alone. I mentioned Jordan's name. He knew about the situation, and expressed his condolences. Then he shared with me his own pain: He had lost his son by suicide. I had wondered if it would have been less painful to accept a death by suicide. Speaking with this man, I realized it would not. Losing a child, regardless of the circumstances, is always unspeakably painful.

There are plenty of books on grief. They offer perspectives to help us cope. Do not look directly at death, turn away, look inwards, and so forth. Focus on positive memories. Any of these can work for a while, but the hard reality must settle in.

Suffering is part of the human condition. Tragedies and accidents happen. But I must look to the future for the well-being of with my wife and daughters. So I will not turn away from the pain of Jordan's death. I will always face it directly. I owe that to Jordan.

Still, questions that were once simple are now more complicated. How many children do you have? I always answer three. Sometimes I explain, other times I do not.

I also wonder what will happen with my regrets. I regret not warning Jordan more about the hazards of mountain climbing or teaching him more about camping in the wilderness. I regret not travelling to Vancouver to spend that Thanksgiving weekend with him. I accept these regrets as part of my life, but I will not allow them to consume me or my family. And I expect a time will come when I can express my regrets and apologies directly to Jordan.

My family and I will find a way to move forward and live in peace without Jordan. We will find tangible ways to never forget him. His presence continues to live on with us and all who knew him. We hold onto many of his possessions, including his car, shoes, furniture, books, photos, and more. Even though they cause pain, we will not put them away. We keep him alive by telling others of the hands that held and shaped them.

Jordan's physical presence is no longer with us. But his spirit will continue to shine forever.

> *When someone you love becomes a memory,*
> *the memory becomes a treasure.*
> —ANONYMOUS

REFERENCES

These are several of the main books, journal papers, and articles that helped shaped the strategies of the search process and my thoughts during the months we searched for Jordan.

Aesop. *Aesop's Fables*. Translated by V. S. Vernon Jones. New York: Barnes and Noble Classic Series, 2003.

Alanis, J., Madeline Brown, James Kitchens et al. "Topography and Behavior Based Movement Modeling for Missing Hikers in Land-Wilderness Settings." Technical Report, Arizona State University, Tempe, 2019.

Beatty, Robert. *Serafina and the Black Cloak*. Glendale: Disney Hyperion, 2015.

Beckey, Fred. *Challenge of the North Cascades*. Seattle: Mountaineers Books, 1996.

Bond, Michael. "Why Humans Totally Freak Out When They Get Lost." San Francisco: Wired Magazine, May 15, 2020. Wire Magazine Ltd, Sheffield, UK.

Bouchard, Dave. *The Seven Sacred Teachings of White Buffalo Calf Woman*. Translated by Nancy Jones. Victoria: Crow Cottage Publishing, 2016.

Cheever, John. *The Stories of John Cheever*. New York: Alfred A. Knopf Publishing, 1978.

Coble, Theresa, Steve Selin, and Beth B. Erickson. "Hiking Alone: Understanding Fear, Negotiation Strategies and Leisure Experience." *Journal of Leisure Research* 35, no. 1 (2003): 1–22.

Delorie, Oliver Luke. *Shinrin-yoku: The Healing Art of Forest Bathing*. New York: Quarto Publishing, 2018.

Doke, Jared. "Analysis of Search Incidents and Lost Person Behavior in Yosemite National Park." Ph.D. Dissertation, University of Kansas, Lawrence, 2012.

Eliot, T. S. "Preface." In *Transit of Venus: Poems by Harry Crosby*, by Harry Crosby. Paris: Black Sun Press, 1931.

Giles, Douglas. "How Can I Be a Better Person? On Virtue Ethics." In *Introduction to Philosophy: Ethics*, 26–35. Vancouver: BC Open Textbook, 2019.

Hesse, Hermann. *Wandering: Notes and Sketches*. Translated by James Wright. New York: The Noonday Press, 1972.

Heth, C. Donald and Edward Cornell. "Characteristics of Travel by Persons Lost in Albertan Wilderness Areas." *Journal of Environmental Psychology* 18, no. 3 (1998): 223–35.

Hill, Kenneth. *Lost Person Behavior*. Ottawa: National Search and Rescue Secretariat of Canada, 1998.

Leach, J. "Survival Psychology: The Won't to Live." *The Psychologist* 24 (2011): 26–9.

Limbaugh, Ronald H. and Kirsten E. Lewis, eds. *John Muir Papers: 1856-1942*. Alexandria, VA: Chadwyk-Healey Inc., 1986.

Moye, Jayme. *Day Hikers are the Most Vulnerable in Survival Situations. Here's Why*. New York: National Geographic, April 11, 2019. https://www.nationalgeographic.com/adventure/article/hikers-survival-tips

Naterer, Jordan, Elena-Iulia Dobre, Ayman Mostafa et al. "Modular Spectrum Utilization for Next-Generation Fixed Transmission Networks," 2021 Biennial Symposium on Communications, Saskatoon, Saskatchewan, June 28–30, 2021.

Oka, Cynthia Dewi. *Salvage.* Evanston: Northwestern University Press, 2017.

Poe, Edgar Allan. *The Raven and Other Poems.* New York: Wiley and Putnam, 2015.

Quackenbush, Thomm. *Holidays with Bigfoot.* Independently Published, 2020.

Roosevelt, Theodore. "Citizenship in a Republic." *Journal des Debats,* Paris, April 23, 1910.

Salter, James. *Light Years.* New York: Penguin Random House, 1995.

Saway, Victorino L. "Indigenous Cultures and Forest Management." XII World Forestry Congress, Quebec City, 2003.

Shah, Tahir. *House of the Tiger King: The Quest for a Lost City.* London: John Murray Press, 2005.

Simard, Suzanne. "Mycorrhizal Networks: Mechanisms, Ecology and Modeling." *Fungal Biology Reviews* 26 (2012): 39–60.

Syilx Nation Siwłkʷ Declaration, Okanagan Nation Alliance, 3535 – 101 Old Okanagan Highway, Westbank, BC, 2014.

Wohlleben, Peter. *The Hidden Life of Trees: What They Feel, How They Communicate—Discoveries from A Secret World.* Vancouver: Greystone Books, 2016.

Wolterstorff, Nicholas. *Lament for a Son.* Grand Rapids: William B. Eerdmans Publishing Company, 1987.

Worton, Holly. *If Trees Could Talk: Life Lessons from the Wisdom of the Woods.* Victoria: Tribal Publishing, 2019.